JOURNAL

OF THE

CONSTITUTIONAL COMMISSION

OF

MICHIGAN.

Printed by order of the Commission, under direction and supervision of

HENRY S. CLUBB,

Clerk of the Constitutional Commission.

BY AUTHORITY.

LANSING:
W. S. GEORGE & CO., STATE PRINTERS AND BINDERS.
1873.

CONTENTS.

PAGE.

OFFICERS AND MEMBERS OF THE CONSTITUTIONAL COMMISSION AND THE POSTOFFICE ADDRESS 2

JOINT RESOLUTION AUTHORIZING THE APPOINTMENT OF A CONSTITUTIONAL COMMISSION 3

JOURNAL OF THE CONSTITUTIONAL COMMISSION OF 1873 5

CERTIFICATE OF THE COMMISSION TO THE GOVERNOR 175

THE CONSTITUTION AS AMENDED AND PROPOSED FOR SUBMISSION.. 177

INDEX TO THE PROPOSED CONSTITUTION 219

GENERAL INDEX 233

APPENDIX CONTAINING:

Report to the Governor iii

Index to changes v

Amended Constitution 1

Present Constitution 43

CONSTITUTIONAL COMMISSION OF 1873.

CHAIRMAN:

SULLIVAN M. CUTCHEON, Ypsilanti, Washtenaw County.

MEMBERS:

ISAAC M. CRANE, Eaton Rapids, Eaton County.
IRA D. CROUSE, Hartland, Livingston County.
JOHN DIVINE, Lexington, Sanilac County.
JAMES R. DEVEREAUX, Houghton, Houghton County.
WILLIAM M. FERRY, Grand Haven, Ottawa County. **[Appointed to** fill vacancy; qualified October 2, 1873.]
EDWIN W. GIDDINGS, Romeo, Macomb County. **[Resigned October** 8, 1873.]
HERSCHEL H. HATCH, Bay City, Bay County.
DAVID H. JEROME, Saginaw City, Saginaw County.
LYMAN G. MASON, Muskegon, Muskegon County. **[Resigned Septem**ber 2, 1873.]
ELIJAH W. MEDDAUGH, Detroit, Wayne County.
SETH C. MOFFATT, Northport, Leelanaw County.
ASHLEY POND, Detroit, Wayne County.
HENRY H. RILEY, Constantine, St. Joseph County.
CHARLES UPSON, Coldwater, Branch County.
HEZEKIAH G. WELLS, Kalamazoo, Kalamazoo County.
EDWIN WILLITS, Monroe, Monroe County.
SOLOMON L. WITHEY, Grand Rapids, Kent County.
LYSANDER WOODWARD, Rochester, Oakland County.

CLERK:

HENRY S. CLUBB, Grand Haven, Ottawa County.

ASSISTANT CLERK:

STEPHEN B. MCCRACKEN, Detroit, Wayne County.

DOORKEEPER AND JANITOR:

WILLIAM D. BURNHAM, Lansing, Ingham County.

CHAIRMAN'S MESSENGER:

DAVID G. S. BARRY, Monroe.

CLERK'S MESSENGER:

FRANK H. JENISON, Lansing, Ingham County.

FLOOR MESSENGERS:

FRANK E. RICE, Saginaw City, Saginaw County.
GEORGE P. BROWN, Kalamazoo, Kalamazoo County.

JOINT RESOLUTION

To Provide for a Commission for the Revision of the Constitution of the State of Michigan.

WHEREAS, The existing constitution of the State of Michigan is defective in many respects, and needs to be amended to conform to the growth and development of the State, and the advanced ideas of the people, as well as in many other respects; therefore,

Resolved by the Senate and House of Representatives of the State of Michigan, That the Governor be and he is hereby authorized and empowered to nominate and appoint eighteen able and discreet citizens, who shall be authorized to examine into and report to the next session, either special or general, of the Legislature of this State, such amendments and revision of the constitution as in their judgment may be necessary for the best interests of the State and the people. Said commission shall assemble in the supreme court rooms, or some other suitable place, in the city of Lansing, at such time as the Governor shall direct, and may remain in session such time as may be necessary to perfect their labors, not exceeding one hundred days in all, and shall be entitled to receive therefor the sum of five dollars per diem for each day actually employed. They shall take the constitutional oath of office to be administered by one of the Judges of the Supreme Court or the Secretary of State; and may elect one of their number chairman. They may appoint a clerk at a compensation not exceeding three dollars per day, and such messengers and assistants as they deem necessary, at a compensation not exceeding two dollars per day, and the State shall pay all expenses of such commission, as near as may be, in the same manner as the expenses of the Legislature are paid. No more than two of such commissioners shall reside in any one congressional district as now organized, and in case of death or resignation of any commissioner, the Governor shall appoint another to fill the vacancy. Such commissioners shall have all the immunities and powers granted to members of the Legislature or the House of Representatives for the purposes necessary to discharge the duty imposed upon them. No proposition or amendment shall be adopted by them or reported by them that is not indorsed and recommended by two-thirds of the whole number of persons upon such commission. They shall cause their work to be laid before the Governor on or before the first day of December, eighteen hundred and seventy-three, and the Governor shall cause the same to be printed for the use of the Legislature, on or before the first day of January, eighteen hundred and seventy-four. The Legislature at its next general or special session may cause such revision, or so much thereof as they may approve, to be submitted to the people for ratification.

Approved April 24, 1873.

JOURNAL

OF THE

CONSTITUTIONAL COMMISSION OF 1873.

LANSING, *August 27, 1873.*

The Commission appointed by the Governor, pursuant to joint resolution No. 19, session laws of 1873, met at the Senate chamber, at the Capitol, Lansing, on Wednesday, August 27th, at noon.

Hon. Daniel Striker called the Commission to order.

Roll called: The following members present:

First District—Ashley Pond of Wayne, and Elijah W. Meddaugh of Wayne.

Second District—Edwin Willits of Monroe, and Sullivan M. Cutcheon of Washtenaw.

Third District—Charles Upson of Branch.

Fourth District—Hezekiah G. Wells of Kalamazoo, and Henry H. Riley of St. Joseph.

Fifth District— ——— ——— ———.

Sixth District—Ira D. Crouse of Livingston.

Seventh District—John Divine of Sanilac.

Eighth District—Herschel H. Hatch of Bay, and David H. Jerome of Saginaw.

Ninth District—Seth C. Moffatt of Leelanaw.

The members present then came forward and took and subscribed the constitutional oath of office, and took their seats.

On motion of Mr. Upson,

Hon. H. G. Wells of Kalamazoo was chosen Chairman *pro tem*.

On motion of Mr. Cutcheon,

Mr. Samuel F. Cook of Washtenaw was chosen Secretary *pro tem.*

ADDRESS OF THE CHAIRMAN, PRO TEM.

The chairman *pro tem.*, on taking the chair, addressed the Commission as follows:

GENTLEMEN OF THE COMMISSION:—I thank you for this favor in honoring me with the position of temporary chairman of a body of citizens of Michigan who are commissioned by his Excellency, Governor Bagley, to report amendments for the revision of the Constitution of the State. We are called here from among the people, not as the representatives of a party, not as political partisans; but it is expected of this assembled Commission that it shall honestly and fairly submit such change in the constitutional law of Michigan as the interests of a great and growing people demand—a people who hold rank in material wealth second to no other State in the Union.

We have, in our large extent of territory, in its extremes, north and south, in what has already been developed, and what may reasonably be expected to be developed in the future, a mining interest second to none on earth; an agricultural and fruit interest which is attracting the attention of the eastern world; a lumber, salt, and fishing interest which, now in its infancy, is measured by the capital of many millions of dollars; a home carrying trade, over our lines of railroad, and a shipping interest connected with the lakes which has increased in value, within a very few years, almost beyond calculation every acre of land within the limits of Michigan: all these interests are to be advanced by wise constitutional enactment.

The powers of your Executive, your Judiciary, and your Legislative departments are connected with all these varied interests, and therefore the weighty responsibility resting on those who propose and submit provisions of Constitutional Law.

While we are dealing with the material interests of our people, we will not, of course, forget that the great, the crowning excellence of our own State of Michigan, is its educational system; its beams of light are flashing, not only over our own pleasant peninsula, but they are streaming out far beyond its boundaries, and the people of other States and countries accord to us the full measure of wisdom in taxing our property to give to their children an intelligence that will enable them to legislate and provide for the future. Let our system of education be fostered and encouraged by the proper action of this Commission.

Thanking you again for the honor conferred upon me, let us now attend to the business before us.

On motion of Mr. Upson,

The Commission took a recess until 3 o'clock this afternoon.

AFTERNOON SESSION.

3 o'clock, P. M.

The Commission met pursuant to adjournment, and was called to order by the Chairman *pro tem.*

Roll called; quorum present.

The following additional members, being present, took and subscribed the oath of office and took their seats:

Third District—Isaac M. Crane of Eaton.

Fifth District—Solomon L. Withey of Kent, Lyman G. Mason of Muskegon.

COMMUNICATION FROM THE SECRETARY OF STATE.

The Chairman *pro tem.* announced the following communication:

STATE DEPARTMENT, MICHIGAN,
SECRETARY'S OFFICE,
Lansing, August 27th, 1873.

To the Chairman of the Commission for the Revision of the Constitution:

SIR:—By direction of the Governor, I herewith transmit eighteen copies of volume one of the laws of 1873 for the use of the Commission.

Very Respectfully,

DANIEL STRIKER,
Secretary of State.

ELECTION OF CHAIRMAN.

On motion of Mr. Meddaugh,

The Commission proceeded to ballot for a presiding officer.

The Chairman *pro tem.* appointed as tellers to canvass the ballot, Messrs. Moffat and Riley.

The ballot having been canvassed the tellers announced that there had been 13 votes cast, of which Mr. S. M. Cutcheon had received seven; Mr. S. L, Withey, three; scattering three.

On motion of Mr. Withey,

The election of Mr. S. M. Cutcheon as permanent chairman, was made unanimous.

THE CHAIRMAN'S ADDRESS.

The Chairman, on taking the chair, said:

GENTLEMEN OF THE COMMISSION,—I am strongly sensible to the great honor you have conferred upon me, in choosing me to preside over your deliberations. I have only to pledge you I will endeavor to discharge the duties of the position to the best of my ability.

ELECTION OF CLERK.

On motion of Mr. Jerome,

The members of the Commission proceeded to ballot for the office of clerk.

Tellers reported the following vote:

For Henry S. Clubb	12
For Samuel F. Cook	1

Mr. Henry S. Clubb subscribed and took the oath of office and took his seat as Clerk of the Commission.

On motion of Mr. Upson,

The Chairman was authorized to appoint two messengers.

On motion of Mr. Moffatt,

The Clerk was authorized to appoint a messenger.

On motion of Mr. Withey,

The Chairman was authorized to appoint a committee on rules.

The Chair announced as committee on rules, Messrs. Withey, Riley, and Willits.

Mr. Hatch moved that the Commission proceed to appoint a Stenographer.

The motion did not prevail.

On motion of Mr. Moffatt,

The Chairman was authorized to appoint a door-keeper.

On motion of Mr. Withey,

The Commission adjourned until 9 o'clock to-morrow morning.

SECOND DAY.

LANSING, *Thursday, August 28, 1873.*

The Commission was called to order at 9 o'clock.

Rev. Mr. Robinson opened the session with prayer.

Roll called: quorum present.

The following additional members being present, subscribed, took the oath of office, and took their seats:

Sixth District—Lysander Woodard, Oakland.

Ninth District—James R. Devereaux, Houghton.

REPORT OF THE COMMITTEE ON RULES.

Mr. Withey, from the committee on rules, made the following report:

To the Constitutional Commission: Your committee to whom was referred the subject of rules for the government of the Constitutional Commission of 1873, respectfully report that they have had the subject under consideration, and recommend the adoption of the following

RULES.

1. The Chairman shall call the Commission to order at the time to which it stands adjourned, and thereupon the roll of members shall be called by the Clerk.

2. Upon the appearance of a quorum, the journal of the preceding day shall be read by the Clerk, unless otherwise ordered, and any mistake therein corrected.

3. After the reading of the journal of the preceding day, the order of business shall be as follows:

I. Presentation of Petitions.
II. Reports of Standing Committees.
III. Reports of Select Committees.
IV. Motions and Resolutions.
V. Third Reading of Articles.
VI. Unfinished Business.
VII. Special Orders of the Day.
VIII. General Orders of the Day.

4. The Chairman shall preserve order and decorum, and shall decide questions of order, subject to an appeal of the Commission.

5. The Chairman shall vote upon all questions taken by yeas and nays, except on appeals from his own decisions, in which case he shall not vote.

6. The Chairman may leave the chair and appoint a member to preside, but not for a longer time than one day, except by leave of the Commission.

7. When two or more members rise at once, the Chairman shall designate the member who is first to speak.

8. All resolutions and motions shall be in writing, when required by the Chairman, and be endorsed by the member introducing the same.

9. When a question shall be under debate, no motion shall be received but the following, to wit:

I. To adjourn;
II. To lay on the table;
III. For the previous question;
IV. To postpone to a day certain;
V. To commit;
VI. To amend;
VII. To postpone indefinitely;

Which several motions shall have precedence, in the order in which they stand arranged.

10. A motion to adjourn shall always be in order; that and the motion to lay on the table shall always be decided without debate.

11. Petitions, memorials, and other papers addressed to the Commission, shall be presented by the Chairman or a member in his place, with a brief statement of the contents, and the name of the member presenting the same endorsed thereon.

12. When the Commission shall have reached the general orders of the day, they shall go into committee of the whole upon such orders, or a particular order designated by a vote of the Commission.

13. The rules of the Commission shall be observed in committee of the whole so far as they may be applicable, except that the yeas and nays shall not be called nor the previous question enforced.

14. A journal of the proceedings in committee of the whole shall be kept, as in Commission.

15. In filling up blanks the largest sum and the longest time shall be first put.

16. All orders, resolutions, or motions shall be entered on the journal of the Commission, with the name of the member moving the same.

17. No rule of the Commission shall be suspended, altered, or amended, without the concurrence of two-thirds of the members present.

18. Upon the call of the Commission, the names of the members shall be called by the Clerk, and the absentees noted; but no excuse shall be made until the Commission shall be fully called over; then the absentees shall be called over the second time, and, if still absent, excuses are to be heard; and if no excuse be made, the absentees may, by order of those present, if there be five members present, be taken into custody by the door-keeper.

19. The rules of parliamentary practice as comprised in "Jefferson's Manual" shall govern the Commission in all cases to which they are applicable, and in which they are not inconsistent with the standing rules and orders of this Commission.

20. The yeas and nays may be called for by any member.

21. A majority of the members shall constitute a quorum.

22. Every article shall receive three several readings previous to its being passed, and the second and third readings shall be on different days.

23. Every article when read a third time and passed, shall be referred, for arrangement only, to the committee on arrangement and phraseology.

24. No proposition or amendment shall be finally adopted without a vote of two-thirds of the members of the Commission, on which the yeas and nays shall be recorded.

25. There shall be six standing committees, composed of three members each, to whom shall be referred the various articles of the Constitution; to

Committee No. 1—Legislative; Boundaries; Seat of Government; and Division of Powers of Government.

Committee No. 2—Judicial; Militia; and Miscellaneous.

Committee No. 3—Finance and Taxation; Salaries; and Exemptions.

Committee No. 4—Corporations; Railroads; and Elections.

Committee No. 5—Executive; State Officers; Counties and Townships; Impeachments and Removals from Office.

Committee No. 6—Education; Amendments and Revisions; and Schedule; to which committee is added Arrangement and Phraseology and Supplies.

Your committee recommend that the Constitution of the State be first referred to the committee of the whole and taken up section by section, as preparatory work.

All of which is respectfully submitted.

S. L. WITHEY,
H. H. RILEY,
EDWIN WILLITS,
Committee on Rules.

LANSING, *Aug. 28, 1873.*

On motion of Mr. Pond,

The report was adopted.

ASSISTANT CLERK AND CHAIRMAN'S MESSENGER.

On motion of Mr. Withey,

The Clerk was authorized to employ an assistant, and the Chairman a Messenger.

APPOINTMENTS.

The Chairman announced the following appointments:

Door-keeper and Janitor—William D. Burnham.

Chairman's Messenger—David S. Barry.

Messengers—Frank Rice, George P. Brown.

The Clerk appointed:

Clerk's Messenger—Frank H. Jenison.

STATIONERY.

On motion of Mr. Willits,

Resolved, That the Clerk of the Commission is hereby authorized and instructed to furnish the Commission with stationery for immediate use.

PRINTING THE DAILY JOURNAL.

On motion of Mr. Upson,

Resolved, That the State Printer be directed to print 800 copies of the Daily Journal of proceedings of this Commission, and to supply five copies to each member and the clerk thereof; also, to send by mail, or otherwise, one copy to every Senator and Representative in the Legislature, every State Officer and member of a State Board, every Senator and Representative in Congress, every Judge of the Supreme, Circuit, and Probate Courts, every County Clerk, every charitable institution, College, University, and incorporated Seminary of learning, and every newspaper in the State of Michigan.

On motion of Mr. Pond,

Resolved, That the committee on supplies be instructed to procure 100 copies of the present Constitution to be printed, for the use of the Commission, in the form usually adopted in the printing of bills for the Legislature.

On motion of Mr. Withey,

The Commission resolved itself into committee of the whole, and proceeded, Mr. Withey in the chair, to consider the present State Constitution.

IN COMMITTEE OF THE WHOLE.

The Constitution of 1850 was considered section by section, to the end of Article IV.

On motion of Mr. Willits,

The committee rose.

IN COMMISSION.

The Chairman took the chair, and

Mr. Withey reported that the committee of the whole had had under consideration the first four articles of the Constitution, had made some progress therein, and asked leave to sit again.

On motion of Mr. Willits,

The report was adopted.

A LECTURE ON NATURAL HISTORY.

The Chairman announced the following communication:

LANSING, *Aug. 28, 1873.*

President of the Constitutional Convention :

I would respectfully request the use of the Senate Chamber this evening, for the purpose of a public lecture on Natural History, by Prof. Beals of the Agricultural College, before the teachers of the Institute now in session in this city.

Very respectfully yours,

E. V. W. BROKAW,

Superintendent City Schools.

On motion of Mr. Withey,

The request was granted.

On motion of Mr. Pond,

The Commission took a recess until 2 o'clock.

AFTERNOON SESSION.

Commission met at two o'clock.

Roll called: Quorum present.

On motion of Mr. Hatch,

The Commission resolved itself into committee of the whole, and proceeded, Mr. Jerome in the chair, to the consideration of the present State Constitution.

IN COMMITTEE OF THE WHOLE.

The reading of the Constitution was resumed at Article V.

On motion of Mr. Meddaugh,

The reading of Sec. 2, Article VI., was dispensed with.

On motion of Mr. Pond,

Article VII., on elections, was passed over.

On motion of Mr. Pond,

The first eight sections of Article X. were passed over.

On motion of Mr. Pond,

Articles XI. and XII. were passed over.

On motion of Mr. Riley,

The committee rose.

IN COMMISSION.

Mr. Jerome reported that the committee of the whole having had under further informal consideration the present Constitution of the State, to and including Article XV., have directed me to report that fact back to the Commission, and ask leave to sit again.

Report adopted.

On motion of Mr. Hatch,

The Commission adjourned until to-morrow morning at 9 o'clock.

THIRD DAY.

LANSING, *Friday, August 29, 1873.*

The Commission was called to order at 9 o'clock.

Roll called: quorum present.

On motion of Mr. Withey,

The reading of yesterday's journal was dispensed with.

COMMITTEE ON FINANCE.

On motion of Mr. Withey,

The Chairman of the Commission was designated as a member of the Committee on Finance and Taxation.

REVISION AND CLASSIFICATION.

On motion of Mr. Willits,

Resolved, That a Committee of Five be appointed on the Revision, Classification, and Arrangement of the Constitution and Schedule as a whole, and that so much of these subjects as are assigned to Committee No. 6 be withdrawn from the consideration of the same.

INCORPORATIONS.

On motion of Mr. Jerome,

Resolved, That the Committee on Corporations be increased to five members.

DAILY SESSIONS.

On motion of Mr. Crouse,

Resolved, That the Sessions of the Commission shall commence at 9 o'clock A. M., and 2.30 o'clock P. M., until otherwise ordered.

On motion of Mr. Withey,

The Commission resolved itself into a committee of the whole and proceeded, Mr. Riley in the Chair, to the consideration of the State Constitution.

IN COMMITTEE OF THE WHOLE.

The consideration of the State Constitution was resumed at Article XVI.

On motion of Mr. Devereaux,

The first six sections of Article XIX. were passed over.

On motion of Mr. Pond,

Article XX. was passed over.

On motion of Mr. Meddaugh,

The schedule was passed over.

On motion of Mr. Withey,

The committee rose.

IN COMMISSION.

The Commission was called to order by the Chairman.

Mr. Riley reported that the committee of the whole had had under consideration the Constitution from Article XV., and asked to be discharged from the further consideration of the subject.

Report accepted and the committee discharged.

The chairman announced the following:

STANDING COMMITTEES.

No. 1. Legislation, Boundaries, Seat of Government, and Division of Powers of Government—Messrs. UPSON, DIVINE, CROUSE.

No. 2. Judicial, Militia, and Miscellaneous—Messrs. WITHEY, HATCH, POND.

No. 3. Finance and Taxation, Salaries and Exemptions—Messrs. JEROME, MASON, UPSON,—CUTCHEON (by vote).

No. 4. Corporations, Railroads, and Elections — Messrs. MEDDAUGH, RILEY, WITHEY, WOODARD, DEVEREAUX.

No. 5. Executive, State Officers, Counties and Townships, Impeachments, and Removals from Office—Messrs. WELLS, CRANE, WOODARD.

No. 6. Education and Supplies—Messrs. WILLITS, MOFFATT, RILEY.

No. 7. Arrangement, Classification, etc.—Messrs. Pond, Hatch, Divine, Moffatt, Crane.

EMPLOYMENT OF A STENOGRAPHER.

Mr. Meddaugh offered the following resolution:

Resolved, That the Commission employ a stenographer, who shall take down and transcribe such of the proceedings of the Commission as the Commission shall direct.

On motion of Mr. Riley,

The Resolution was laid on the table.

APPOINTMENT OF ASSISTANT CLERK.

The Chair announced the following communication from the Clerk:

Senate Chamber,
Lansing, Aug. 28, 1873.

To the Chairman of the Constitutional Convention:

Mr. Chairman:—I have this day appointed Mr. S. B. McCracken of Detroit, as Assistant Clerk to the Constitutional Commission, pursuant to resolution passed this forenoon.

Very respectfully yours,

HENRY S. CLUBB,
Clerk of the Commission.

PRINTING THE CONSTITUTION.

Mr. Withey moved to rescind the resolution adopted yesterday, ordering the Constitution printed in bill form, and to substitute the following:

Resolved, That the Committee on Supplies be instructed to procure 200 copies of the present Constitution, and a like number of the Constitution proposed in 1867, to be printed for the use of the Commission, in the form usually adopted in printing bills for the Legislature, to be printed on one side only of the leaf;

Which motion prevailed.

EXCUSED.

On motion of Mr. Withey,

Mr. Divine was excused from attendance until one week from next Monday.

PRINTING THE RULES.

On motion of Mr. Upson,

Resolved, That the Clerk be instructed to cause a sufficient number of lists of the committees appointed, with the rules adopted by the Commission, to be printed for the use of the members.

LEGISLATIVE DEPARTMENT.

Mr. Jerome moved that the committee on the Legislative Department be requested to consider and report upon the expediency of amending Section 2, Article IV., as follows:

1st. Provide for the election of thirty-two Senators.

2d. At the first session after the adoption of this amendment, said Senators shall be divided by lot into three classes, as follows:

First class to hold office for two years. Second class to hold office for four years. Third class to hold office for six years.

3d. After said classification Senators shall be elected for six years.

The motion prevailed.

REFERENCE TO COMMITTEES.

The chairman announced the reference of the several divisions of the Constitution to the appropriate committees.

ADJOURNMENT.

On motion of Mr. Riley,

The Commission adiourned until to-morrow morning at 9 o'clock.

FOURTH DAY.

LANSING, *Saturday, August 30, 1873.*

Mr. Willits called the Commission to order at 9 o'clock.

Roll called: Not a quorum present.

On motion of Mr. Jerome,

The Commission adjourned until half past two o'clock, P. M., on Monday next.

FIFTH DAY.

LANSING, *Monday, September 1, 1873.*

The Commission was called to order at 2:30 o'clock, by Mr. Willits, Chairman *pro tem.*

Roll called: not a quorum present.

On motion of Mr. Riley,

The Commission adjourned until half-past two o'clock p. m., to-morrow.

SIXTH DAY.

LANSING, *Tuesday, Sept. 2, 1873.*

The Commission was called to order at 2:30 o'clock.

Roll called: quorum present.

On motion of Mr. Moffatt,

The reading of the daily journal was dispensed with until otherwise ordered.

EDUCATION.

By the committee on education:

The committee on education, to whom was referred

Article XIII. of the State Constitution,

Respectfully report that they have had the same under consideration, and have directed me to report the same back to the Commission with amendments thereto, recommending that the amendments be concurred in, and that the article, when so amended, do pass, and ask to be discharged from the further consideration of the subject.

EDWIN WILLITS, *Chairman.*

Report accepted and committee discharged.

The article was read first and second time, ordered printed, referred to the committee of the whole, and placed on the general order.

SPECIFIC TAXES.

On motion of Mr. Moffatt,

Resolved, That the Committee on Finance and Taxation be instructed to inquire into the expediency of abolishing all specific taxes.

STATE PRISON IN THE UPPER PENINSULA.

On motion of Mr. Devereaux,

Resolved, That the Legislative committee consider the propriety of inserting an article in the Constitution of the State of Michigan, authorizing the Legislature to establish a State Prison at some central point in the Upper Peninsula.

COMMISSION JOURNAL IN OCTAVO FORM.

On motion of Mr. Crane,

The State printer was instructed to print five hundred and twenty-five copies of the library edition of the journal of the Commission.

SCHOOL LAWS OF THE STATE.

The Chairman submitted the following:

OFFICE OF SUPT. OF PUBLIC INSTRUCTION,
Lansing, August 29, 1873.

HON. S. M. CUTCHEON,
Chairman of Constitutional Commission:

SIR,—I transmit herewith eighteen copies of the School

Laws, revised edition of 1873, for the use of the Commission.

Very respectfully yours,
DANIEL B. BRIGGS,
Supt. of Public Instruction.

ADJOURNMENT.

On motion of Mr. Willits,

The Commission adjourned.

SEVENTH DAY.

LANSING, *Sept. 3, 1873.*

The Commission was called to order at 9 o'clock, by the Chairman.

Roll called: quorum present.

EXECUTIVE DEPARTMENT.

By the committee on executive department:

The committee on executive department to whom was referred

Article V. of the State Constitution,

Respectfully report that they have had the same under consideration, and have directed me to report the same back to the Commission, with amendments thereto, recommending that the amendments be concurred in, and that the Article, when so amended, do pass, and ask to be discharged from the further consideration of the subject.

H. G. WELLS, *Chairman.*

Read twice, ordered printed, placed on the general order, and referred to the committee of the whole.

PRINTING.

On motion of Mr. Jerome,

Resolved, That unless otherwise ordered, all propositions introduced by members of the Commission be printed in full in the journal, and that all Articles, or amendments reported by committees, be ordered printed in bill form, placed upon the general order, and referred to the committee of the whole.

LEAVE OF ABSENCE.

On motion of Mr. Riley,

Leave of absence was granted for two days for Messrs. Hatch and Upson.

On motion of Mr. Willits,

Indefinite leave of absence was granted to Messrs. Meddaugh and Pond.

On motion of Mr. Withey,

Leave of absence was granted to Mr. Mason for to-day.

ANNUAL SESSIONS.

Mr. Devereaux offered the following:

Resolved, That the Committee on legislative power be instructed to report in favor of annual sessions of the Legislature.

Mr. Moffatt moved to lay the resolution on the table;

Which motion did not prevail.

The question recurring on the adoption of the resolution,

Mr. Moffatt demanded the yeas and nays.

The resolution did not prevail, as follows:

YEAS.

Mr. Devereaux,	Mr. Riley,	Mr. Withey.	
Jerome,			4

NAYS.

Mr. Crane,	Mr. Moffatt,	Mr. Willits,	
Cutcheon,	Wells,	Woodard.	6

INSTRUCTION IN THE INDUSTRIAL ARTS.

On motion of Mr. Wells,

Resolved, That the committee on education be instructed to inquire into the expediency of requiring, by constitutional enactment, that the Legislature shall provide for instruction in the science of architecture, in mechanical drawing, and in other of the industrial arts.

LICENSING THE SALE OF LIQUORS.

On motion of Mr. Crane,

Resolved, That the legislative committee be requested to report to the Commission the expediency of so amending Sec. 47 of Article 4 of the existing Constitution of this State, as to empower the Legislature to authorize the granting of licenses for the sale of spirituous liquors upon the following conditions:

1st. That the question of license or no license shall be submitted to the electors of any city, village, or town, in the manner to be provided by law;

2d. If a majority of such electors are in favor of licensing the traffic in their respective municipalities, then the proper authorities of such municipality to have the exclusive control of the granting of licenses, and the moneys arising therefrom to enter into the general fund of such city, etc.;

3d. When the electors, etc., shall be opposed to licensing the traffic, then as to such city, village, etc., prohibitory laws to be in force.

SPECIAL LEGISLATION.

Mr. Riley offered the following resolution:

Resolved, That the legislative committee be instructed to report the following to stand as one of the sections in the legislative department:

The Legislature shall not pass local or special laws in any of the following enumerated cases, that is to say: For

1st. Divorcing any named party;

2d. Changing the names of persons or places;

3d. Laying out, opening, altering, working, obstructing, or vacating roads, highways, streets, or alleys, or public grounds, or buildings, or repairing bridges, or for draining swamps or other low lands;

4th. Regulating internal affairs of towns or counties;

5th. Regulating the practice in courts of justice, or regulating the jurisdiction of justices of the peace, police magistrates, or constables;

6th. Providing for changes of venue in civil or criminal cases;

7th. Incorporating cities or villages, or changing or amending the charter of any city or village;

8th. Providing for the election of members of boards of supervisors;

9th. Summoning and impaneling grand or petit jurors;

10th. Providing for the management and support of common schools;

11th. Regulating the rate of interest on money;

12th. The opening and conducting of any election, or designating the place of voting;

13th. The sale or mortgage of real estate belonging to minors or others under disability;

14th. Protection of game or fish;

15th. Chartering or licensing ferries or toll bridges;

16th. Remitting fines, penalties, or forfeitures;

17th. Creating, increasing, or decreasing fees, per centages, or allowances of public officers during the term for which said officers are elected or appointed;

18th. Changing the law of descent;

19th. Granting to any corporation, association, or individual the right to lay down railroad track, or amending charters for any such purpose;

20th. Granting to any corporation, association, or individual any special or exclusive privilege, immunity, or franchise whatever;

21st. Declaring any named person of age;

22d. Authorizing any named minor to sell, lease, or incumber his or her property;

23d. Extending the time for the assessment or collection of

taxes, or otherwise relieving any assessor or collector of taxes from the due performance of his official duties;

25th. Giving effect to any informal will or deed;

26th. Legalizing, except as against the State, the unauthorized or invalid acts of any officer;

27th. Punishing crimes or misdemeanors;

28th. Legitimatizing any person not born in lawful wedlock;

29th. Adopting by any person any named person as his child or heir;

30th. The exception of any named locality from the operation of a general law.

On motion of Mr. Willits,

The resolution was ordered printed in bill form and laid on the table.

FEMALE SUFFRAGE.

On motion of Mr. Willits,

Resolved, That the committee on elections is directed to inquire into the expediency of so amending the Article of the present Constitution entitled "Elections," so as to read as follows:

The Legislature of 1875 shall by law provide a registration in their respective towns, wards, and election districts, at the time of the registration of the qualified voters of the State for the annual township elections of 1877, of all the females who have the same qualifications as too age, citizenship, and residence as males in this Constitution; which said registration shall be in a separate book, to be provided for that purpose, and on the day of the annual township elections for the year one thousand eight hundred and seventy-seven, the question whether the word "male" shall be stricken out of this Constitution, where it is a qualification for voting, shall be submitted to the females so registered; and if a majority of the females so registered in the whole State shall vote in favor of the same, the word "male," where it occurs in said Article as a qualification for voting, shall no longer be a part of this Constitution. The Legislature aforesaid shall also provide for a correct canvass of said registration, and the votes cast as aforesaid on said proposition.

ADDITIONAL SENATE DISTRICT.

On motion of Devereaux,

Resolved, That the committee on legislative matters be asked to inquire into the justice of increasing the senatorial districts in the State of Michigan, so as to permit the Upper Peninsula two Senators to represent it at Lansing.

On motion of Mr. Crane,

The Commission adjourned.

AFTERNOON SESSION.

The Commission was called to order at 2:30 P. M., by the Chairman.

APPEARED AND QUALIFIED.

The following additional member being present, took and subscribed the oath of office, and took his seat:

Seventh District—Edwin W. Giddings, of Macomb.

LEAVE OF ABSENCE.

On motion of Mr. Withey,

Further leave of absence was granted to Mr. Mason for the balance of the present week, on account of sickness in his family.

ADJOURNMENT.

On motion of Mr. Willits,

The Commission adjourned.

EIGHTH DAY.

LANSING, *September 4, 1873.*

The Commission was called to order at 9 o'clock, by the Chairman.

Roll called: quorum present.

FINANCE AND TAXATION.

By the committee on finance and taxation:

The committee on finance and taxation, to whom was referred Article IX., on salaries,

Respectfully report that they have had the same under consideration, and have directed me to report the same back to the Commission with amendment theretc, recommending that the amendment be concurred in, and that the Article, when so amended, do pass, and ask to be discharged from the further consideration of the subject.

D. H. JEROME,
Chairman of Committee.

Report accepted and committee discharged.

The article was read a first and second time, ordered printed, referred to the committee of the whole, and placed on the general order.

THE WORK OF THE COMMISSION.

Mr. Moffatt offered the following:

Resolved, That it is the sense of this Commission that we amend and not revise the Constitution of 1850.

The resolution was not adopted.

SUBSCRIPTIONS OF STOCK BY MUNICIPAL CORPORATIONS.

Mr. Withey offered the following resolution:

Resolved, That the committee on the legislative department be instructed to inquire into the propriety of reporting a section that "the Legislature shall not authorize any county, city, township, or muncipality to become a stockholder in, or lend its credit, or make any donation to any private company, corporation, or association."

The resolution was adopted.

FEMALE SUFFRAGE.

Mr. Crouse offered the following resolution:

Resolved, That the committee on elections be instructed to inquire into the expediency of striking out the word "male," wherever it occurs in section 1, article 7, of the Constitution of this State; also, the words "Nor while confined in any public prison," in section 5 of the same article.

On motion of Mr. Crouse,

The resolution was laid on the table.

TRIALS BY JURY.

Mr. Withey offered the following resolution:

Resolved, That the committee on the legislative department be instructed to inquire into the expediency of reporting a section that "the right of trial by jury shall be inviolate, but the Legislature may provide for juries in civil causes composed of any number of jurors not less than six, and that the agreement of not less than two-thirds of any jury in any civil case, shall be sufficient for verdict."

The resolution was adopted.

GENERAL ORDER.

On motion of Mr. Withey,

The Commission resolved itself into committee of the whole, on the general order, and proceeded, Mr. Crane in the chair, to consider the report of the committee on education, being general order No. 1, Article XIII., on education.

After some time spent therein the committee rose, and

Mr. Crane reported that the committee of the whole had had under consideration Article XIII., had made some progress therein, and asked leave to sit again.

Report accepted and leave granted.

RULE FOURTEEN RESCINDED.

Mr. Crane moved to rescind rule fourteen ;

Two-thirds of the members present having voted in favor of the motion,

Rule fourteen was rescinded.

On motion of Mr. Devereaux,

The Commission took a recess until 2:30 o'clock this afternoon.

AFTERNOON SESSION.

Commission was called to order at 2:30 o'clock by the Chair man.

Roll called ; quorum present.

PROCEEDINGS IN COMMITTEE OF THE WHOLE.

On motion of Mr. Jerome,

The clerk was instructed to omit from the journal of this morning, proceedings in committee of the whole.

GENERAL ORDER.

On motion of Mr. Jerome,

The Commission resolved itself into committee of the whole on the general order, and proceeded, Mr. Crane in the chair, to the consideration of Article XIII., on education.

After some time spent therein, the committee rose, and the Commission was called to order by the Chairman.

REPORT OF THE COMMITTEE OF THE WHOLE.

The committee of the whole, to whom was referred Article XIII., as reported by the committee on education,

Respectfully report that they have had the same under consideration, and have directed me to report the same back to the Commission, with amendments thereto, recommending that the amendments be concurred in, and ask to be discharged from the further consideration of the subject.

ISAAC M. CRANE,
Chairman of Committee.

Report accepted and committee discharged.

The amendments were concurred in.

PRINTING THE AMENDED ARTICLE.

Mr. Moffatt moved that the article, as amended, be printed and placed on the order of third reading.

The motion prevailed.

Mr. Withey moved that the action of the committee of the whole, in regard to Article XIII. of the present Constitution be printed as a substitute.

The motion was informally agreed to.

ADJOURNMENT.

On motion of Mr. Willits,

The Commission adjourned.

NINTH DAY.

LANSING, *Friday, September 5, 1873.*

The Commission was called to order at 9 o'clock by the Chairman.

Roll called: quorum present.

JUDICIAL DEPARTMENT.

By the committee on the judicial department:

The committee on the judicial department, to whom was referred Article VII. of the Constitution,

Respectfully report that they have had the same under consideration, and have directed me to report the same back to the Commission with amendments thereto, recommending that the amendments be concurred in, and that the article when so amended do pass, and ask to be discharged from the further consideration of the subject.

S. L. WITHEY,
Chairman of Committee.

Report accepted and committee discharged.

The article was read a first and second time, ordered printed, referred to the committee of the whole, and placed on the general order.

FEMALE SUFFRAGE.

Mr. Crouse moved that the resolution offered by him yesterday, relative to female suffrage, be taken from the table, and that the same be referred to the committee on elections.

The motion prevailed.

SPECIAL LEGISLATION.

Mr. Willits moved that the resolution offered by Mr. Riley on Wednesday, proposing an article relative to special legislation, which was ordered printed and laid on the table, be taken from the table and placed on the general order.

The motion prevailed.

COMMITTEE OF THE WHOLE.

On motion, the Commission resolved itself into committee of the whole, and proceeded, Mr. Moffatt in the chair, to the consideration of general orders.

After some time spent therein, the committee rose, and, through their chairman, made the following report:

REPORT OF THE COMMITTEE OF THE WHOLE.

The committee of the whole, to whom wss referred Article V., relating to Executive Department,

Respectfully report that they have had the same under consideration, and have directed me to report the same back to the Commission with amendments thereto, recommending that the amendments be concurred in, and that the article, when so amended, do pass, and ask to be discharged from the further consideration of the subject.

S. C. MOFFATT,
Chairman of Committee.

Report accepted and committee discharged.

On motion of Mr. Jerome,

The amendments made to the article by the committee were concurred in.

On motion of Mr. Upson,

The article was ordered reprinted, and placed on the order of third reading.

LEAVES OF ABSENCE.

Mr. Withey asked and obtained leave of absence for himself until Wednesday next.

Mr. Crane asked and obtained leave of absence for himself until to-morrow noon.

Mr. Giddings asked and obtained leave of absence for himself until Wednesday next.

RAILROAD CONSOLIDATION.

Mr. Pond offered the following:

Resolved, That the committee on corporations be requested to report the following to stand as a section in the article upon corporations, to wit:

Sec. —. No railroad corporation shall be consolidated with, or shall acquire or hold stock in any other railroad corporation owning or controlling any parallel or competing line of road, nor shall any railroad corporation purchase or lease any such parallel or competing road.

The resolution was adopted.

GENERAL ELECTIONS.

Mr. Crane offered the following resolution:

Resolved, That the legislative committee be requested to inquire into the expediency of the following amendment to section one of Article XX.:

Add to said section the following words: "And for the purpose of submitting such amendments, the annual township meetings shall be taken and deemed to be a general election."

The resolution was adopted.

RECESS.

On motion of Mr. Upson,

A recess was taken until half-past two o'clock P. M.

AFTERNOON SESSION.

The Commission was called to order pursuant to adjournment.

Roll called: quorum present.

GENERAL ORDER.

On motion of Mr. Riley,

The Commission resolved itself into committee of the whole on the general order, Mr. Upson in the chair, and after some time spent therein, the committee rose and through their chairman made the following report:

REPORT OF THE COMMITTEE OF THE WHOLE.

The committee of the whole, to whom was referred Article IX. of salaries, general order No. 3,

Respectfully report that they have had the same under consideration, and have directed me to report the same back to the Commission without amendment, and recommend that the article do pass, and ask to be discharged from the further consideration of the subject.

CHAS. UPSON, *Chairman.*

Report accepted and committee discharged.

Mr. Jerome moved to amend by adding the following to the article, to stand as section 3:

Sec. 3. The compensation of the members of the Legislature shall be three dollars a day for actual attendance; and when absent on account of sickness [for the first sixty days of the session of the year one thousand eight hundred and fifty-one, and for the first forty days of every subsequent session, and nothing thereafter]; *but the Legislature may allow extra compensation to the members from the territory of the Upper Peninsula, not exceeding two dollars per day during the session.* When convened in extra session, their compensation shall be three dollars a day for the first twenty days, and nothing thereafter; and they shall legislate on no other subjects than those expressly stated in the Governor's proclamation, or submitted to them by special message. They shall be entitled to ten cents, and no more, for every mile actually traveled, going to and returning from the place of meeting, on the usually traveled route; and for stationery and newspapers, not exceeding five dollars for each member during any session. Each member shall be entitled to one copy of the laws, journals and documents of the Legislature of which he was a member; but shall not receive, at the expense of the State, books, newspapers, or other perquisites of office, not expressly authorized by this Constitution.

Which motion prevailed.

The article, as thus amended, was placed on the order of third reading.

REPORT OF THE COMMITTEE OF THE WHOLE.

The committee of the whole, to was referred resolution in reference to legislative limitations, general order No. 4,

Respectfully report that they have had the same under consideration, and have directed me to report the same back to the Commission with several amendments thereto, recommending that the amendments be concurred in, and that the resolution when so amended do pass, and ask to be discharged from the further consideration of the subject.

CHAS. UPSON,
Chairman of Committee.

Report accepted and committee discharged.

The resolution was then adopted as follows:

Resolved, That the legislative committee be instructed to report the following to stand as one of the sections in the legislative department:

The Legislature shall not pass local or special laws in any of the following enumerated cases, that is to say: For

1st. Divorcing any named party or upon the subject of divorce;

2d. Changing the names of persons or places;

3d. Laying out, opening, altering, working, obstructing, or vacating roads, highways, streets, or alleys, or public grounds, or buildings, or repairing bridges, or for draining swamps or other low lands;

4th. Regulating internal affairs of towns or counties;

5th. Regulating the practice in courts of justice, or regulating the jurisdiction of justices of the peace, or constables;

6th. Providing for changes of venue in civil or criminal cases;

7th. Incorporating cities or villages;

8th. Providing for the election or appointment of members of boards of supervisors;

9th. Summoning and impaneling grand or petit jurors;

10th. Providing for the management and support of common schools;

11th. Regulating the rate of interest on money;

12th. The opening and conducting of any election, or designating the place of voting;

13th. The sale or mortgage of real estate belonging to minors or others under disability;

14th. Protection of game or fish;

15th. Chartering or licensing ferries or toll bridges;

16th. Remitting fines, penalties, or forfeitures;

17th. Creating, increasing, or decreasing fees, percentages, or allowances of public officers during the term for which said officers are elected or appointed;

18th. Changing the law of descent;

19th. Granting to any corporation, association, or individual the right to lay down railroad track, or amending charters for any such purpose;

20th. Granting to any corporation, association, or individual any special or exclusive privilege, immunity, or franchise whatever;

21st. Declaring any named person of age;

22d. Authorizing any named minor to sell, lease, or incumber his or her property;

23d. Extending the time for the assessment or collection of taxes, or otherwise relieving any assessor or collector of taxes from the due performance of his official duties;

24th. Giving effect to any informal will or deed;

25th. Legalizing, except as against the State, the unauthorized or invalid acts of any officer;

26th. Punishing crimes or misdemeanors;

27th. Adopting by any person any named person as his child or heir;

28th. Nor shall the Legislature except any named locality from the operation of a general law.

LEAVES OF ABSENCE.

On motion of Mr. Woodward,

Indefinite leave of absence was granted to Mr. Crouse, on account of the death of a brother.

Mr. Woodard asked and obtained leave of absence for himself from to-morrow noon until Tuesday morning.

Mr. Pond asked and obtained leave of absence for himself until Thursday next.

Mr. Upson asked and obtained leave of absence for himself until Thursday morning next.

Mr. Meddaugh asked and obtained leave of absence for himself until Thursday morning next.

ADJOURNMENT.

On motion of Mr. Devereaux,

The Commission adjourned.

TENTH DAY.

LANSING, *Saturday, September 6, 1873.*

The Commission was called to order at 9 o'clock by Mr. Moffatt, Chairman *pro tem.*

Roll called: not a quorum present.

On motion of Mr. Riley,

The Commission adjourned until Monday afternoon, at 2:30 o'clock.

ELEVENTH DAY.

LANSING, *Monday, September 8, 1873.*

The Commission was called to order at 2:30 o'clock by Mr. Riley, Chairman *pro tem.*

Roll called: not a quorum present.

On motion of Mr. Hatch,

The Commission adjourned.

TWELFTH DAY.

LANSING, *Tuesday, September 9, 1873.*

The Commission was called to order at 9 o'clock by the Chairman.

Roll called: quorum present.

PREAMBLE AND BILL OF RIGHTS.

Mr. Hatch moved that the subject of Preamble and Bill of Rights be referred to the judiciary committee;

Which motion prevailed.

FOREIGN CORPORATIONS.

Mr. Willits offered the following resolution:

Resolved, That the committee on corporations are instructed to inquire into the expediency of reporting the following section to the article on corporations:

SEC. —. Corporations organized out of this State may be permitted to do business in this State under such limitations as may be prescribed by law; but no other or greater privilege shall at any time be granted to, or claimed by, any such corporation than are or shall be granted or belong to like corporations of this State; and such foreign corporations, and the corporators and stockholders thereof, shall be subject to all liabilities of like corporations, and the corporators and stockholders thereof, in this State, and may be required to furnish in this State ample security for such liabilities.

The resolution was adopted.

QUALIFICATIONS FOR OFFICE.

Mr. Willits offered the following resolution:

Resolved, That the Committee on Miscellaneous Provisions are instructed to inquire into and report on the expediency of reporting a section as follows:

SEC. —. No person shall be elected or appointed to fill any State, county, township, city, or village office in this State who shall not possess the qualifications of an elector: *Provided,* That females of the age, and other qualifications, except sex, of electors, may be appointed to the offices to which males are eligible by appointment.

The resolution was adopted.

PUBLIC OFFICERS AND RAILWAYS.

Mr. Willits offered the following resolution:

Resolved, That the Committee on Miscellaneous Provisions, are instructed to inquire into and report on the expediency of adding to the article on Miscellaneous Provisions the following section:

SEC —. No person while holding any office under the constitution or laws of this State shall accept any gratuitous service or pass from any railroad company, nor any commutation of such service at less rates than are at the same time offered to the public.

The resolution was not adopted.

GENERAL ORDER.

On motion of Mr. Hatch the Commission resolved itself into committee of the whole on the general order, Mr. Wells in the chair, and after some time spent therein the committee rose, and through their chairman submitted the following report:

REPORT OF THE COMMITTEE OF THE WHOLE.

The committee of the whole, to whom was referred Article VII., as reported by the committee on the judiciary,

Respectfully report that they have had the same under consideration, have made some progress therein, and have directed me to report that fact to the Commission, and asked leave to sit again.

H. G. WELLS, *Chairman.*

Report accepted and leave granted.

ADJOURNMENT.

On motion of Mr. Devereaux,

The Commission adjourned.

AFTERNOON SESSION.

The Commission was called to order by the chairman.

Roll called: quorum present.

REPORTS OF COMMITTEES.

By the committee on counties:

The committee on counties, to whom was referred Article X. of the Constitution of Michigan,

Respectfully report that they have had the same under consideration, and have directed me to report the same back to the Commission with amendment thereto, recommending that the amendment be concurred in, and that the article when so amended do pass, and ask to be discharged from the further consideration of the subject.

H. G. WELLS,
Chairman of Committee.

Report accepted and committee discharged.

The article was read a first and second time, ordered printed, referred to the committee of the whole, and placed on the general order.

By the committee on townships:

The committee on townships, to whom was referred Article XI. of the constitution of Michigan,

Respectfully report that they have had the same under consideration, and have directed me to report the same back to the Commission with amendment thereto, recommending that the amendment be concurred in, and that the article when so amended do pass, and ask to be discharged from the further consideration of the subject.

H. G. WELLS,
Chairman of Committee.

Report accepted and committee discharged.

The article was read first and second time, ordered printed, referred to the committee of the whole, and placed on the general order.

EXEMPTING UPPER PENINSULA FROM SPECIAL LEGISLATIVE PROHIBITIONS.

Mr. Devereaux offered the following resolution:

Resolved, That the Committee on Legislation be instructed to consider the expediency of exempting the Upper Peninsula of Michigan from the prohibitions relating to special legislation.

The resolution was adopted.

MINORITY REPRESENTATION.

Mr. Devereaux offered the following resolution:

Resolved, That the committee on elections be instructed to inquire and report upon the propriety of adopting a system of cumulative voting, with a view to give representation to minorities.

The resolution was adopted.

LEAVE OF ABSENCE.

On motion of Mr. Riley,

Indefinite leave of absence was granted to Mr. Willits.

ADJOURNMENT.

On motion of Mr. Devereaux,

The Commission adjourned.

THIRTEENTH DAY.

LANSING, *Wednesday, September 10, 1873.*

The Commission was called to order at 9 o'clock, by the Chairman.

Roll called: quorum present.

LEAVE OF ABSENCE.

On motion of Mr. Crane,

Mr. Mason was granted indefinite leave of absence, on account of sickness.

REPORTS OF STANDING COMMITTEES.

By the committee on impeachments and removals from office:

The committee on impeachments and removals from office, to whom was referred Article XII., impeachments and removals from office, respectfully report that they have had the same under consideration, and have directed me to report the same back to the Commission with amendment thereto, recommending that the amendment be concurred in, and that the article when so amended do pass, and ask to be discharged from the further consideration of the subject.

H. G. WELLS,
Chairman of Committee.

Report accepted and committee discharged.

The article was read a first and second time, ordered printed, referred to the committee of the whole, and placed on the general order.

By the committee on exemptions:

The committee on exemptions, to whom was referred

Article XVI., on exemptions,

Respectfully report that they have had the same under consideration, and have directed me to report the same back to the Commission with amendments thereto, recommending that the amendments be concurred in, and that the article when so amended do pass, and ask to be discharged from the further consideration of the subject.

D. H. JEROME,
Chairman of Committee.

Report accepted and committee discharged.

The article was read a first and second time, ordered printed, referred to the committee of the whole, and placed on the general order.

By the committee on finance and taxation:

The committee on finance and taxation, to whom was referred Article XIV., on finance and taxation,

Respectfully report that they have had the same under consideration, and have directed me to report the same back to the Commission with amendments thereto, recommending that the amendments be concurred in, and that the article when so amended do pass, and ask to be discharged from the further consideration of the subject.

D. H. JEROME,
Chairman of Committee.

Report accepted and committee discharged.

The article was read a first and second time, ordered printed, referred to the committee of the whole, and placed on the general order.

PARDONS.

Mr. Hatch offered the following resolution:

Resolved, That the following propositions and regulations be embodied in and made a part of Article V., entitled "Executive Department," viz:

"Whenever application shall be made to the Governor for the pardon of one under sentence of imprisonment for life, upon conviction for willful and deliberate murder, such application may be referred by the Governor to the Supreme Court, and notice thereof shall be given to the Attorney General.

The Supreme Court shall fix a time and place for hearing such application, and may order the testimony of witnesses, touching the merits of such application, to be taken either orally in open court, or upon deposition.

If the said court is of opinion that under the principles, hereinafter stated, the said prisoner should be pardoned, or his sentence mitigated, such opinion shall be entered upon the journal of said court, and certified to the Governor. The Governor may in his discretion grant the pardon recommended, or refuse it altogether.

The Governor, in the cases above specified, shall have no power to grant a pardon without taking the opinion of said Supreme Court in relation thereto in the manner hereinbefore provided, nor shall he have power to grant a pardon or mitigate the sentence of any prisoner in such case, to any greater extent than that recommended in the opinion of said court.

In the cases above specified, no pardon or mitigation of sentence shall be granted unless it shall be made to appear:

1st. That there was some mistake of law, or of fact made by the court or jury who tried the cause, and which being correctly understood would dictate an acquittal, or conviction for a less offense;

2d. That the punishment imposed is disproportionate to the moral guilt of the prisoner; or

3d. That there are strong and controlling considerations relating to the prisoner which, under the dictates of humanity, require his enlargement or relief.

The resolution was adopted.

LIMITATION OF MUNICIPAL INDEBTEDNESS.

Mr. Hatch offered the following resolution:

Resolved, That the committee on finance be instructed to inquire into the propriety of adopting the following section:

SEC. —. No county, township, city, village, school district, municipal or other public corporation shall have power to become indebted to an amount exceeding ——— per cent of the assessed valuation of the property within such county, township, or other corporation; and in the construction of this section, all public corporations, excepting counties, townships, and school districts, embracing the same territory, shall be taken to be one corporation.

The resolution was adopted.

EDUCATION.

Article XIII., relative to education, being first on the order,

Mr. Jerome moved that the Article be taken from the order of third reading and referred to the committee of the whole, together with the substitute therefor,

Which motion prevailed.

SALARIES.

Article IX., relative to salaries, being next on the order of third reading,

Mr. Riley, by unanimous consent, moved to amend the article by striking out the word "salary" where the same occurs respectively in the fourth line of section one, and in the second line of section two, and insert in lieu thereof, in each case, the word "salaries;"

Which motion prevailed.

Mr. Jerome, by unanimous consent, moved to further amend the article by adding thereto two new sections, to stand as sections four and five, as follows:

SEC. 4. The President of the Senate and Speaker of the House of Representatives shall be entitled to the same per diem compensation and mileage as members of the Legislature, and no more;

SEC. 5. The Lieutenant Governor and President *pro tempore* of the Senate, when performing the duties of Governor, shall receive the same compensation as the Governor;

Which motion prevailed.

Mr. Withey moved to re-commit the article to the committee on salaries, with instructions to amend by striking out the word "three" in all cases where the same occurs before the word "dollars," in section three, and insert in lieu thereof in each case the word "four;"

Which motion did not prevail.

Mr. Moffatt moved to re-commit the article to the committee on salaries, with instructions to amend the same by striking out the word "three" in all cases where the same occurs before the word "dollars," in section three, and insert in lieu thereof in each case the word "five;"

Which motion prevailed.

Mr. Crane moved further to instruct the committee to strike out the provision relating to mileage;

Which motion did not privailed.

GENERAL ORDER.

On motion of Mr. Withey,

The Commission resolved itself into committee of the whole, on the general order, Mr. Woodard in the chair, and after some time spent therein the comittee rose and through their chairman made the following report:

REPORT OF THE COMMITTEE OF THE WHOLE.

The committee of the whole have had under consideration

Article VII. of the Judicial Department, and having made some progress therein, have directed me to report that fact to the Commission, and ask leave to sit again.

LYSANDER WOODWARD, *Chairman.*

Report accepted and leave granted.

RECESS.

On motion of Mr. Giddings,

The Commission took a recess until 2:30, P. M.

AFTERNOON SESSION.

The Commission was called to order by the chairman at 2.30.

Roll called; quorum present.

GENERAL ORDER.

On motion of Mr. Moffatt,

The Commission resolved itself into committee of the whole on the general order, and after some time spent therein, the committee rose, and through their chairman, made the following report:

REPORT OF THE COMMITTEE OF THE WHOLE.

The committee of the whole have had under consideration,

Article VII. of the Judicial Department,

Have made sundry amendments thereto, and have directed me to report the same back to the Commission, recommending that the amendments be concurred in, and that the article when so amended do pass, and ask to be discharged from the further consideration of the subject.

L. WOODWARD,

Chairman of Committee.

Report accepted and committee discharged.

Mr. Jerome moved that the article be reprinted and placed on the order of third reading.

Which motion prevailed.

ADDITION TO RULES.

Mr. Moffatt moved to add a new rule to the rules of the Commission, providing that amendments may be entertained to articles on the order of third reading, when supported by a majority of the members present;

Which motion prevailed.

LEAVES OF ABSENCE.

On motion of Mr. Withey,

Mr. Crane was granted leave of absence for to-morrow.

Mr. Withey offered the following resolution:

Resolved, That no further leave of absence be granted to members of the Commission, unless for reasons deemed imperative.

The resolution was adopted.

On motion of Mr. Crane,

The Commission adjourned.

FOURTEENTH DAY.

LANSING, *Thursday, September 11, 1873.*

The Commission was called to order at 9 o'clock, by the Chairman.

Roll called: quorum present.

LEAVE OF ABSENCE.

On motion of Mr. Meddaugh,

Mr. Pond was granted further leave of absence until Tuesday of next week, on account of imperative business engagements arising before his connection with the Commission.

On motion of Mr. Upson,

Mr. Meddaugh was granted leave of absence from and after to-day, until Tuesday of next week, for reasons similar to those in the case of Mr. Pond.

AMENDMENTS OF RULES.

Mr. Riley offered the following resolution:

Resolved, That Rule 23 be so amended as to read as follows:

23. Every article when read a third time, and perfected by amendments, shall, before it is put on its passage, be referred to the committee on phraseology, and after its passage shall be referred to the committee on arrangement and classification.

Two-thirds of the members present voting in the affirmative, the resolution was adopted.

APPOINTMENT OF JUDGES.

Mr. Hatch offered the following resolutions:

Resolved, That the article on the judicial department be so amended as to provide for the appointment of the judges of the Supreme Court by the Governor by and with the advise and consent of the Senate;

Resolved, That the article on judicial department be so amended as to provide for the appointment of the judges of the Circuit Courts by the Governor by and with the advise and consent of the Senate;

Mr. Upson offered the following as a substitute:

Resolved, That the Committee on the Judiciary be, and they are hereby instructed to propose an amendment to the article on the Judicial Department, providing for the appointment of the Judges of the Supreme and Circuit Courts by the Governor, by and with the advice and consent of the Senate, such amendment to be submitted to the electors as a separate proposition.

Which motion prevailed by yeas and nays as follows:

YEAS.

Mr. Cutcheon,	Mr. Jerome,	Mr. Upson,	
Divine,	Moffatt,	Woodward,	
Giddings,	Riley,		8

NAYS.

Mr. Crouse,	Mr. Hatch,	Mr. Wells,	
Devereaux,	Meddaugh,	Withey,	6

The question recurring on the adoption of the substitute, the same was adopted, by yeas and nays, as follows:

YEAS.

Mr. Crouse,	Mr. Hatch,	Mr. Upson,	
Cutcheon,	Jerome,	Wells,	
Divine,	Meddaugh,	Withey,	
Devereaux,	Moffatt,	Woodward,	
Giddings,	Riley,		14

NAYS. 0

EXECUTIVE DEPARTMENT.

Article V. of the Executive Department came up on the order of third reading.

Mr. Hatch asked leave to offer an amendment to the article.

Leave being granted,

Mr. Hatch moved to add the following to section eleven, to stand as a part of said section;

"Whenever application shall be made to the Governor for the pardon of one under sentence of imprisonment for life, upon conviction for willful and deliberate murder, such application may be referred by the Governor to the Supreme Court, and notice thereof shall be given to the Attorney General.

The Supreme Court shall fix a time and place for hearing such application, and may order the testimony of witnesses, touching the merits of such application, to be taken either orally in open court, or upon deposition.

If the said court is of opinion that under the principals, hereinafter stated, the said prisoner should be pardoned, or his sentence mitigated, such opinion shall be entered upon the journal of said court, and certified to the Governor. The Governor may in his discretion grant the pardon recommended, or refuse it altogether.

The Governor, in the cases above specified, shall have no power to grant a pardon without taking the opinion of said Supreme Court in relation thereto in the manner hereinbefore provided, nor shall he have power to grant a pardon or mitigate the sentence of any prisoner in such case, to any greater extent than that recommended in the opinion of said court.

In the cases above specified, no pardon or mitigation of sentence shall be granted unless it shall be made to appear:

1st, That there was some mistake of law, or of fact made by the court or jury who tried the cause, and which being correctly understood would dictate an acquittal, or conviction for a less offense;

2d, That the punishment imposed is disproportionate to the moral guilt of the prisoner; or

3d, That there are strong and controlling considerations relating to the prisoner which, under the dictates of humanity, require his enlargement or relief.

Which motion did not prevail.

The article was read a third time and referred to the committee on phraseology.

COMPENSATION TO MEMBERS OF THE LEGISLATURE.

The committee on finance and taxation to whom was recommitted Article IX., respectfully report that they have amended the same in accordance with the instruction of the Commission, and ask to be discharged from the further consideration of the subject.

D. H. JEROME, *Chairman.*

Report accepted and committee discharged.

The question being on concurring in the amendment made to the article by the committee,

Mr. Meddaugh moved that the subject be referred to the committee on legislative department.

Mr. Jerome moved to lay the motion on the table,

Which motion prevailed.

RECESS.

On motion of Mr. Woodward,

The Commission took a recess until 2:30 P. M.

AFTERNOON SESSION.

The Commission was called to order at 2:30 o'clock by the Chairman.

Roll called: quorum present.

COMPENSATION OF MEMBERS OF THE LEGISLATURE.

Mr. Jerome moved to take from the table the motion of Mr. Meddaugh, to refer the report of the committee on finance and taxation relative to compensation of members of the Legislature, submitted at the forenoon session, to the committee on legislative department.

The motion prevailed.

Mr. Meddaugh, with the consent of the committee, withdrew his motion.

The question being on concurring in the amendment made to Article IX., relative to salaries, by the committee, the same was not concurred in.

Mr. Upson asked leave to offer an amendment to the article.

Leave being granted,

Mr. Upson moved to amend the article by striking therefrom sections three, four, and five;

Which motion prevailed.

The article was then referred to the committee on phraseology.

GENERAL ORDER.

On motion of Mr. Jerome,

The Commission resolved itself into committee of the whole on the general order, Mr. Hatch in the chair, and after some time spent therein, the committee rose, and through their chairman made the following report:

REPORT OF THE COMMITTEE OF THE WHOLE.

The committee of the whole have had under consideration Article X., of Counties,

Have made sundry amendments thereto, and have directed me to report the same back to the Commission, recommending that the amendments be concurred in, and that the article, when so amended, do pass, and ask to be discharged from the further consideration of the subject.

The committee of the whole have also had under consideration Article XI., of Townships,

Have made no amendments thereto, and have directed me to report the same back to the Commission, recommending that it do pass, and ask to be discharged from the further consideration of the subject.

H. H. HATCH,
Chairman of Committee.

Report accepted and committee discharged.

On motion of Mr. Upson,

The amendments made to Article X. were concurred in, the article ordered reprinted, and placed on the order of third reading.

Article XI. was placed on the order of third reading.

ADJOURNMENT.

On motion of Mr. Jerome,

The Commission adjourned.

FIFTEENTH DAY.

LANSING, *Friday, September 12, 1873.*

The Commission was called to order at 9 o'clock by the Chairman.

Roll called: quorum present.

CORPORATIONS.

By the committee on corporations, railroads, and elections:

The committee on corporations, railroads, and elections, to whom was referred Article XV. of the State Constitution,

Respectfully report that they have had the same under consideration, and have directed me to report the same back to the Commission with amendments thereto, recommending that the amendments be concurred in, and that the article when so amended do pass, and ask to be discharged from the further consideration of the subject.

E. W. MEDDAUGH, *Chairman.*

Report accepted and committee discharged.

The article was read a first and second time, ordered printed, referred to the committee of the whole, and placed on the general order.

TOWNSHIPS.

Article XI. of Townships, being on the order of third reading, the same was read a third time, when

Mr. Woodward, leave being granted, moved to amend the same by inserting in the fourth line of section one, after the word "district," "and such other officers as the Legislature may by law provide;"

Which motion prevailed.

The article was referred to the committee on phraseology.

LEAVE OF ABSENCE.

On motion of Mr. Devereaux,

Mr. Crane was granted leave of absence for the day.

GENERAL ORDER.

On motion of Mr. Riley,

The Commmission resolved itself into committee of the whole, on the general order, Mr. Crouse in the chair, and after some time spent therein, the committee rose and through their chairman made the following report:

REPORT OF THE COMMITTEE OF THE WHOLE.

The committtee of the whole have had under consideration

Article XII., of Impeachments and Removals from Office, and

Article XVI., of Exemptions;

Have made sundry amendments thereto, and have directed me to report the same back to the Commission, recommending that the amendments be concurred in, and that the articles, when so amended, do pass, and ask to be discharged from the further consideration of the subject.

The committee of the whole have also had under consideration

Article XIV., of Finance and Taxation,

Have made some progress therein, but not having gone through therewith, have directed me to report that fact to the Commission, and ask leave to sit again.

IRA D. CROUSE, *Chairman.*

Report accepted.

The amendments made to the two first named articles were concurred in, except the first amendment to section two, Article XVI., striking out the words, "Not exceeding in value," and inserting in lieu thereof the words, "Not less in value than."

The question being on concurring in said amendment,

Mr. Jerome demanded the yeas and nays.

The amendment was concurred in by yeas and nays as follows:

YEAS.

Mr. Divine,	Mr. Moffatt,	Mr. Wells,	
Devereaux,	Riley,	Withey,	
Hatch,			7

NAYS.

Mr. Crouse,	Mr. Giddings,	Mr. Upson,	
Cutcheon,	Jerome,	Woodard,	6

Articles XII. and XVI. were placed on the order of third reading.

The request of the committee as to Article XIV. was granted.

RECESS.

On motion of Mr. Riley,

The Commission took a recess until 2:30 P. M.

AFTERNOON SESSION.

The Commission was called to order by the chairman at 2:30.

RECONSIDERED.

Mr. Hatch moved to reconsider the vote by which the Commission concurred in the first amendment to section two of Article XVI.;

Which motion prevailed.

The question being on concurring, the amendment was not concurred in.

GENERAL ORDER.

On motion of Mr. Withey,

The Commission resolved itself into committee of the whole on the general order, Mr. Crouse in the chair, and after some time spent therein, the committee rose, and through their chairman made the following report:

REPORT OF THE COMMITTEE OF THE WHOLE.

The committee of the whole have had under consideration Article XIV., of Finance and Taxation.

Have made sundry amendments thereto, and have directed me to report the same back to the Commission, recommending that the amendments be concurred in, and that the article, when so amended, do pass, and ask to be discharged from the further consideration of the subject.

IRA D. CROUSE,
Chairman of Committee.

Report accepted and committee discharged.

SPECIFIC TAXATION.

Mr. Moffatt offered the following resolution:

Resolved, That the article on finance and taxation be referred to the committee on finance and taxation, with instructions to amend the same so as to abolish specific taxation on property.

The resolution was not adopted, by yeas and nays, as follows:

YEAS.

Mr. Devereaux,	Mr. Moffatt.	Mr. Woodard,	3

NAYS.

Mr. Crouse,	Mr. Hatch,	Mr. Upson,	
Cutcheon,	Jerome,	Wells,	
Divine,	Riley,	Withey,	
Giddings,			10

On motion of Mr. Upson,

Article XIV. was ordered re-printed and placed on the order of third reading.

LEAVE OF ABSENCE.

Mr. Giddings asked and obtained leave of absence for himself, until Tuesday next.

ADJOURNMENT.

On motion of Mr. Upson,

The Commission adjourned.

SIXTEENTH DAY.

Lansing, *Saturday, September 13, 1873.*

The Commission was called to order at 9 o'clock, by the Chairman.

Roll called: quorum present.

BILL OF RIGHTS.

By the committee on bill of rights:

The committee on the judiciary, to whom was referred Article II., Bill of Rights,

Respectfully report that they have had the same under consideration, and have directed me to report the same back to the Commission with amendments thereto, recommending that the amendments be concurred in, and that the article when so amended do pass, and ask to be discharged from the further consideration of the subject.

S. L. WITHEY,
Chairman of Committee.

Report accepted and committee discharged.

CITIES.

By the committee on cities:

The committee on corporations, to whom was referred Article XVI., of "Cities,"

Respectfully report that they have had the same under consideration, and have directed me to report the same back to the Commission, with amendments thereto, recommending that the amendments be concurred in, and that the article when so amended do pass, and ask to be discharged from the further consideration of the subject.

E. W. MEDDAUGH,
Chairman of Committee.

Report accepted and committee discharged.

PREAMBLE.

The committee on the judiciary, to whom was referred the subject of preamble,

Respectfully report, that they have had the same under consideration, and have directed me to report the following, and recommend that the same do pass, and ask to be discharged from the further consideration of the subject.

S. L. WITHEY, *Chairman.*

Report accepted and committee discharged.

The articles and preamble were read a first and second time, ordered printed, referred to the committee of the whole, and placed on the general order.

APPOINTMENT OF JUDGES.

By the committee on judiciary department:

The committee on the judiciary department, to whom was

referred the resolution relating to an amendment of the article on judicial department, so as to provide for the appointment of judges,

Respectfully report that they have had the same under consideration, and have directed me to report the same back to the Commission, with a draft of such amendment, and recommending that the amendment be passed, and ask to be discharged from the further consideration of the subject.

H. H. HATCH,
for the Chairman of Committee.

Report accepted and committee discharged.

The amended section was ordered printed and referred to the committee of the whole.

LEGISLATION—BOUNDARIES—SEAT OF GOVERNMENT—DIVISION OF POWERS OF GOVERNMENT.

By the committee on legislation, boundaries, seat of government, and division of powers of government.

The committee on legislation, boundaries, seat of government, and division of powers of government, respectfully submit the following report of articles under those respective heads, to stand as Articles I., III., and IV., of the amended constitution.

CHARLES UPSON, *Chairman.*

The articles were read a first and second time, ordered printed, referred to the committee of the whole, and placed on the general order.

MOTIONS AND RESOLUTIONS.

Mr. Crouse offered the following resolution:

Resolved, That the committee on miscellaneous provisions be instructed to inquire into the expediency of providing that there be no distinction on account of sex with regard to the acquisition, possession, enjoyment, and disposition of property.

The resolution was adopted.

POWER TO INCREASE SUBJECTS OF TAXATION.

Mr. Jerome offered the following resolution:

Resolved, That the Clerk be directed, before its printing, to add at the end of Section 13, Article XIV., the following:

"The specification of the objects and subjects of taxation shall not deprive the Legislature of the power to require other subjects or objects to be taxed, in such manner as may be consistent with the principles of taxation fixed in this Constitution."

The resolution was adopted.

TIME FOR NEXT SESSION.

Mr. Hatch moved that when the Commission adjourn it be until Monday afternoon next;

Which motion prevailed.

ENROLLING CLERK.

Mr. Riley offered the following resolution:

Resolved, That the committe on arrangement and classification be authorized to employ an enrolling clerk, whose duty shall be to enroll each article of the Constitution as soon as the same is finally passed and ready for that purpose.

The resolution was adopted.

LEAVE OF ABSENCE.

Mr. Woodward asked and obtained leave of absence for himself until Tuesday morning.

COUNTIES.

Article X., of Counties, was read a third time.

On motion of Mr. Withey,

The article was laid on the table.

IMPEACHMENTS.

Article XII., of Impeachments and Removals from Office, was read a third time.

Mr. Upson, leave being granted, moved to amend the article by striking out of section eight all after the word "session," where the same occurs the second time in the sixth line of said section;

Which motion prevailed.

Mr. Upson moved to further amend the article, by striking out section eight and inserting the corresponding section of the present constitution;

Which motion prevailed.

The article was referred to the committee on phraseology.

EXEMPTIONS.

Article XVI., of exemptions, was read a third time.

On motion of Mr. Hatch,

The article was laid on the table.

DISPOSITION OF FINES.

By Mr. Crane presented the memorial of Geo. W. Squire, treasurer of Eaton Co., relative to disposition of fines.

On motion of Mr. Crane,

Referred to the committee on finance and taxation.

ADJOURNMENT.

On motion of Mr. Devereaux,

The Commission adjourned.

SEVENTEENTH DAY.

LANSING, *Monday, September 15, 1873.*

The Commission was called to order at 2:30 o'clock, by Mr. Withey.

Roll called: quorum present.

PETITIONS.

Mr. Crane presented the remonstrance of E. C. Manchester, Dr. J. V. Spencer, Dr. S. B. Thayer, and 31 other legal voters, and 20 ladies of Battle Creek, against omitting from the amended constitution the words, "but no money shall be appropriated for the payment of any religious services in either House of the Legislature," as the same stands in section 24 of Article IV., of the present constitution.

The remonstrance was received and ordered printed in the journal. It is as follows:

To the Honorable the Commission for Revising the Constitution of Michigan, in session at Lansing:

The undersigned, residents of Battle Creek, in the State of Michigan, have been advised that by the report of your committee on the article relating to the legislative department, it is proposed to omit from section 24 of said article, as it stands in the present Constitution, the words "but no money shall be appropriated for the payment of any religious services in either House of the Legislature."

Your memorialists respectfully represent that there are very many persons and voters in the State who would desire, and would petition for, an explicit declaration in the organic law, that the State government in all of its departments, and all institutions established by it, and maintained at the public expense, are purely secular, and that the State shall not directly or indirectly patronize or recognize any particular system of religious belief or practice. They would refrain from doing so, however, rather than provoke discussion on points of difference in a way to endanger the ultimate success of the good work which the people of the State have confidence will be presented for their acceptance at your hands.

In this spirit your memorialists would most respectfully but earnestly remonstrate against any change in the Constitution that may seem to be a concession in the opposite direction, and especially against the proposed change spoken of in the first sentence of this memorial, believing that such changes would awaken an opposition that might endanger the results of your labors.

Dated September 15, 1873.

Mr. Crane moved that the committee on exemptions be

instructed to report an amendment to section 4 of Article XVI., by adding to the said section the following:

"And the husband of any married woman shall not be liable for or on account of any debt or obligation of his wife contracted before her marriage, or contracted by her in relation to her sole property after marriage;"

Which motion prevailed.

GENERAL ORDER.

On motion of Mr. Moffatt,

The Commission resolved itself into committee of the whole on the general order, and after some time spent therein, the committee rose, and through their chairman, made the following report:

REPORT OF THE COMMITTEE OF THE WHOLE.

The committee of the whole have had under consideration, Article XIII., of Education,

Have made sundry amendments thereto, and have directed me to report the same back to the Commission, recommending that the amendments be concurred in, and that the article when so amended do pass, and ask to be discharged from the further consideration of the subject.

S. C. MOFFATT,
Chairman of Committee.

Report accepted and committee discharged.

The amendments made to the article were concurred in except as to the amendment by which the word "four" was inserted in lieu of the word "three," in the first line of section four.

The question recurring on concurring in said amendment, the same was not concurred in.

The article was placed on the order of third reading.

LEAVE OF ABSENCE.

Mr. Crouse asked and obtained leave of absence for himself until Thursday morning next.

ADJOURNMENT.

On motion of Mr. Upson,

The Commission adjourned.

EIGHTEENTH DAY.

LANSING, *Tuesday, September 16, 1873.*

The Commission was called to order at 9 o'clock, by the Chairman.

Roll called: quorum present.

MILITARY DEPARTMENT.

By the committee on military department:

The committee on judiciary, to whom was referred Article XIII., entitled "Military Department,"

Respectfully report that they have had the same under consideration, and have directed me to report the same back to the Commission without amendment, and recommend that the same do pass, and ask to be discharged from the further consideration of the subject.

S. L. WITHEY, *Chairman.*

Report accepted and committee discharged.

The article was referred to the committee of the whole, and placed on the general order.

THIRD READING OF ARTICLES—EDUCATION.

Article XIII., of Education,

Having been read a third time,

Mr. Pond asked leave to offer an amendment to the article.

Leave being granted.

Mr. Pond moved to amend the article by striking out of section two, to and including the word "office," and inserting in lieu thereof the following;

"The supervision and control of the University shall be

vested in a Board of Regents, to consist of the two *ex officio* members, herein provided for, and of eight elective members. The terms of office of the elective members —";

Mr. Wells moved that the article be reprinted and laid upon the table.

Which motion prevailed.

Mr. Withey moved that the vote by which the article was thus disposed of be reconsidered ;

Which motion prevailed.

The article was then referred to the committee on arrangement and phraseology, with instructions to have the same reprinted when revised by them.

JUDICIAL DEPARTMENT.

Article VII., of the Judicial Department, having been reached,

On motion of Mr. Hatch,

The same was laid on the table.

GENERAL ORDER.

On motion of Mr. Withey,

The Commission resolved itself into committee of the whole on the general order, and after some time spent therein the committee rose, and through their chairman made the following report:

REPORT OF THE COMMITTEE OF THE WHOLE.

The committee of the whole have had under consideration Article XV., of Corporations;

Have made sundry amendments thereto, and have directed me to report the same back to the Commission, recommending that the amendments be concurred in, and that the article when so amended do pass, and ask to be discharged from the further consideration of the subject.

The committee of the whole have also had under consideration

The preamble to the constitution;

Have made no amendments thereto, and have directed me to report the same back to the Commission, recommending that it do pass, and ask to be discharged from the further consideration of the subject.

CHAS. UPSON,
Chairman of Committee.

Report accepted and committee discharged.

The amendments made to Article XV. were concurred in, the article ordered reprinted, and placed on the order of third reading.

The preamble was placed on the order of third reading.

RECESS.

On motion of Mr. Riley,

The Commission took a recess until 2:30, P. M.

AFTERNOON SESSION.

The Commission was called to order at 2:30 P. M., by the Chairman.

Roll called: quorum present.

MUNICIPAL INDEBTEDNESS.

Mr. Hatch offered the following resolution:

Resolved, That the clerk cause to be printed and transmitted a circular letter to the principal cities and villages of the State requesting from them answers to the following questions:

First—What is the total assessed valuation in your municipality this year?

Second—What is the total amount of the indebtedness of your municipality now outstanding?

Third—What is the total amount of indebtedness of the school districts, board of water-works, and other public corporations within your municipality now outstanding?

The resolution was adopted.

LICENSING THE SALE OF LIQUORS.

Mr. Upson presented the following:

To the Commission for revising the State Constitution, now assembled in the city of Lansing:

I hereby certify that the following report of a committee appointed by the Michigan Annual Conference of the Methodist Episcopal Church, in conference assembled, in the city of Ionia, was adopted September 15th, 1873:

Your committee appointed to memorialize the Commission appointed by the Governor to advise amendments to the present constitution of the State, and now in session in the city of Lansing, on the subject of temperance, present the following resolution, viz:

Resolved, As the sense of this Conference, that no change in the constitutional provision in relation to the traffic in intoxicating drinks is desirable.

G. B. JOCELYN,
D. D. GILLETT.

J. I. BUELL, *Secretary of Conference.*

Ordered laid on the table and printed in the journal.

GENERAL ORDER.

On motion of Mr. Hatch,

The Commission resolved itself into committee of the whole on the general order, Mr. Divine in the chair, and after some time spent therein the committee rose, and through their chairman made the following report:

REPORT OF THE COMMITTEE OF THE WHOLE.

The committee of the whole have had under consideration Article I. of Boundaries,

Article III. of the Division of the Powers of Government,

Have made no amendments thereto, and have directed me to report the same back to the Commission, recommending that the article do pass, and ask to be discharged from the further consideration of the subject.

The committee of the whole have also had under consideration Article V., of the Legislative Department.

Have made some progress therein, but not having gone through therewith, have directed me to report that fact to the Commission, and ask leave to sit again.

JOHN DIVINE, *Chairman.*

Report accepted.

Articles I. and III. were placed on the order of third reading.

As to Article V. the committee had leave to sit again.

LEAVE OF ABSENCE.

Mr. Crane asked and obtained leave of absence for himself indefinitely.

ADJOURNMENT.

On motion of Mr. Devereaux,

The Commission adjourned.

NINETEENTH DAY.

LANSING, *Wednesday, September 17, 1873.*

The Commission was called to order at 9 o'clock, by the Chairman.

Roll called: quorum present.

RAILROADS.

By the committee on corporations, railroads, and elections:

The committee on corporations, railroads, and elections, to whom was referred Article XIX.–A., of the State Constitution,

Respectfully report that they have had the same under consideration, and have directed me to report the same back to the Commission with amendments thereto, recommending that the amendments be concurred in, and that the article as amended do pass, and ask to be discharged from the further consideration of the subject.

E. W. MEDDAUGH, *Chairman.*

Report accepted and committee discharged.

The article was read a first and second time, ordered printed, referred to the committee of the whole, and placed on the general order.

LIABILITY OF HUSBANDS.

By the committee on finance and taxation:

The committee on finance and taxation, to whom was referred the proposition to amend Section 4, Article XVI., as to the liability of husbands for the debts of their wives, according to the following resolution, adopted on the 15th inst.:

Resolved, That the committee on exemptions be instructed to report an amendment to Section 4, of Article XVI., by adding to the said section the following:

"And the husband of any married woman shall not be liable for or on account of any debt or obligation of his wife contracted before her marriage, or contracted by her in relation to her sole property after marriage;"

Respectfully report that they have considered the same, and have instructed me to report herewith the amendment, recommending that the same be adopted, and ask to be discharged from the further consideration of the subject.

D. H. JEROME, *Chairman.*

Report accepted and committee discharged.

The amendment was concurred in.

ELIGIBILITY OF WOMEN FOR OFFICE.

Mr. Withey offered the following:

Resolved, That the committee on election be instructed to inquire into the expediency of incorporating a provision in said article, in substance, that every woman above the age of twenty-one years, who shall have resided in this State three months, and in any township or ward ten days, shall be eligible to any office under the laws of the State, except as otherwise provided in section five of article four.

The resolution was adopted.

BOUNDARIES AND SEAT OF GOVERNMENT.—DIVISION OF POWERS, PREAMBLE.

Article I., of Boundaries and Seat of Government; Article III., of the Division of the Powers of Government; and the preamble to the Constitution, were severally read a third time, and referred to the committee on phraseology.

GENERAL ORDER.

On motion of Mr. Moffatt,

The Commission resolved itself into committee of the whole, on the general order, Mr. Divine in the chair, and after some time spent therein, the committee rose, and through their chairman, made the following report:

REPORT OF THE COMMITTEE OF THE WHOLE.

The committee of the whole have had under further consideration Article IV., of the Legislative Department;

Have made some progress therein, but not having gone through therewith, have directed me to report that fact to the Commission, and ask leave to sit again.

JOHN DIVINE, *Chairman.*

Report accepted and leave granted.

RECESS.

On motion of Mr. Upson,

The Commission took a recess until 2:30 P. M.

AFTERNOON SESSION.

The Commission was called to order at 2:30 by the chairman.

Roll called; quorum present.

LEAVE OF ABSENCE.

On motion of Mr. Jerome,

Mr. Withey was granted indefinite leave of absence, on account of the sickness of Hon. W. D. Foster.

GENERAL ORDER.

On motion of Mr. Hatch,

The Commission resolved itself into committee of the whole on the general order, Mr. Divine in the chair, and after some time spent therein the committee rose, and through their chairman made the following report:

REPORT OF THE COMMITTEE OF THE WHOLE.

The committee of the whole have had under further consideration Article IV., of the Legislative Department,

Have made some progress therein, but not having gone through therewith, have directed me to report that fact to the Commission, and ask leave to sit again.

JOHN DIVINE, *Chairman.*

Report accepted and leave granted.

ADJOURNMENT.

On motion of Mr. Riley,

The Commission adjourned.

TWENTIETH DAY.

LANSING, *Thursday, Sept. 18, 1873.*

The Commission was called to order at 9 o'clock. by the Chairman.

Roll called: quorum present.

ELECTIVE FRANCHISE—WOMAN'S SUFFRAGE.

By the committee on corporations, railroads, and elections:

The committee on corporations, railroads, and elections, to whom was referred Article III., Elective Franchise,

Respectfully report that they have had the same under consideration, and have directed me to report the same back to the Commission with amendments thereto, recommending that the amendments be concurred in, and that the article when so amended do pass.

The committee have also considered the matters embraced in the several resolutions referred to them relative to providing for woman's suffrage, and have instructed me to report against adding any such provision to the constitution at present.

The committee ask to be discharged from the further consideration of the subject.

E. W. MEDDAUGH, *Chairman.*

Report accepted and committee discharged.

The article was read a first and second time, ordered printed, referred to the committee of the whole, and placed on the general order.

SALARIES, IMPEACHMENTS, TOWNSHIPS, EXECUTIVE.

By the committee on arrangement and phraseology:

The committee on arrangement and phraseology, to whom was referred

Article IX., of Salaries;

Article XII., of Impeachments and Removals from Office;

Article XI., of Townships;

Article V., of the Executive Department;

Respectfully report that they have had the same under consideration, and have directed me to report the same back to the Commission with amendments thereto, recommending that the amendments be concurred in, and that articles when so amended do pass, and ask to be discharged from the further consideration of the subject.

H. H. HATCH,
Acting Chairman of Committee.

Report accepted and committee discharged.

The amendments made to article IX. were concurred in.

The article was ordered printed and placed on the order of final passage.

The amendments made to Article XII. were concurred in, except those in line one of section two, substituting the word "if" for "when," and striking out the words "or otherwise" in line two of section five.

The article was re-referred to the committee on arrangement and phraseology.

Amendments made to Articles V. and XI. were concurred in, and the articles ordered printed and placed on the order of final passage.

BOUNDARIES, DIVISION OF POWERS, PREAMBLE.

Article I. of Boundaries,

Article III. of the Division of the Powers of the Government, and

The Preamble to the Constitution,

Having been read a third time, were referred to the committee on arrangement and phraseology.

GENERAL ORDER.

On motion of Mr. Hatch,

The Commission resolved itself into committee of the whole on the general order, Mr. Divine in the chair, and after some time spent therein, the committee rose, and through their chairman made the following report:

REPORT OF THE COMMITTEE OF THE WHOLE.

The committee of the whole have had under further consideration Article IV., of the Legislative Department;

Have made sundry amendments thereto, and have directed me to report the same back to the Commission, recommending that the amendments be concurred in.

The committee also recommend that the article be re-committed to the committee on the legislatve department, with instructions to amend section two so as to provide that the Legislature shall divide the State into sixteen senatorial districts, each of which shall choose two senators, and that so soon as the Senate first elected under the provisions of this article shall meet, it shall cause the senators from each district to be divided by lot into two classes of one each; the classes to be numbered first and second. The seats of the senators of the first class shall be vacated at the end of two years; of the second class at the end of four years; and after the first election there shall, biennially, be elected one senator in each district.

JOHN DIVINE,
Chairman of Committee.

The amendments made to the article were concurred in.

The question recurring on recommitting the article to the committee on the legislative department, with instructions as recommended by the committee,

Mr. Moffatt demanded the yeas and nays.

The recommendation of the committee was concurred in by yeas and nays as follows:

YEAS.

Mr. Crane,	Mr. Hatch,	Mr. Riley,	
Cutcheon,	Jerome,	Wells,	
Devereaux,	Meddaugh,	Willits,	
Giddings,			10

NAYS.

Mr. Divine,	Mr. Pond,	Mr. Woodward,	
Moffatt,	Upson,		5

The article was ordered reprinted, and recommitted to the committee on legislative department.

Mr. Wells offered the following resolution:

Resolved, That the committee on the legislative department be instructed to report the following as a substitute for section 23 of Article V.:

SEC. 23. The Legislature shall not pass local or special laws in any of the following enumerated cases, for,

1st. Divorcing any named party, or upon the subject of divorce.

2d. Incorporating cities and villages.

3d. Extending the time for the assessment or collection of taxes.

4th. Changing the name of any person.

5th. Adopting by any person any named person as his child or heir.

6th. Authorizing the sale or conveyance of any real estate belonging to any person.

7th. Vacating or altering any road laid out by the commissioners of highways, or any street, alley, or public ground in any city, village, or in any recorded town plat.

On motion of Mr. Wells,

The resolution was laid on the table.

EVENING SESSIONS.

Mr. Devereaux offered the following resolution:

Resolved, That hereafter, the Commission employed to revise the Constitution of the State of Michigan, in addition to its daily labors, shall sit in session at least four evenings in the week for the purpose of completing its work, and protecting the pockets of the tax-payers of this glorious commonwealth.

The resolution was not adopted.

RECESS.

On motion of Mr. Hatch,

The Commission took a recess until 2:30 P. M.

AFTERNOON SESSION.

The Commission was called to order at 2:30 by the chairman.

Roll called: quorum present.

The regular order of business was resumed.

STATE FAIR.

Mr. Woodward offered the following resolution:

Whereas, One of the greatest industrial exhibitions known to the history of Michigan is being held at Grand Rapids, Michigan, and to the end that members of this Commission may attend said exhibition,

Resolved, That when this Commission adjourn to-day, Sept. 18th, it adjourn to meet on the 22d day of Sept., 1873, at 9 o'clock, A. M.

The resolution was not adopted.

SENATORS IN UPPER PENINSULA.

Mr. Devereaux offered the following resolution :

Resolved, That the legislative committee in modifying Article No. IV. be further instructed to provide for two senators in the upper Peninsula of Michigan.

On motion of Mr. Devereaux the resolution was laid on the table.

GENERAL ORDER.

On motion of Mr. Willits,

The Commission resolved itself into committee of the whole on the general order, and after some time spent therein, the committee rose, and through their chairman made the following report:

REPORT OF THE COMMITTEE OF THE WHOLE.

The committee of the whole have had under consideration Article XVI., of Cities and Villages; Article XIX.–A., of Railroads.

Have made sundry amendments thereto, and have directed me to report the same back to the Commission, recommending that the amendments be concurred in, and that the articles when so amended do pass, and ask to be discharged from the further consideration of the subject.

J. R. DEVEREAUX,
Chairman of Committee.

Report accepted and committee discharged.

The amendments were concurred in, and the articles ordered reprinted, and placed on the order of third reading.

ADJOURNMENT.

On motion of Mr. Crane,

The Commission adjourned.

TWENTY-FIRST DAY.

LANSING, *Friday, September 19, 1873.*

The Commission was called to order at 9 o'clock, by the Chairman.

Roll called: quorum present.

IMPEACHMENTS—BOUNDARIES—PREAMBLE.

By the committee on arrangement and phraseology:

The committee on arrangement and phraseology, to whom was referred

Article XII., of Impeachments and Removals from Office;

Article I., of Boundaries and Seat of Government;

Preamble to the Constitution,

Respectfully report that they have had the same under consideration, and have directed me to report the same back to the Commission with amendments thereto, recommending that the amendments be concurred in, and that the articles when so amended do pass, and ask to be discharged from the further consideration of the subject.

ASHLEY POND,
Chairman of Committee.

Report accepted and committee discharged.

The amendments were concurred in, and the articles ordered reprinted and placed on the order of final passage.

LEAVE OF ABSENCE.

On motion of Mr. Moffatt,

Mr. Woodward was granted leave of absence until Monday next.

IMPROVEMENT OF STREAMS.

Mr. Jerome offered the following resolution:

Resolved, That the committee on corporations be requested to consider the propriety of so amending the article on corporations as to provide for the improvement of streams, in substance as follows:

Corporations may be created for the purpose of improving the navigation of the streams of the State for public use. Such corporations may be authorized by law to take private property for such purpose when necessary, upon making just compensation therefore, and to collect tolls for the use of such improvement; but such authority shall not interfere with the right of the public to use any such stream for any purpose for which it was capable of being used before such improvement was made.

The resolution was adopted.

ADJOURNMENT OF THE COMMISSION.

Mr. Riley offered the following resolution:

Resolved, That this Commission adjourn on Friday, the 26th day of September to the — day of October ensuing.

On motion of Mr. Jerome, the resolution was laid on the table.

Mr. Crane offered the following resolution:

Resolved, That the committee on judiciary be instructed to inquire into the expediency of incorporating a provision in substance that any married woman may, by deed, or other proper conveyance, release to the husband all her claim, right or title to dower in the estate of her husband, and such conveyance shall be as effectual to bar the dower of the wife in the estate of her husband as a jointure settled on her with her assent before marriage.

The resolution was adopted.

EXEMPTIONS FROM TAXATION.

Mr. Upson presented the following memorial:

HILLSDALE, MICH., Sept. 18, 1873.

To the Honorable Commission for the Revision of the Constitution of the State of Michigan:

The undersigned would respectfully represent: that there have recently been published in the N. Y. Independent a series of editorial articles favoring "uniform taxation of all property," without exception in favor of religious or other societies.

Many honest and astute men concur in the opinions on the subject so ably enforced by the editor of that journal. The subject is respectfully suggested for your consideration.

Our State law, in carrying out the laws of Congress, provides for the assessment of the shares of stock in the National banks in this wise: That the taxes on shares owned by residents outside this State shall, as a last resort, be paid by the banks themselves; that the taxes on the shares of residents shall be assessed to the owners in the townships or wards where they reside. Why not have the same provision in relation to insurance, or other companies organized under the laws of this State which do not pay a special tax directly into the treasury of the State, in lieu of all other taxes? By law, as it now exists, the Michigan State Insurance Company (*e. g.*) is assessed in the township or ward where its principal office is situated (Adrian). The assessment is merely nominal. The company has a large amount of assessable property. When the assessor approaches a stockholder in this insurance company and asks him for the amount of his "moneys and credits," he frequently claims exemption on account of stock owned in insurance companies and assessed to the company elsewhere. This virtually proves an exemption in favor of such stockholders.

I would also call the attention of your honorable body to the exemptions of county farms from assessment. These farms sometimes have an area of 200 or 300 acres, and occupy a large space in the school or highway district where they are situated. The schools and roads in such districts suffer, unless the owners of the residue of the property in these districts submit to much heavier taxes than they would be subjected to were it not for this non-taxable territory, and the personal property pertaining to it.

I would suggest, also, for reasons that will readily occur to the Commission, that for the purpose of ascertaining the taxes in fractional school districts, the assessment be required to be taken by "district assessors," instead of by township supervisors. This would promote uniform valuations within the limits of such fractional districts.

These hints are thrown out to the wisdom of the Commission to determine whether they shall be incorporated on the Constitution, or "rejected" to the discretion of the Legislature.

Very respectfully,

WM. R. MONTGOMERY.

On motion of Mr. Hatch,

The memorial was ordered printed in the journal, and laid on the table.

FINANCE AND TAXATION.

Article XIV., of Finance and Taxation, was read a third time.

Mr. Jerome moved that the same be re-committed to the committee of the whole and placed on the general order.

Which motion prevailed.

COUNTIES.

Article X., of Counties, was read a third time.

Mr. Upson, leave being granted, moved to amend the article by adding the following, to stand as a proviso to section :

Provided, That nothing herein contained shall be so construed as to prevent the Legislature from organizing any county composed wholly of islands within the territory of the State, or discontinuing any such county, and attaching the same to the nearest county or counties on the main land.

The motion prevailed.

Mr. Riley, leave being granted, moved to amend the article by inserting after the word "law," in the third line of section two, the following: "The Legislature may provide for the appointment by the Governor, of prosecuting attorneys, by and with the advice and consent of the Senate."

The motion prevailed.

Mr. Pond, leave being granted, moved to amend the article by striking out section nine.

Which motion prevailed.

Mr. Crane, leave being granted, moved to amend the article by adding after the word "law," in the second line of section one, the following: "In which their powers of taxation, borrowing money, and contracting debts shall be restricted."

The motion prevailed.

Mr. Wells, leave being granted, moved to amend the article by adding the following, to stand as a part of section six:

"A board of supervisors, consisting of one from each township, and two in each village having a population of not less than ten thousand, shall be established, with such powers as shall be prescribed by law."

The motion prevailed.

The article was referred to the committee on phraseology.

CORPORATIONS.

Article XV., of Corporations, was read a third time.

Mr. Willits, leave being granted, moved to amend the article by striking out all of line three, in section eight, after the word "franchises," and all of line four in said section, and inserting in lieu thereof the following: "Foreign corporations may be permitted to do business in this State under such limitations and restrictions as may be prescribed by law, but shall at all times be subject to all restrictions and limitations imposed, and shall have no greater rights than are conferred upon domestic corporations of like character;"

Which motion prevailed.

The article was referred to the committee on phraseology.

RECESS.

On motion of Mr. Devereaux,

The Commission took a recess until 2:30 P. M.

AFTERNOON SESSION.

The Commission was called to order by the chairman at 2:30.

Roll called: quorum present.

GENERAL ORDER.

On motion of Mr. Hatch,

The Commission resolved itself into committee of the whole on the general order, Mr. Moffatt in the chair, and after some time spent therein, the committee rose and through their chairman made the following report:

REPORT OF THE COMMITTEE OF THE WHOLE.

The committtee of the whole have had under consideration,

Provisions relating to the appointment of judges to be separately submitted, and to stand as sections 2, 6, 7, 12, and 13 of Article VII., entitled "Judicial Department."

Article XIV., of Finance and Taxation,

Have made sundry amendments thereto, and have directed me to report the same back to the Commission, recommending that the amendments be concurred in, and that the sections and articles when so amended do pass, and ask to be discharged from the further consideration of the subject.

S. C. MOFFATT,
Chairman of Committee.

Report accepted and committee discharged.

The amendments made by the committee were concurred in, except as to the amendment striking out the last clause of section six of the sections relating to the appointment of judges.

The said amendment was concurred in by yeas and nays, as follows:

YEAS.

Mr. Crane,	Mr. Moffatt,	Mr. Upson,	
Divine,	Pond,	Willits,	
Devereaux,	Riley,		8

NAYS.

Mr. Crouse,	Mr. Giddings,	Mr. Jerome,	
Cutcheon,	Hatch,	Meddaugh,	6

The sections and article were ordered printed and placed on the order of third reading.

ADJOURNMENT.

On motion of Mr. Hatch,

The Commission adjourned.

TWENTY-SECOND DAY.

LANSING, *Saturday, September 20, 1873.*

The Commission was called to order at 9 o'clock, by the Chairman.

On motion of Mr. Crouse,

The Commission adjourned until Monday afternoon at 2.30 o'clock.

TWENTY-THIRD DAY.

LANSING, *Monday, September 22, 1873.*

The Commission was called to order at 2:30 o'clock by the Chairman.

Roll called: no quorum present.

A CALL OF THE HOUSE.

On motion of Mr. Crane, a call of the house was ordered.

The roll being called,

Messrs. Devereaux, Giddings, Hatch, and Jerome were found to be absent without leave.

The bar of the Commission was ordered closed and the door-keeper was dispatched after absentees.

The door-keeper reported Mr. Devereaux at the bar of the Commission.

On motion of Mr. Moffatt,

Mr. Devereaux was allowed to come within the bar of the Commission and render his excuse for being absent without leave.

Mr. Devereaux having rendered his excuse, stating that his absence was occasioned by illness,

Mr. Riley moved that all further proceedings under call be dispensed with;

Which motion prevailed.

ADJOURNMENT.

On motion of Mr. Crane,

The Commission adjourned.

TWENTY-FOURTH DAY.

LANSING, *Tuesday, September 23, 1873.*

The Commission was called to order at 9 o'clock by the Chairman.

Roll called: quorum present.

LEAVE OF ABSENCE.

On motion of Mr. Pond,

Mr. Meddaugh was granted indefinite leave of absence on account of sickness.

On motion of Mr. Divine,

Mr. Giddings was granted indefinite leave of absence on account of important and necessary business.

TENURE OF REAL ESTATE BY CORPORATIONS.

The Chairman presented to the Commission communications from the Ludington Lumber Company of Chicago, and of John Mason Loomis of the same place, adverse to the proposed provision limiting the title to lands held by corporations, but not actually occupied by them, to ten years.

Referred to the committee on corporations.

SENATORIAL DISTRICTS.

By the committee on the legislative department:

The committee on the legislative department, to whom was re-committed Article IV., Legislative Department, heretofore reported by them, with instructions to amend the same in regard to the arrangement of senatorial districts, and the elective classification of Senators, respectfully report back the same with the following amendment, in accordance with said instructions, striking out section two of said article, and substituting the following amended section to stand in place thereof:

SEC. 2. The Senate shall consist of thirty-two members. At its first session after the adoption of this amended constitution, the Legislature shall divide the State into sixteen senatorial districts, each of which shall choose two Senators. As soon as the Senate first elected under the provisions of this article shall meet, it shall cause the Senators from each senatorial district to be divided by lot into two classes, to be numbered first and second. The seats of the Senators of the first class shall be vacated at the end of two years; of the second class at the end of four years, and after the said first election there shall be elected biennially one Senator in each of said senatorial districts, who shall hold his office for four years.

CHAS. UPSON,
Chairman of Committee.

The amendment was concurred in, the amended section read a first and second time, and referred to the committee on phraseology.

GENERAL ELECTIONS.

By the committee on legislative department:

The committee on the legislative department, who were requested by resolution, introduced by the gentleman from Eaton, and adopted by the Commission, as follows, viz.:

Resolved, That the legislative committee be requested to inquire into the expediency of the following amendment to section one of Article XX.:

Add to said section the following words: "And for the purpose of submitting such amendments, the annual township meetings shall be taken and deemed to be a general election;"

Respectfully report that in their judgment the amendment proposed is a judicious and proper one, and that its adoption would relieve the section of all doubts as to its construction, and would settle a question that has been much discussed in times past. It would also give an opportunity to submit amendments promptly after they have been discussed and passed upon by the legislature, and at an election where there are not usually exciting political contests agitating the public mind and calling public attention away from the consideration of such proposed amendment. But as the article in question has not been submitted to your committee to report upon, your committee recommend that the proposed amendment thereto be referred to the committee on arrangement, phraseology, etc., with instructions to amend section one of Article XX., by adding the said amendment to it, and respectfully ask to be discharged from further consideration of the subject.

CHARLES UPSON,
Chairman.

Report accepted and committee discharged.

The amended section was read twice and referred to the committee on phraseology.

PRIVATE PROPERTY FOR PUBLIC USE.

Mr. Willits offered the following resolution:

Resolved, That the committee on miscellaneous provisions be instructed to inquire into the propriety of reporting two sections, in substance as follows:

SEC. —. The private property of no person shall be taken for public use without just compensation therefor. When private property is taken for the use or benefit of the public, the necessity for using such property, except when to be used for the State, and the just compensation therefor shall be ascercertained by such tribunal as the legislature shall designate or create.

SEC. —. Private property may be taken as provided in section —, for private roads, and for right of way for corporations; but the compensation shall be first paid to the owner by the person or corporation benefited by such taking. All corporations which are or shall be common carriers, may take sufficient of the lands of either persons or corporations for right of way, depots, stations, turnouts, repair shops, docks, and wharves; but whenever this right may infringe upon the franchises or encroach upon the lands of any incorporated company, except railroad crossings, it shall first be determined in such manner as the legislature shall prescribe, that the land or franchises so proposed to be taken are not necessary for the exclusive use of such corporation, and will not prevent it in the exercise of its franchises.

The resolution was adopted.

RAILROADS.

Article XIX.–A. of Railroads was read a third time.

Mr. Jerome, leave being granted, moved to amend section one of the article by striking out all after the word "legislature," in the first line, to, but not including, the word "shall," in the third line.

Mr. Upson moved to amend the amendment by striking out

the word "shall," in the first line, and inserting in lieu thereof the word "may;"

Which motion prevailed.

The question recurring on the motion as amended, the same was not adopted, by yeas and nays, as follows:

YEAS.

Mr. Crane,	Mr. Hatch,	Mr. Wells,
Devereaux,	Jerome,	5

NAYS.

Mr. Cutcheon,	Mr. Pond,	Mr. Willits,
Divine,	Riley,	Woodward,
Moffatt,	Upson,	8

Mr. Willits moved to substitute for section one the following:

SEC. 1. The Legislature may, from time to time, pass laws establishing reasonable maximum rates of charges for the transportation of passengers and freight on different railroads in this State, and shall prohibit running contracts between such railroad companies whereby discrimination is made in favor of either of such companies as against other companies owning connecting or intersecting lines of railroads.

The motion prevailed.

Mr. Jerome, leave being granted, moved to amend the article by striking out section two;

Which motion did not prevail.

Mr. Willits, leave being granted, moved to amend the article by striking out, in first line of section three, the words "owning or operating a railroad," and insert in lieu thereof the following words: "doing business;"

Which motion prevailed.

Mr. Willits offered the following amendment: Add after the word "assets," in fifth line of section three, the following words: "which book shall at all times be open to the inspection of any stockholder, and of such officer or officers of the State as shall be designated by law.

The motion prevailed.

Mr. Crane moved to amend the article by striking out section four.

The motion prevailed.

Mr. Hatch moved to amend the article by striking out section five.

Pending which motion,

On motion of Mr. Hatch,

The Commission took a recess till 2:30.

AFTERNOON SESSION.

The Commission was called to order by the chairman at 2:30.

Roll called: quorum present.

LEAVE OF ABSENCE.

On motion of Mr. Willits,

Leave of absence was granted Mr. Woodward until to-morrow.

RAILROADS.

The consideration of Article XIX—A, on Railroads, was resumed. Pending the question on striking out section 5,

On motion of Mr. Crane, the article was recommitted to the committee of the whole and placed on the general order.

CITIES AND VILLAGES.

Article XVI., of Cities and Villages, was read a third time.

Mr. Pond, leave being granted, moved to amend the same by striking out the second section.

The motion prevailed.

The article was referred to the committee on phraseology.

LEGISLATIVE DEPARTMENT.

Article V. of the Legislative Department was read a third time.

Mr. Jerome, leave being granted, moved to amend the article by adding to section two the following; "In making the first apportionment under this section, the Upper Peninsula shall constitute one district;"

Which motion prevailed, by yeas and nays, as follows:

YEAS.

Mr. Crane,	Mr. Devereaux,	Mr. Riley,	
Crouse,	Hatch,	Wells,	
Cutcheon,	Jerome,	Willits,	9

NAYS.

Mr. Divine,	Mr. Pond,	Mr. Upson,	
Moffat,			4

Mr. Wells, leave being granted, moved to amend the article by substituting the following in place of section twenty-two:

SEC. 22. The Legislature shall not pass local or special laws in any of the following enumerated cases, for,

1st. Divorcing any named party, or upon the subject of divorce;

2d. Incorporating cities and villages;

3d. Extending the time for the assessment or collection of taxes;

4th. Changing the name of any person;

5th. Adopting by any person any named person as his child or heir;

6th. Authorizing the sale or conveyance of any real estate belonging to any person;

7th. Vacating or altering any road laid out by the commissioners of highways, or any street, alley, or public ground in any city, village, or in any recorded town plat.

The motion did not prevail.

Mr. Riley, leave being granted, moved to amend the article by striking out the word "three," wherever the same is used with reference to the compensation of members of the Legislature, and inserting in lieu thereof the word "four."

Mr. Hatch moved to amend by inserting the word "five."

The motion did not prevail.

The question recurring on Mr. Riley's amendment, it was adopted.

Mr. Crouse, leave being granted, moved to amend the article by adding to section two the following: "In organizing the senatorial districts in the Lower Peninsula, the Legislature shall so arrange them that each district shall contain as nearly as may be an equal number of inhabitants, and shall consist of convenient and contiguous territory;"

Which motion prevailed.

The article was referred to the committee on phraseology.

LOCAL OPTION.

The committee on the legislative department, who were requested to report to the Commission in pursuance of the following resolutions, viz:

Resolved, That the legislative committee be requested to report to the Commission the expediency of so amending Sec. 47 of Article IV. of the existing constitution of this State, as to empower the Legislature to authorize the granting of licenses for the sale of spirituous liquors upon the following conditions:

1st, That the question of license or no license shall be submitted to the electors of any city, village, or town, in the manner to be provided by law;

2d, If a majority of such electors are in favor of licensing the traffic in their respective municipalities, then the proper authorities of such municipality to have the exclusive control of the granting of licenses, and the moneys arising therefrom to enter into the general fund of such city, etc.;

3d, When the electors, etc., shall be opposed to licensing the traffic, then, as to such city, village, etc., prohibitory laws to be in force;

Respectfully report that, in their judgment, any law on that subject ought to be uniform in its operation throughout the State, and not be left to local option to determine whether or not it shall be in force in each particular locality, and thus be a constant occasion for political excitement at each recurring township or city election. There is also something repugnant to the moral sense of the community in the idea of licensing, and thus apparently legalizing a traffic which is so prolific of evil to individuals and to society, although the real object of such licensing may be the regulation of, or restraining to some extent, this business.

The fact that the present State law is not practically enforced in many parts of the State, may be a proper argument to be addressed to the Legislature, which can at any time change the law and remedy these defects which experience may point out, by further legislation.

So far as regulating the traffic or raising a revenue therefrom if the business is allowed to be carried on, the changes that have already been proposed in other parts of the constitution by the Commission, have made ample provision, and if the public sentiment demands the repeal of the present prohibitory law, the Legislature has now, as it always has had, the power to change it, and allow the traffic to be carried on, and may impose such taxation thereon, and under such regulations as it sees fit.

The regulation of the traffic and the raising of revenue therefrom, under the late decision of the Supreme Court, would seem, under the present constitution, to be within the control of the Legislature, and under the proposed changes made by the Commission, there can certainly be no question of the power of the legislature in this regard.

A majority of your committee are therefore of opinion that it is not expedient to amend section 47, of Article IV., as proposed by said resolution, and they report back said resolution, and ask to be discharged from the further consideration of the subject.

CHARLES UPSON,
JOHN DIVINE.

Report accepted and committee discharged.

Mr. Crouse, of the committee, asked leave to present a minority report at some future time.

Leave granted.

EDUCATION.

By the committee on phraseology, etc.:

The committee on phraseology, etc., to whom was referred Article XIII., entitled, Education,

Respectfully report that they have had the same under consideration, and have directed me to report the same back to the Commission with amendments thereto, recommending that the amendments be concurred in, and that the article when so amended do pass, and ask to be discharged from the further consideration of the subject.

ASHLEY POND,
Chairman of Committee.

Report accepted and committee discharged.

The amendments were concurred in, and the article ordered printed, and placed on the order of final passage.

LEAVE OF ABSENCE.

Mr. Upson asked and obtained leave of absence for himself until Tuesday morning next.

ADJOURNMENT.

On motion of Mr. Wells,

The Commission adjourned.

TWENTY-FIFTH DAY.

LANSING, *Wednesday, September 24, 1873.*

The Commission was called to order at 9 o'clock, by the Chairman.

Roll called: quorum present.

CORPORATIONS.

By the committee on phraseology:

The committee on phraseology, to whom was referred Article XV. entitled, of Corporations,

Respectfully report that they have had the same under consideration, and have directed me to report the same back to the Commission with amendment thereto, recommending that the amendment be concurred in, and ask to be discharged from the further consideration of the subject.

H. H. HATCH,
For Chairman of Committee.

Report accepted and committee discharged.

The amendments were concurred in and the article ordered printed, and placed on the order of final passage.

LICENSING THE SALE OF LIQUORS.

Mr. Crane offered the following resolution:

Resolved, That the committee on the legislative department be instructed to inquire into the expediency of framing a section to be submitted separately, and if adopted, to stand in the place of section 47 of Article IV. of the present constitution, in manner following:

SEC. 47. The Legislature shall, at their first session after the adoption of this amendment, pass all necessary laws regulating the granting of licenses for the sale of spirituous and intoxicating liquors, or for imposing a special tax upon the traffic in the same.

The resolution was adopted.

FINANCE AND TAXATION.

Article XIV., of Finance and Taxation, was read a third time.

Mr. Riley, leave being granted, moved to amend the article by adding the following, to stand as a part of section eight: "The Legislature shall provide by law for rejecting all claims against the State, unless presented within a time to be therein fixed."

The motion prevailed by yeas and nays as follows:

YEAS.

Mr. Crane,	Mr. Hatch,	Mr. Riley,	
Divine,	Jerome,	Wells,	
Deveraux,	Moffatt,		8

NAYS.

Mr. Crouse,	Meddaugh,	Woodward,	
Cutcheon,	Willits,		5

The article was referred to the committee on phraseology.

GENERAL ORDER.

On motion of Mr. Woodward,

The Commission resolved itself into committee of the whole, on the general order, and after some time spent therein, the committee rose and through their chairman made the following report:

REPORT OF THE COMMITTEE OF THE WHOLE.

The committee of the whole have had under consideration

Article II., Bill of Rights; and

Article III. of the Elective Franchise;

Have made sundry amendments thereto, and have directed me to report the same back to the Commission, recommending that the amendments be concurred in, and that the articles when so amended do pass, and ask to be discharged from the further consideration of the subject.

L. WOODWARD,
Chairman of Committee.

Report accepted and committee discharged.

The amendments made to the articles were concurred in.

Mr. Hatch moved that Article III. be referred back to the committee on elections, with instructions to strike out the word "male" wherever the same occurs in section one;

The motion did not prevail by yeas and nays as follows:

YEAS.

Mr. Crouse,	Mr. Willits,	2

NAYS.

Mr. Crane,	Mr. Hatch,	Mr Pond,
Cutcheon,	Jerome,	Riley,
Divine,	Meddaugh,	Wells,
Devereaux,	Moffatt,	Woodward, 12

The articles were placed on the order of third reading.

RECESS.

On motion of Mr. Riley,

The Commission took a recess until 2:30 P. M.

AFTERNOON SESSION.

The Commission was called to order by the Chairman at 2:30.

Roll called: quorum present.

LEGISLATIVE.—FINANCE.—COUNTIES.—EXEMPTIONS.

By the committee on phraseology:

The committee on phraseology, to whom was referred Article IV. of the Legislative Department, Article XIV. of Finance and Taxation, Article X., Counties, and Article XVI., Exemptions,

Respectfully report that they have had the same under consideration, and have directed me to report the same back to the Commission with amendments thereto, recommending that the amendments be concurred in, and ask to be discharged from the further consideration of the subject.

ASHLEY POND,
Chairman of Committee.

Report accepted and committee discharged.

The amendments made to the articles by the committee were concurred in.

The articles were ordered printed and placed on the order of final passage.

JUDICIAL DEPARTMENT—EXEMPTIONS.

On motion of Mr. Moffatt,

Article VII. of the Judicial Department was taken from the table and placed on the order of third reading.

Article XIV. of Exemptions, was taken from the table, and referred to the committee on phraseology.

LIMITATION OF AMOUNTS IN ACTION.

Mr. Crane offered the following resolution:

Resolved, That the judiciary committee be instructed to inquire into the expediency of adopting a provision limiting the right of trial by jury in civil causes in courts of record, to cases where the amount in controversy shall exceed the sum of twenty-five dollars.

The resolution was adopted.

ARTICLE ON AMENDMENTS.

On motion of Mr. Pond, the committee on the judicial department was instructed to report back the article relative to amendments to the constitution.

Mr. Pond, from the committee on the judicial department, reported verbally that the committee had had under consideration the article relative to amendments, had made no amendments thereto, and asked to be discharged from the further consideration of the subject.

Report accepted and committee discharged.

The article was referred to the committee on education.

SCHEDULE.

Mr. Hatch moved that a special committee of three be appointed on schedule, but desired to be excused from serving on said committee.

The motion prevailed.

The Chairman appointed as such committee, Messrs. Riley, Wells, and Willits.

ADJOURNMENT.

On motion of Mr. Riley,

The Commission adjourned.

TWENTY-SIXTH DAY.

LANSING, *Thursday, September 25, 1873.*

The Commission was called to order at 9 o'clock by the Chairman.

Roll called: quorum present.

IMPROVEMENT OF STREAMS.

By the committee on corporations:

The committee on corporations, to whom was referred a resolution instructing the committee to consider the propriety of so amending the article on corporations of the State constitution as to provide for the improvement of streams,

Respectfully report that they have had the matter under consideration, and have instructed me to report the same back to the Commission, without recommendation.

E. W. MEDDAUGH, *Chairman.*

Report accepted and committee discharged.

On motion of Mr. Jerome,

The proposed section was ordered printed in bill form, referred to the committee of the whole, and placed on the general order.

STATE OFFICERS.

By the committee on State officers:

The committee on State officers, to whom was referred Article VIII., of State Officers,

Respectfully report that they have had the same under consideration, and have directed me to report the same back to the Commission with amendment thereto, recommending that the amendment be concurred in, and that the article when so amended do pass, and ask to be discharged from the further consideration of the subject.

H. G. WELLS,
Chairman of Committee.

Report accepted and committee discharged.

The article was read a first and second time, ordered printed, referred to the committee of the whole, and placed on the general order.

AMENDMENT AND REVISION.

By the committee on education, etc.:

The committee on education, etc., to whom was referred Article XX., entitled Amendment and Revision of the Constitution,

Respectfully report that they have had the same under consideration, and have directed me to report the same back to the Commission with amendments thereto, recommending that the amendments be concurred in, and that the same when so amended do pass, and ask to be discharged from the further consideration of the subject.

EDWARD WILLITS,
Chairman of Committee.

Report accepted and committee discharged.

The article was read a first and second time, ordered printed, referred to the committee of the whole, and placed on the general order.

By the committee on judiciary;

The committee on judiciary, to whom was referred the resolutions of Mr. Willets,

Respectfully report that they have had the same under consideration, and have directed me to report the same back to the Commission with amendment thereto, recommending that the amendment be concurred in, and that the same when so amended do pass, and ask to be discharged from the further consideration of the subject.

H. H. HATCH,
For Chairman of Committee.

Report accepted and committee discharged.

The resolutions were read a first and second time, ordered printed, referred to the committee of the whole, and placed on the general order.

SCHEDULE.

By the special committee on Schedule:

The special committee to whom was referred the schedule of the Constitution of 1850,

Respectfully report that they have had the same under consideration, and have directed me to report the same back to the Commission and that the schedule when so amended do pass, and ask to be discharged from the further consideration of the subject.

H. H. RILEY,
Chairman of Committee.

Report accepted and committee discharged.

The schedule was read a first and second time, ordered printed, referred to the committee of the whole, and placed on the general order.

GENERAL ELECTIONS.

By the committee on phraseology, etc.:

The committee on phraseology, etc., to whom was referred Proposed amendment to Section 1, Article XX;

Respectfully report that they have had the same under consideration, and have directed me to report the same back to the Commission without amendment, and ask to be discharged from the further consideration of the subject.

ASHLEY POND,
Chairman.

Report accepted and committee discharged.

On motion of Mr. Pond,

The proposed amendment was laid on the table.

LICENSING THE SALE OF LIQUORS.

By the minority of the committee on Legislative Department:

The undersigned, member of the legislative committee, to which committee was referred the following:

Resolved, That the legislative committee be requested to report to the Commission the expediency of so amending Sec. 47 of Article IV. of the existing constitution of this State, as to empower the Legislature to authorize the granting of licenses upon the following conditions:

1st, That the question of license or no license shall be submitted to the electors of any city, village, or town, in the manner to be provided by law;

2d, If a majority of such electors are in favor of licensing the traffic in their respective municipalities, then the proper authorities of such municipality to have the exclusive control of the granting of licenses, and the moneys arising therefrom to enter into the general fund of such city, etc.;

3d, When the electors, etc., shall be opposed to licensing the traffic, then, as to such city, village, etc., prohibitory laws to be in force;

Would respectfully submit the following minority report:

That, while there may exist some valid objections to the principle of local option set forth in the above resolutions, the undersigned cannot agree with the majority of this committee as to the reasons set forth in the report made by them for rejecting the above resolutions.

The present constitution expressly forbids the Legislature making any laws granting license for the sale of spirituous liquors, thus embarrassing the action of that body, and *absolutely* preventing them from passing any laws in regard to such traffic, so that the State may derive some revenue therefrom.

The experience of the past has shown that the prohibitory law is impracticable, and has *utterly* failed to accomplish the end so fondly anticipated by its projectors. While it has been in force the sale of intoxicating liquors has been carried on, intemperance has increased, rather than diminished, and the law-making power has been powerless, except to insist upon prohibitory laws.

The sentiment of the majority, in their report, that "There is also something *repugnant* to the moral sense of the community in the idea of licensing, and thus apparently legalizing a traffic which is so prolific of evil to individuals and to society, although the real object of such licensing may be the regulation of, or restraining, to some extent, this business," is not accepted by the majority of the people of this State, and is, indeed, the subject of sentimental theories, and of no practical importance whatever. The Federal government *ignores* such notions of "repugnance to the moral sense of the communities," and reaps a great revenue from a tax imposed upon this traffic. And the people of this State, after testing for some twelve years the virtues of the prohibitory laws, in 1867, by some 14,000 majority, voted against prohibition, and in favor of a license system.

The opinion of the majority of the committee, that under existing laws, as interpreted by the Supreme Court, ample power exists in the Legislature to raise a revenue upon this traffic is hardly correct, as will be readily seen by examination of the decision of the Supreme Court referred to, and with present laws. And if the power to tax the traffic exist,—if the policy of the existing law be to tolerate a system so "repugnant to the moral sense of the community," why not place the subject beyond all doubt, and where it will be fully understood, and its benefits secured to the people?

The principle of the above resolutions is to refer this whole subject to the people. If any municipality choose to abandon all attempts at the exploded theory of prohibition, and impose a tax upon this traffic and keep it within proper bounds, there seems no good reason why this right should be denied them, simply because their neighbor still insists upon the illusion of prohibition.

Theoretically, the plan suggested in the resolution seems just; in practice, inconveniences may result. Of this, the undersigned is unable to say. But that the organic law should be changed in this regard, is obvious, for the following reasons:

1st, Because the present prohibitory law has failed to suppress the traffic;

2d, Because, with the existing constitutional provision, the Legislature is prohibited from passing a license law;

3d, Because the people of the State desire a change of the law;

4th, For the reason that the cause of temperance will be advanced by a well guarded law imposing a tax upon the traffic.

The undersigned, therefore, trusts that the Commission will take this subject under serious consideration, and adopt some provision upon this subject that will meet the wants of the people and the necessities of the occasion.

And for that purpose, the undersigned offers the following as a substitute for Sec. 36 of Article IV:

License may be granted for the sale of ardent spirits or other intoxicating liquors, by the several township boards, and the city and village authorities of the several cities and villages in this State; but no person or persons shall so engage without a license, under penalty of three hundred dollars for the first offense, and of five hundred dollars, or imprisonment for one year, one or both, as the Legislature may provide by law; and the several authorities shall grant no license, without the person or persons obtaining the same shall have first paid into the treasury of such township, city, or village the sum of three hundred dollars, or more, as the Legislature may provide by law, and in no case shall any person or persons obtaining a license sell such liquors to any insane or idiotic person, pauper, or common drunkard, under penalty of forfeiting his or their license. All such license fees shall be applied to, and become a part of, the primary school fund.

The Legislature shall enforce, by appropriate legislation, the provisions of this article.

All of which is respectfully submitted.

IRA D. CROUSE.

Report accepted and committee discharged.

On motion of Mr. Meddaugh,

The report was laid on the table.

JUDICIAL DEPARTMENT.

Article VII., of the Judicial Department, was read a third time.

Mr. Hatch, leave being granted,

Moved to amend the article by substituting for the second section the second section of printed number thirty-five;

Which motion prevailed by yeas and nays as follows:

YEAS.

Mr. Crane,	Mr. Hatch,	Mr. Riley,	
Crouse,	Jerome,	Wells,	
Cutcheon,	Meddaugh,	Willits,	
Divine,	Moffatt,	Withey,	
Devereaux,	Pond,	Woodward,	15

NAYS. 0

Mr. Hatch moved to amend the article by substituting for section six the corresponding section of printed number thirty-five;

Which motion prevailed.

Mr. Hatch moved to amend the last substituted section by adding thereto the following: "Each of the judges of the Supreme Court may perform the duties of a circuit judge;"

Which motion did not prevail.

Mr. Meddaugh moved to amend the article by substituting for section seven the corresponding section of printed number thirty-five;"

Which motion prevailed.

Mr. Riley moved to amend the article by adding the following to section eight:

"The Legislature may provide for the trial of causes, at any term of any circuit court, by any attorney at law, to be appointed by the circuit judge, or by stipulation of parties, so that more than one trial may progress at the same time and place; but the judge of the circuit shall in all cases sign the record."

The motion did not prevail, by yeas and nays as follows:

YEAS.

Mr. Crouse,	Mr. Hatch,	Mr. Willits,	
Divine,	Riley,		5

NAYS.

Mr. Crane,	Mr. Meddaugh,	Mr. Wells,	
Cutcheon,	Moffatt,	Withey,	
Devereaux,	Pond,	Woodward,	
Jerome,			10

Mr. Pond moved to amend the article by adding to section nine the following:

"The appellate jurisdiction of said courts shall not extend to any case in which the amount or value of the thing in controversy is less than twenty-five dollars, exclusive of costs, except upon allowance of an appeal or writ of *certiorari* by the judge of the court entitled to exercise such appellate jurisdiction."

Which motion prevailed.

Mr. Middaugh moved to substitute for section thirteen the corresponding section of printed number thirty-five.

Which motion prevailed.

The article was referred to the committee on phraseology.

ELECTIVE FRANCHISE.

Article III., of the Elective Franchise, was read a third time and referred to the committee on phraseology.

BILL OF RIGHTS.

Article II., Bill of Rights, was read a third time.

Mr. Woodward offered the following as a substitute for section two:

SEC. 2. No law shall be passed respecting the establishment of a religion, or r tricting the free exercise thereof. No person shall be compelled to attend, erect, or support any place of religious worship, or to pay tithes, taxes, or other rates, for the support of any minister of the gospel or teacher of religion; but this section shall not be so construed as to relieve any person from any specific pecuniary obligation voluntarily assumed.

The substitute was not adopted.

Mr. Pond moved to amend the article by striking out all of section seven after the word "record," in the fourth line.

The motion prevailed by yeas and nays as follows:

YEAS.

Mr. Crane,	Mr. Pond,	Mr. Willits,	
Divine,	Riley,	Woodward,	
Meddaugh,	Wells,		8

NAYS.

Mr. Crouse,	Mr. Hatch,	Mr. Moffatt,	
Cutcheon,	Jerome,	Withey,	
Devereaux,			7

RECESS.

On motion of Mr. Crane,

The Commission took a recess until 2:30 P. M.

AFTERNOON SESSION.

The Commission was called to order by the chairman at 2:30.

Roll called: quorum present.

BILL OF RIGHTS.

The consideration of Article II., Bill of Rights, was resumed on the order of third reading.

Mr. Pond moved to amend the article by striking out section twenty-three.

The motion did not prevail, by yeas and nays, as follows:

YEAS.

Mr. Meddaugh,	Mr. Pond,	Mr. Wells,	
Moffatt,	Riley,	Willits,	6

NAYS.

Mr. Crouse,	Mr. Devereaux,	Mr. Withey,	
Cutcheon,	Hatch,	Woodward,	
Divine,	Jerome,		8

The article was referred to the committee on phraseology.

GENERAL ORDER.

On motion of Mr. Hatch,

The Commission resolved itself into committee of the whole on the general order, Mr. Divine in the chair, and after some time spent therein the committee rose, and through their chairman made the following report:

REPORT OF THE COMMITTEE OF THE WHOLE.

The committee of the whole have had under consideration Article XIX.–A., of Railroads;

Have made sundry amendments thereto, and have directed me to report the same back to the Commission, recommending that the amendments be concurred in, and that the article when so amended do pass, and ask to be discharged from the further consideration of the subject.

JOHN DIVINE,
Chairman of Committee.

Report accepted and committee discharged.

The amendments made to the article by the committee of the whole were concurred in, except as to those by which sections five and seven were struck out.

The amendment by which section five was stricken out was not concurred in, by yeas and nays, as follows:

YEAS.

Mr. Crane,	Mr. Hatch,	Mr. Wells,	
Crouse,	Jerome,	Woodward,	
Devereaux,			7

NAYS.

Mr. Cutcheon,	Mr. Moffatt,	Mr. Willets,	
Divine,	Pond,	Withey,	
Meddaugh,	Riley,		8

The amendment by which section seven was stricken out was concurred in, by yeas and nays, as follows:

YEAS.

Mr. Crane,	Mr. Jerome,	Mr. Willits,	
Cutcheon,	Meddaugh,	Withey,	
Divine,	Pond,	Woodward,	
Hatch,			10

NAYS.

Mr. Crouse,	Mr. Moffatt,	Mr. Wells,	
Devereaux,	Riley,		5

The article was ordered printed and placed on the order of third reading.

JUDICIAL—BILL OF RIGHTS—ELECTIVE FRANCHISE.

By the committee on phraseology:

The committee on phraseology, to whom was referred

Article VII., of Judicial Department;

Article II., Bill of Rights;

Article III., of the Elective Franchise;

Respectfully report that they have had the same under consideration, and have directed me to report the same back to the Commission with amendments thereto, recommending that the amendments be concurred in, and ask to be discharged from the further consideration of the subject.

ASHLEY POND,

Chairman of Committee.

Report accepted and committee discharged.

The amendments were concurred in, and the articles ordered printed, and placed on the order of final passage.

ADJOURNMENT.

On motion of Mr. Crane,

The Commission adjourned.

TWENTY-SEVENTH DAY.

LANSING, *Friday, September 26, 1873.*

The Commission was called to order at 9 o'clock, by the Chairman.

CITIES AND VILLAGES.

By the committee on phraseology:

The committee on phraseology, to whom was referred

Article XVI., entitled Cities and Villages,

Respectfully report that they have had the same under consideration, and have directed me to report the same back to the Commission without amendment, and ask to be discharged from the further consideration of the subject.

H. H. HATCH,
Chairman of Committee.

Report accepted and committee discharged.

The article was ordered printed and placed on the order of final passage.

LEAVE OF ABSENCE.

Mr. Willits asked and obtained leave of absence for Mr. Riley until Tuesday next.

Mr. Hatch asked and obtained leave of absence for himself indefinitely;

Also, for Mr. Jerome until Tuesday next.

ADJOURNMENT.

On motion of Mr. Withey,

The Commission adjourned until Tuesday next, at 2 o'clock P. M.

TWENTY-EIGHT DAY.

LANSING, *Tuesday, September 30, 1873.*

The Commission was called to order at 9 o'clock by the Chairman.

Roll called: quorum present.

LEAVE OF ABSENCE.

Mr. Meddaugh asked and obtained indefinite leave of absence for Mr. Giddings on account of necessary business.

RAILROADS.

Article XIX.-A, of Railroads was read a third time.

Mr. Meddaugh, leave being granted, moved to amend the article, by adding after the words "received by it," in the third line of section four, the words, "equal to seventy-five per cent of the par value of such bonds or evidences of indebtedness;"

Which motion did not prevail, by yeas and nays as follows:

YEAS.

Mr. Meddaugh, Mr. Pond, Mr. Upson,
Moffatt, Riley, Willits, 6

NAYS.

Mr. Crane, Mr. Devereaux, Mr. Wells,
Cutcheon, Jerome, Woodward, 6

Mr. Devereaux, leave being granted, moved to amend the article by striking out section five;

Which motion did not prevail by yeas and nays as follows:

YEAS.

Mr. Crane, Mr. Jerome, Mr. Woodward,
Devereaux, Wells, 5

NAYS.

Mr. Crouse,	Mr. Moffatt,	Mr. Upson,
Cutcheon,	Pond,	Willits,
Meddaugh,	Riley,	8

Mr. Woodward, leave being granted, moved to amend the article by striking out of the second line of section five, the words "holding or exercising any civil office or appointment;"

Which motion prevailed.

Mr. Devereaux, leave being granted, moved to amend the article by striking out of section one all after the word "laws" in the first line, to and including the word "and" in the second line, and also by striking out all of said section after the word "State" in the third line;

Which motion did not prevail, by yeas and nays, as follows:

YEAS.

Mr. Crane,	Mr. Jerome,	Mr. Woodward, 5
Devereaux,	Wells,	

NAYS.

Mr. Crouse,	Mr. Moffatt,	Mr Upson,
Cutcheon,	Pond,	Willits, 8
Meddaugh,	Riley,	

The article was referred to the committee on phraseology.

GENERAL ORDER.

On motion of Mr. Willits,

The Commission resolved itself into committee of the whole on the general order, Mr. Pond in the chair, and after some time spent therein, the committee rose, and through their chairman made the following report:

REPORT OF THE COMMITTEE OF THE WHOLE.

The committee of the whole have had under consideration Article VIII. of State Officers;

Article XX. of Amendments and Revision of the Constitution;

Article ——. of the Improvement of Streams; and

The Schedule;

Have made sundry amendments thereto, and have directed me to report the same back to the Commission, recommending that the amendments be concurred in, and that the sections and articles when so amended do pass, and ask to be discharged from the further consideration of the subject.

The committtee of the whole have also had under consideration

Article XVII. of the Militia;

Have made no amendments thereto, and have directed me to report the same back to the Commission, recommending that it do pass, and ask to be discharged from the further consideration of the subject.

The committee of the whole have also had under consideration

Certain sections relating to the taking of private property for public and private use, and have directed me to report the same back to the Commission, with a recommendation that it be referred back to the committee on miscellaneous provisions.

ASHLEY POND,
Chairman of Committee.

Report accepted and committee discharged.

The amendments made to the three first named articles were concurred in, and the articles ordered printed, and placed on the order of third reading.

Article XVII. was placed on the order of third reading.

On motion of Mr. Moffatt,

The schedule was recommitted to the committee on that subject.

The recommendation of the committee as to the last named sections was concurred in.

RAILROADS.

By the committee on phraseology:

The committee of phraseology to whom was referred

Article XIX.–A;

Respectfully report that they have had the same under consideration, and have directed me to report the same back to the commission without amendment, and ask to be discharged from further consideration of the subject.

ASHLEY POND,
Chairman.

Report accepted and committee discharged.

The article was ordered printed, and placed on the order of final passage.

ADJOURNMENT.

On motion of Mr. Crouse,

The Commission adjourned.

TWENTY-NINTH DAY.

LANSING, *Wednesday, October 1, 1873.*

The Commission was called to order at 9 o'clock, by the Chairman.

Roll called: quorum present.

CORPORATIONS OTHER THAN MUNICIPAL.

Mr. Pond moved that

Article XVI., of Corporations other than municipal, and Article XIX.–A, of Railroads, be referred back to the committee on phraseology, with instructions to combine the same into a single article;

Which motion prevailed.

The committee on phraseology thereupon submitted the following report:

The committee on phraseology, to whom was referred

Act XIX.–A, and Article XVI.,

Respectfully report that they have had the same under consideration, and have directed me to report the same back to the Commission, the several sections thereof combined into a single article, to stand as article XV., of Corporations other than Municipal, and ask to be discharged from the further consideration of the subject.

ASHLEY POND,
Chairman of Committee.

Report accepted and committee discharged.

The combined article was ordered printed, and placed on the order of final passage.

MILITIA.

Article XVII., of the Militia, was read a third time, ordered printed, and placed on the order of final passage.

AMENDMENT AND REVISION OF THE CONSTITUTION.

Article XX., of Amendment and Revision of the Constitution, was read a third time, and referred to the committee on phraseology.

FINAL PASSAGE.

On the order of final passage the Commission considered, as in committee of the whole, Articles I., II., III., and IV.

During the consideration of the last named article,

Mr. Moffatt moved to amend the same by substituting for section two the corresponding section as originally reported by tho committee on legislative department;

The motion did not prevail, by yeas and nays as follows:

YEAS.

Mr. Meddaugh, Mr. Moffatt, Mr. Pond,
Woodward, 4

NAYS.

Mr. Crane,	Mr. Devereaux,	Mr. Wells,	
Crouse,	Jerome,	Willits,	
Cutcheon,	Riley,	Withey,	9

Mr. Woodward moved to amend the article by substituting the word "three" in place of "four" in the first line of section fifteen, relating to the compensation of members of the Legislature.

The motion did not prevail, by yeas and nays as follows:

YEAS.

Mr. Wells,	Mr. Woodward,	2

NAYS.

Mr. Crane,	Mr. Meddaugh,	Mr. Riley,	
Crouse,	Moffatt,	Willits,	
Cutcheon,	Pond,	Withey,	
Devereaux,			10

RECESS.

On motion of Mr. Devereaux,

The Commission took a recess until 2:30 P. M.

AFTERNOON SESSION.

The Commission was called to order by the chairman at 2:30.

Roll called: quorum present.

AMENDMENT AND REVISION OF THE CONSTITUTION.

By the committee on phraseology, etc.:

The committee on phraseology, etc., to whom was referred Article XX., entitled "Amendment and Revision of the Constitution,"

Respectfully report that they have had the same under consideration, and have directed me to report the same back to the Commission without amendment, and ask to be discharged from the further consideration of the subject.

ASHLEY POND, *Chairman.*

Report accepted and committee discharged.

The article was ordered printed, and placed on the order of final passage.

RESTRICTING LOCAL TAXATION.

By the committee on finance and taxation:

The committee on finance and taxation, to whom was referred a resolution directing an inquiry into the expediency of restricting municipal corporations from creating debts, respectfully report that, after considering the subject, together with the financial condition of many of the cities of the State, they have directed me to report herewith a section providing for such limitation at ten per cent of their assessed valuation.

They also herewith report a statement from the financial exhibits furnished by several of the prominent cities of the State.

Respectfully submitted.

D. H. JEROME, *Chairman.*

Report accepted and committee discharged.

The proposed section is as follows:

SEC. 2. Hereafter no city shall become indebted to an amount exceeding ten per cent of its assessed valuation, including debts incurred by and for school districts within the corporate limits of such city.

The financial exhibit referred to in the report is as follows

CITIES.	VALUATION.	CITY DEBT.	SCHOOL DEBT.	TOTAL.
Owosso	$241.570	None.	$40,000	$40,000
Bay City	1,712,550	$327,000	76,000	403,000
Saginaw	1,917,000	247,000	49,000	296,000
Niles	884,580	26,000	12,500	38,500
Holland	348,990	11,500	......	11,500
Battle Creek	980,560	8,300	78,000	86,300
Coldwater	1,000,000	4,000	6,000	10,000
Adrian	1,774,607	47,000	55,250	102,250
Monroe	953,647	33,000	500	33,500
Grand Haven	547,510	......	34,000	34,000
Grand Rapids	4,551,250	139,700	49,500	189,200
East Saginaw	3,204,663	565,393	50,000	615,393
Detroit	27,091,645	901,400	900,000	1,801,400

LICENSING THE SALE OF LIQUORS.

By the committee on legislative department:

The committee on the legislative department, who were instructed as follows, viz.:

"*Resolved,* That the committee on the legislative department be instructed to inquire into the expediency of framing a section to be submitted separately, and if adopted, to stand in the place of section 47 of Article IV. of the present constitution, in manner following:

"SEC. 47. The Legislature shall, at their first session after the adoption of this amendment, pass all necessary laws regulating the granting of licenses for the sale of spirituous and intoxicating liquors, or for imposing a special tax upon the traffic in the same;"

Respectfully report that in the absence of one of their number, they are unable to agree upon any recommendation for or against the proposition contained in the said resolution, and they therefore report back the said proposed section in the form of a separate proposition, to be submitted at the time of the submission of the proposed amended constitution, without any recommendation in regard to the same, and ask to be discharged from the further consideration of the subject.

CHAS. UPSON,
IRA D. CROUSE.

Report accepted and committee discharged.

The proposed section is as follows:

At the election when this amended constitution shall be submitted to the electors of this State for adoption or rejection, there shall also be submitted to such electors the following proposition, to stand, in case of its adoption, as Section 47 of Article IV., in the present constitution of this State, in place of said section 47 in said Article IV., as it now stands, and of section 36 in said Article IV., in said proposed amended constitution, if adopted, viz.:

"SECTION 47. The Legislature shall, at its first session after the adoption of this section, pass all necessary laws regulating the granting of licenses for the sale of spirituous and intoxicating liquors, or for imposing a special tax upon the traffic in the same."

Said section shall be separately submitted to the electors of this State for their adoption or rejection in form following, to-wit:

A separate ballot may be given by every person having the right to vote, to be deposited in a separate box.

Upon the ballots given for said separate section shall be written, printed, or partly written, the words "License—Yes;" and upon the ballots given against the adoption in like manner the words, "License—No."

If at said election a majority of the votes for and against said section shall contain the words "License—Yes," then there shall be inserted as section 47, in the said article IV., the said proposed section 47, in the place of section 47 as contained in the present constitution, and of section 36 in said article in the proposed amended constitution.

The proposed section was ordered printed in bill form, referred to the committee of the whole, and placed on the general order.

Mr. Woodward moved that the proposed section embodied in the report of the minority of the committee on the legislative department, presented on the 25th of September, be taken from the table and printed, and referred to the committee of the whole, and placed on the general order;

Which motion prevailed.

The said section, proposed to stand as section 36 of Article IV., is as follows:

SEC. 36. License may be granted for the sale of ardent spirits or other intoxicating liquors, by the several township boards, and the city and village authorities of the several cities and villages in this State; but no person or persons shall so engage without a license, under penalty of three hundred dollars for the first offense, and of five hundred dollars, or imprisonment for one year, one or both, as the Legislature may provide by law; and the several authorities shall grant no license, without the person or persons obtaining the same shall have first paid into the treasury of such township, city, or village, the sum of three hundred dollars, or more, as the Legislature may provide by law, and in no case shall any person or persons obtaining a license sell such liquors to any insane or idiotic person, paupers, or common drunkards, under penalty of forfeiting his or their license. All such license fees shall be applied to, and become a part of, the primary school fund.

The Legislature shall enforce, by appropriate legislation, the provisions of this article.

STATE OFFICERS.

Article VIII., of State Officers, was read a third time and referred to the committee on phraseology.

IMPROVEMENT OF STREAMS.

Printed number fifty-five, embodying provisions relating to the improvement of streams, was read a third time and referred to the committee on miscellaneous provisions, to be embodied in the article on that subject.

FINAL PASSAGE.

The Commission resumed the consideration of articles on the order of final passage, as in committee of the whole, Mr. Meddaugh in the chair, and had under further consideration,

Article V., of the Executive Department, and

Article VI., of the Judicial Department,

To which sundry amendments were made.

STATE OFFICERS.

By the committee on phraseology, etc.:

The committee on phraseology, etc., to whom was referred Article VIII.,

Respectfully report that they have had the same under consideration, and have directed me to report the same back to the Commission without amendment, and ask to be discharged from the further consideration of the subject,

ASHLEY POND, *Chairman.*

Report accepted and committee discharged.

The article was ordered printed, and placed on the order of final passage.

ADJOURNMENT.

On motion of Mr. Riley,

The Commission adjourned.

THIRTIETH DAY.

LANSING, *Thursday, October 2, 1873.*

The Commission was called to order at 9 o'clock by the Chairman.

Roll called: quorum present.

MUNICIPAL CORPORATIONS.

Mr. Pond moved that Article X., of Counties, Article XI., of Townships, and Article XVI., of Cities and Villages, be consolidated into a single article, to stand as Article X., of Municipal Corporations.

Which motion prevailed.

LEAVE OF ABSENCE.

Mr. Moffatt asked and obtained indefinite leave of absence for himself on account of necessary business.

FINAL PASSAGE.

On this order, the Commission, as in committee of the whole, had under consideration

Article VI., of the Judicial Department;

Article VIII., of the Elective Franchise;

Article IX., of Salaries;

Article X., of Municipal Corporations, to and including section twelve.

ADJOURNMENT.

On motion of Mr. Devereaux,

The Commission adjourned until 3 o'clock p. m.

AFTERNOON SESSION.

At three o'clock p. m., there being no quorum present,

On motion of Mr. Pond,

The Commission adjourned.

THIRTY-FIRST DAY.

LANSING, *Friday, October 3, 1873.*

The Commission was called to order at 9 o'clock, by the Chairman.

Roll called: quorum present.

IMPROVEMENT OF STREAMS.

By the committee on judiciary:

The committee on judiciary, to whom was referred printed bill No. 55, relative to the improvement of streams,

Respectfully report that they have had the same under consideration, and have directed me to report the same back to the Commission without amendment, and without recommendation, and ask to be discharged from the further consideration of the subject.

S. L. WITHEY, *Chairman.*

Report accepted and committee discharged.

The bill was laid on the table.

MISCELLANEOUS PROVISIONS.

The committee on judiciary, to whom was referred Article XIX., on Miscellaneous Provisions,

Respectfully report that they have had the same under consideration, have amended the same, and have directed me to report the same back to the Commission, and recommend that the same do pass, and ask to be discharged from the further consideration of the subject.

S. L. WITHEY, *Chairman.*

Report accepted and committee discharged.

The article was read twice, ordered printed, referred to the committee of the whole, and placed on the general order.

ADJOURNMENT.

Mr. Withey moved,

That when the Commission adjourn to-day, it be until Tuesday of next week, at 2 o'clock p. m.

Mr. Riley moved to amend by making the adjournment until the first Tuesday in November;

Mr. Pond moved a substitute fixing the time for the 13th of October, at 2:30 o'clock.

After some debate,

Mr. Withey, with the consent of the Commission, withdrew his motion.

Mr. Withey moved, as the sense of the Commission, that it hold its sessions continuously until its work is completed.

Which motion prevailed.

FINAL PASSAGE.

On the order of final passage the Commission considered, as in committee of the whole,

Article X., of Municipal Corporations;

Article XII., of Impeachments and Removals from Office;

Article XIII., of Education;

Article XIV., of Finance and Taxation.

During the consideration of Article XIII.,

Mr. Meddaugh moved to amend the same by inserting the word "general" before the word "supervision," in the ninth line of section two, and also by striking out of said ninth line the words "and control."

The motion did not prevail, by yeas and nays as follow:

YEAS.

Mr. Crouse,	Mr. Meddaugh,	Mr. Wells,	
Devereaux,	Upson,	Woodward,	6

NAYS.

Mr. Crane,	Mr. Jerome,	Mr. Riley,	
Cutcheon,	Pond,	Willits,	6

FINANCE AND TAXATION.

The consideration of Article XIV., on Finance and Taxation, was proceeded with to section 13, the question pending being on an amendment proposed by Mr. Wells, prohibiting the exemption of church property from taxation.

LEAVE OF ABSENCE.

On motion of Mr. Jerome,

Mr. Withey was granted leave of absence indefinitely.

NEW MEMBER.

The Chairman presented the following communication:

LANSING, *October 2, 1873*

HON. S. M. CUTCHEON, *Prest. of Constitutional Commission:*

SIR—Hon. Wm. M. Ferry this day appeared before me and subscribed to the oath of office as a member of the Constitutional Commission.

Very respectfully,

DANIEL STRIKER,

Secretary of State.

RECESS.

On motion of Mr. Devereaux,

Commission took a recess until 2:00 p. m.

AFTERNOON SESSION.

The Commission was called to order by the chairman at 2 o'clock.

Roll called: quorum present.

CORPORATIONS OTHER THAN MUNICIPAL.

On motion of Jerome,

Article XI., of Corporations other than Municipal, was made the special order for Wednesday next at 9 o'clock.

FINAL PASSAGE.

The Commission resumed the consideration of articles on the order of final passage, as in committee of the whole.

Article XIV., of Finance and Taxation, being under consideration, the pending amendment, relative to prohibiting the exemption of church property from taxation, was adopted.

Article X., on Municipal Corporations, was considered and amended.

PRINTING OF AMENDED ARTICLES.

The clerk was directed to have such articles as have been considerably amended, and are on the order of final passage, printed.

ADJOURNMENT.

Mr. Woodward moved that when the Commission adjourn it be until Wednesday next at 9 o'clock;

Which motion prevailed.

On motion of Mr. Crane,

The Commission adjourned.

THIRTY-SECOND DAY.

LANSING, *Wednesday, October 8, 1873.*

The Commission was called to order at 9 o'clock by the Chairman.

Roll called: quorum present.

SPECIAL ORDER.

Mr. Pond moved that the special order, being the consideration of

Article XI., of Corporations other than Municipal,

Be deferred until the afternoon session.

Which motion prevailed.

MISCELLANEOUS PROVISIONS.

On motion of Mr. Jerome,

The Commission resolved itself into committee of the whole, on the general order, and after some time spent therein, the committee rose and through their chairman made the following report:

REPORT OF THE COMMITTEE OF THE WHOLE.

The committee of the whole have had under consideration,

Article XIX., Miscellaneous Provisions.

Have made some progress therein, but not having gone through therewith, have directed me to report that fact to the Commission, and ask leave to sit again.

D. H. JEROME, *Chairman.*

Report accepted and leave granted.

RECESS.

On motion of Mr. Devereaux,

The Commission took a recess until 2:00 P. M.

AFTERNOON SESSION.

The Commission was called to order by the chairman at 2 o'clock.

Roll called: quorum present.

MISCELLANEOUS.—LICENSES.—RESTRICTIONS.

On motion of Mr. Hatch,

The Commission resolved itself into committee of the whole on the general order, and after some time spent therein the committee rose, and through their chairman made the following report:

REPORT OF THE COMMITTEE OF THE WHOLE.

The committee of the whole have had under further consideration,

Article XIX., Miscellaneous Provisions;

Also,

Printed number 63, being a proposed substitute for section 47 of Article IV.;

Also,

Printed number 59, relative to licenses;

Have made sundry amendments thereto, and have directed me to report the same back to the Commission, recommending that the amendments be concurred in, and ask to be discharged from the further consideration of the subject.

D. H. JEROME, *Chairman.*

The amendments were concurred in, except as to the amendment by which section 10 of Article XIX. was stricken out, and the substitute reported by the committee to printed number 63.

ELIGIBILITY OF WOMEN FOR OFFICE.

Mr. Hatch moved that Article XIX. be referred back to the committee on miscellaneous provisions, with instructions to report the following as a substitute for section 10:

SEC. 10. Women may hold office under such restrictions and limitations as may be prescribed by law.

The motion did not prevail, by yeas and nays as follows:

YEAS.

Mr. Hatch,	Mr. Willits,	Mr. Withey,	
Wells,			4

NAYS.

Mr. Crane,	Mr. Divine,	Mr. Upson,	
Cutcheon,	Jerome,	Woodward,	
Devereaux,	Pond,		8

The question being on concurring in the amendment by which section ten was stricken out, the same was concurred in, by yeas and nays as follows:

YEAS.

Mr. Crane,	Mr. Divine,	Mr. Upson,	
Cutcheon,	Jerome,	Woodward,	
Devereaux,	Pond,		8

NAYS.

Mr. Hatch	Mr. Willits,	Mr. Withey,	
Wells,			4

The question being on concurring in the substtoitute printed number 63, the same was not concurred in, by yeas and nays as follows:

YEAS.

Mr. Devereaux,	Mr. Jerome,	Mr. Withey,	
Hatch,	Wells,	Woodward,	6

NAYS.

Mr. Crane,	Mr. Divine,	Mr. Upson,	
Cutcheon,	Pond,	Willits,	6

On motion of Mr. Upson,

Printed number 63, relative to the sale of liquors, was amended as agreed to in committee of the whole.

Article XIX. was placed on the order of third reading.

Printed number 63 was ordered re-printed, and placed on the order of third reading.

Printed number 59 was laid on the table.

RESIGNATION OF COMMISSIONER GIDDINGS.

The Chairman announced a dispatch from the Hon. E. W. Giddings, a member of the Commission from the seventh Congressional district, tendering his resignation on account of imperative business engagements.

CORPORATIONS OTHER THAN MUNICIPAL.

The special order for the afternoon, being the consideration of Article XI., of Corporations other than Municipal, having been informally passed,

Mr. Jerome moved that the same be made the special order for to-morrow at 9 o'clock;

Which motion prevailed.

ADJOURNMENT.

On motion of Mr. Jerome,

The Commission adjourned.

THIRTY-THIRD DAY.

LANSING, *Thursday, October 9, 1873.*

The Commission was called to order at 9 o'clock by the Chairman.

Roll called: quorum present.

CONTROL OF UNIVERSITY FUNDS.

Mr. Wells presented a petition of Amberg & Helmer, Stebbins & Coon, and 102 others of Battle Creek, relative to the management and control of the University and its funds;

Referred to the committee on education.

The petition is as follows:

To the Constitutional Commission:

The undersigned, citizens and voters of Battle Creek, beg leave to represent that they are decidedly opposed to any attempt on the part of your Commission, to change the Constitution so as to give control of the University and its funds into the hands of the Regents, as contemplated in the amendment of Mr. Pond, of Wayne. We are of the opinion that the University should, by right, remain under the control of the people, who furnish it with subsistence.

MISCELLANEOUS PROVISIONS.

Article XIX., Miscellaneous Provisions, was read a third time.

Mr. Wells, leave being granted, moved to amend the article by restoring section 10, to and including the word "eligible," in the third line, and to add thereto the following: "To the office of county superintendent of schools, school inspector, and other school offices;"

Which motion prevailed.

The article was referred to the committee on phraseology.

FINAL PASSAGE.

The Commission took up the consideration of articles on the order of final passage.

Article I., of Boundaries and Seat of Government,

Was passed, two-thirds of the Commission voting therefor, by yeas and nays as follows:

YEAS.

Mr. Crane,	Mr. Ferry,	Mr. Upson,	
Crouse,	Hatch,	Wells,	
Cutcheon,	Jerome,	Willits,	
Devereaux,	Meddaugh,	Withey,	
Divine,	Pond,	Woodward,	15

NAYS. 0

Article II., Bill of Rights, was passed, two-thirds of the Commission voting therefor, by yeas and nays, as follows:

YEAS.

Mr. Crane,	Mr. Ferry,	Mr. Upson,	
Crouse,	Hatch,	Wells,	
Cutcheon,	Jerome,	Willits,	
Devereaux,	Meddaugh,	Withey,	
Divine,	Pond,	Woodward,	15

NAYS. 0

Article III., of Boundaries and Seat of Government,

Was passed, two-thirds of the Commission voting therefor, by yeas and nays as follows:

YEAS.

Mr. Crane,	Mr. Ferry,	Mr. Upson,	
Crouse,	Hatch,	Wells,	
Cutcheon,	Jerome,	Willits,	
Devereaux,	Meddaugh,	Withey,	
Divine,	Pond,	Woodward,	15

NAYS. 0

The articles were referred to the committee on phraseology for engrossment.

CORPORATIONS OTHER THAN MUNICIPAL.

On motion of Mr. Hatch,

The Commission resolved itself into committee of the whole on the special order, Mr. Willits in the chair, and after some time spent therein the committee rose, and through their chairman made the following report:

REPORT OF THE COMMITTEE OF THE WHOLE.

The committee of the whole have had under consideration Article XI., of Corporations other than Municipal,

Have made some progress therein, but not having gone through therewith, have directed me to report that fact to the Commission, and ask leave to sit again.

EDWIN WILLITS,
Chairman.

Report accepted and leave granted.

RECESS.

On motion of Mr. Hatch,

The Commission took a recess until 2:00 P. M.

AFTERNOON SESSION.

The Commission was called to order by the Chairman at 2:00 o'clock.

Roll called: quorum present.

SPECIAL ORDER.

On motion of Mr. Hatch,

The Commission resolved itself into committee of the whole on the special order, and after some time spent therein, the committee rose and through their chairman made the following report:

REPORT OF THE COMMITTEE OF THE WHOLE.

The committee of the whole have had under further consideration,

Article XI., of Corporations other than Municipal,

Have made sundry amendments thereto, and have directed me to report the same back to the Commission, recommending that the amendments be concurred in, and that the article when so amended do pass, and ask to be discharged from the further consideration of the subject.

EDWIN WILLITS, *Chairman.*

Report accepted and committee discharged.

On motion of Mr. Willits,

The article was laid on the table.

FINAL PASSAGE.

The Commission took up the order of final passage.

Article V. of the Judicial Department,

Was passed, two-thirds of the members of the Commission voting therefor, by yeas and nays, as follows:

YEAS.

Mr. Crane,	Mr. Hatch,	Mr. Upson,	
Crouse,	Jerome,	Wells,	
Cutcheon,	Meddaugh,	Willits,	
Devereaux,	Pond,	Withey,	
Divine,	Riley,	Woodward,	
Ferry,			16

NAYS. 0

SENATORIAL DISTRICTS.

Article IV., of the Legislative Department, being on its final passage,

Mr. Meddaugh, leave being granted, moved to amend the same by striking out section two, and inserting in lieu thereof, the following:

SEC. 2. The Senate shall consist of thirty-two members. But, after the year 1875, the Legislature may increase the number to thirty-three, by authorizing the election of two Senators in that portion of the State now included within the limits of the Thirty-second Senatorial District. Senators shall be elected for four years, and by single districts. At the first election after the adoption of this amended Constitution, Senators in the odd-numbered districts shall be elected for two years, and in the even-numbered districts for four years. Such districts shall be numbered from one to thirty-three inclusive, each of which shall choose one Senator. No county shall be divided in the formation of Senate districts, unless such county shall be equitably entitled to two or more Senators.

The motion prevailed, by yeas and nays, as follows:

YEAS.

Mr. Crane,	Mr. Meddaugh,	Mr. Upson.	
Cutcheon,	Pond,	Woodward.	8
Divine,	Riley,		

NAYS.

Mr. Crouse,	Mr. Jerome,	Mr. Willits,	
Devereaux,	Wells,	Withey.	
Hatch,			7

The article was then passed, two-thirds of the members of the Commission voting therefor, as follows:

YEAS.

Mr. Crane,	Mr. Hatch,	Mr Upson,	
Crouse,	Jerome,	Wells,	
Cutcheon,	Meddaugh,	Willits,	
Devereaux,	Pond,	Withey,	
Divine,	Riley,	Woodward.	15

NAYS. 0

The articles were referred to the committee on phraseology, for engrossment.

ADJOURNMENT.

On motion of Mr. Crane,

The Commission adjourned.

THIRTY-FOURTH DAY.

LANSING, *Friday, October 10, 1873.*

The Commission was called to order at 9 o'clock, by the Chairman.

Roll called: quorum present.

PUBLIC HEALTH.

The Chairman laid before the Commission the following communication from the State Board of Health:

LANSING, *October 9th, 1873.*

Hon. S. M. Cutcheon, President of the Constitutional Commission:

SIR—In this memorial the undersigned petitioners respectfully suggest that as for the individual man, one of the primary laws of nature is self-preservation, so, also, one of the first duties of the State is the protection of the lives and health of the people, and we ask your honorable body to consider the propriety of embodying in the proposed new Constitution some recognition of the principle sought to be expressed in the paragraph herewith respectfully submitted.

Very Respectfully,

R. C. KEDZIE,
HOMER O. HITCHCOCK,
HENRY B. BAKER,

Committee from the State Board of Health on "Legislation in the interests of Public Health."

SEC.—. The Legislature shall pass all laws necessary for the protection of the lives and health of the people; especially such laws as shall best guard the people from dangers to life and health which arise from the aggregation of persons in organized society, and which as individuals they are unable to avoid or control.

Mr. Wells presented to the Commission the following memorial:

LANSING, *October 8th, 1873.*

To the Honorable Constitutional Commission:

The undersigned, members of the State Board of Health, a committee of said board on "Poisons, explosives, chemicals, accidents, and special sources of danger to life and health," also a committee on "Legislation in the interests of public health," would respectfully petition the Constitutional Commission to embody in the organic law of the State, some safeguard for the lives and persons of our citizens, when traveling on railroads, steamboats, and other public conveyances. The law ordains that "The State Board of Health shall have the general supervision of the interests of the life and health of the citizens of this State." Charged with so grave a responsibility, we trust that you will not consider us as officiously thrusting ourselves forward in thus calling your attention to causes which annually destroy the life, or dreadfully mutilate the persons of a large number of the citizens of this State. The duties assigned us by the law would seem to leave us no option in the case.

We need not bring before you in detail the list of such accidents. Every newspaper, almost, brings the report of sudden and violent death by railroad accidents, or steamers wrecked. The State Board of Health are convinced that many of these so-called accidents arise from preventable causes. A broken rail, or an unusual storm on the lakes, is often alleged as justifiable excuse for such accidents, and an inscrutable Providence is often held responsible for results springing from human recklessness. In our opinion, Providence should be relieved of much of this responsibility, and the guilty human agents should be held to a stern account by the law. A railroad track knowingly left in a dangerous condition, or a steamboat which leaves harbor in unseaworthy condition, should not be charged to the account of Providence. The improvidence of man should not be charged to the Providence of God.

We recognize the propriety of those provisions in the organic law of the State that throw the strong arm of its sanction around vested rights, and give security to capital. But should not equal sanction be thrown around human life?

No one would accuse railroad directors or steamboat owners of a personal and wanton disregard of human life; but these forms of capital must trust the responsibility for the safety of the traveling public to its subordinates; these subordinates, from the nature of the case, are assigned to specified duties, and when any emergency arises, such officials too often will ask not, "Is there danger to life or person?" but "Is it my special duty to avert that danger?"—and thus shifting the responsibility on some other, perhaps absent, functionary, a train is left unwarned, to rush into the very jaws of death, or a steamboat founders within sight of port, with all its precious freight of human life.

The question arises, how shall we make railroad and steamboat lines, and other public carriers, responsible for the destruction of life, and injury of person—such as would be visited with swift punishment if inflicted by an individual? We must demand from capital some security for the lives of those with respect to whom capital seeks employment; and in the opinion of this committee, the only feasible way is to hold capital responsible in the only way that capital can be influenced, viz., the *danger of loss.* Then capital will seek to guard itself from loss, and some assurance of safety will be given to the traveling public. We come before you to plead for the safety of the poor and unprotected against the rapacity of organized wealth. We would not undermine capital, but we would make life sacred.

We ask therefore your honorable body to embody in the constitution a provision whereby the stockholders of any railroad, or steamboat, or other public carrier, shall forfeit some adequate sum of money for every life destroyed by preventable causes in their management, or by the carelessness, or inefficiency of any of their employes.

If it should be objected that such action would be in the nature of special legislation, we would respectfully ask if any subject can be of more general interest than the protection of the lives and persons of our citizens? The question may arise: why not leave to the legislature the enacting of laws for this protection of person and life? One reason for desiring the engrafting of such provision in the constitution, is that in enforcing such law, enacted by the legislature, the question of its constitutionality would first have to be settled, and years of litigation might ensue before the law would have its full force. Some railroads at the East have said that they design to make litigation for securing personal rights so costly that no man would dare to go to law with a railroad; and thus justice is overborne by the insolence of money. By placing this provision in the constitution, the only question which would come before the courts, would be those of fact, and not of the validity of the law.

We ask this action out of no hostility to railroad or steamboat managers, or other public carriers, but we ask it in the name of that enlighted humanity which holds life sacred unless forfeited by crime. We beseech you not to permit the security of life to be small in order to make the dividends on capital large.

Respectfully submitted.

R. C. KEDZIE,
H. O. HITCHCOCK,
HENRY B. BAKER,

"*Committee on Poisons, Explosives, Chemicals, Accidents, and Special Sources of Danger to Life and Health;*" *and* "*Committee on Legislation in the Interests of Public Health.*"

The communication and memorial were laid on the table.

FINAL PASSAGE.

The Commission took up the consideration of articles on the order of final passage.

Article VI., of the Judicial Department,

Being under consideration.

Mr. Woodward, leave being granted, moved to amend the same so as to make judges of the Supreme and Circuit Courts elective.

The motion did not prevail, by yeas and nays, as follows:

YEAS.

Mr. Crouse,	Mr. Woodward,		2

NAYS.

Mr. Devereaux,	Mr. Meddaugh,	Mr. Wells,	
Ferry,	Pond,	Willits,	
Hatch,	Riley,	Withey,	
Jerome,	Upson,		11

The article was then passed, two-thirds of the members of the Commission voting therefor, by yeas and nays, as follows:

YEAS.

Mr. Crane,	Mr. Hatch,	Mr. Upson,	
Crouse,	Jerome,	Wells,	
Cutcheon,	Meddaugh,	Willits,	
Devereaux,	Pond,	Withey,	
Ferry,	Riley,	Woodward,	
			15

NAYS. 0

Article VII., of the Elective Franchise,

Was passed, two-thirds of the members of the Commission voting therefor, by yeas and nays, as follows:—

YEAS.

Mr. Crane,	Mr. Hatch,	Mr. Upson,	
Cutcheon,	Jerome,	Wells,	
Devereaux,	Meddaugh,	Willits,	
Divine,	Pond,	Withey,	
Ferry,	Riley,	Woodward,	15

NAYS.

Mr. Crouse,			1

Article VIII., of State Officers,

Was passed, two-thirds of the members of the Commission voting therefor, by yeas and nays, as follows:

YEAS.

Mr. Crane,	Mr. Hatch,	Mr. Upson,
Crouse,	Jerome,	Wells,

Mr. Cutcheon,	Mr. Meddaugh,	Mr. Willits,	
Devereaux,	Pond,	Withey,	
Divine,	Riley,	Woodward,	
Ferry,			16

NAYS. 0

Article IX., of Salaries,

Was passed, two-thirds of the members of the Commission voting therefor, by yeas and nays, as follows:

YEAS.

Mr. Crane,	Mr. Hatch,	Mr. Upson,	
Crouse,	Jerome,	Wells,	
Cutcheon,	Meddaugh,	Willits,	
Devereaux,	Pond,	Withey,	
Divine,	Riley,	Woodward,	15

NAYS. 0

The articles were referred to the committee on phraseology for engrossment.

Article X., of Municipal Corporations,

Being under consideration, pending a motion to amend by Mr. Willits,

On motion of Mr. Devereaux,

The Commission took a recess until 2.00 P. M.

AFTERNOON SESSION.

The commission was called to order by the Chairman at 2 o'clock.

Roll called: quorum present.

MISCELLANEOUS PROVISIONS.

By the committee on phraseology:

The committee on phraseology, to whom was referred

Article XIX., Miscellaneous Provisions,

Respectfully report that they have had the same under consideration, and have directed me to report the same back to the Commission with amendment thereto, recommending that the amendment be concurred in, and ask to be discharged from the further consideration of the subject. The committee also recommend that the numbering of the article be changed, to stand as Article XVII.

ASHLEY POND,
Chairman of Committee.

Report accepted and committee discharged.

The amendment was concurred in, and the article was ordered printed and placed on the order of final passage.

FINAL PASSAGE.

The Commission resumed the consideration of articles on the order of final passage.

Article X., of Municipal Corporations, having been further considered,

On motion of Mr. Pond,

The same was referred to the committee on corporations, with instructions to report a provision limiting the amount of indebtedness that may be incurred by municipalities.

Article XII., of Impeachments and Removals from Office,

Was passed, two-thirds of the members of the Commission voting therefor, by yeas and nays, as follows:

YEAS.

Mr. Crane,	Mr. Ferry,	Mr. Upson,	
Crouse,	Jerome,	Wells,	
Cutcheon,	Meddaugh,	Willits,	
Devereaux,	Pond,	Withey,	
Divine,	Riley,	Woodward,	15

NAYS. 0

Article XIII., of Education,

Being under consideration,

Mr. Upson, leave being granted, moved to amend the same so as to restore substantially the provision of the present constitution relative to the control of the University.

The motion did not prevail, by yeas and nays, as follows:

YEAS.

Mr. Crane,	Mr. Meddaugh.	Mr. Withey,	
Crouse,	Upson,	Woodward,	
Deveraux,	Wells,		8

NAYS.

Mr. Cutcheon,	Mr. Hatch,	Mr. Riley,	
Divine,	Jerome,	Willitts,	
Ferry,	Pond,		8

The Article was passed, two-thirds of the members of the Commission voting therefor, by yeas and nays, as follows:

YEAS.

Mr. Crane,	Mr. Ferry,	Mr. Riley,	
Cutcheon,	Hatch,	Wells,	
Deveraux,	Jerome,	Willits,	
Divine,	Pond,	Withey,	12

NAYS.

Mr. Crouse,	Mr. Upson,	Mr. Woodward,	
Meddaugh,			4

Article XIV. of Finance and Taxation,

Being under consideration,

Mr. Withey, leave being granted, moved to amend the same by striking from section thirteen the clause prohibiting the exemption of church property from taxation.

The motion did not prevail, by yeas and nays, as follows:

YEAS.

Mr. Cutcheon,	Mr. Jerome,	Mr. Withey,	
Divine,	Pond,	Woodward,	
Hatch,	Riley,		8

NAYS.

Mr. Crane,	Mr. Ferry,	Mr. Wells,	
Crouse,	Meddaugh,	Willits,	
Devereaux,	Upson,		8

The question being upon the final passage of the article, the same was not passed, two-thirds of the members of the Commission not voting therefor, by yeas and nays, as follows:

YEAS.

Mr. Crane,	Mr. Ferry,	Mr. Upson,	
Crouse,	Meddaugh,	Wells,	
Devereaux,	Pond,	Willits,	9

NAYS.

Mr. Cutcheon,	Mr. Jerome,	Mr. Withey,
Divine,	Riley,	Woodward,
Hatch,		7

Mr. Cutcheon moved that the vote by which the article was lost be reconsidered;

Which motion prevailed.

Mr. Cutcheon moved that the article be recommitted to the committee on finance and taxation, with instructions to strike out the provision relating to the taxation of church property

The motion prevailed, by yeas and nays, as follows:

YEAS.

Mr. Crane,	Mr. Hatch,	Mr. Riley,
Cutcheon,	Jerome,	Withey,
Devereaux,	Pond,	Woodward,
Divine,		10

NAYS.

Mr. Crouse,	Mr. Meddaugh,	Mr. Wells,
Ferry,	Upson,	Willits, 6

Mr. Jerome, from the committee on finance, leave being granted, reported the article back, amended according to instructions, recommending that the amendment be concurred in.

The amendment was concurred in, by yeas and nays, as follows:

YEAS.

Mr. Crane,	Mr. Hatch,	Mr. Riley,
Cutcheon,	Jerome,	Willits,
Devereaux,	Meddaugh,	Withey,
Divine,	Pond,	Woodward, 12

NAYS.

Mr. Crouse,	Mr. Upson,	Mr. Wells,
Ferry,		4

The article being upon its final passage, the same was passed, two-thirds of the members of the Commission voting therefor, by yeas and nays, as follows:

YEAS.

Mr. Crane,	Mr. Hatch,	Mr. Upson,	
Cutcheon,	Jerome,	Willits,	
Devereaux,	Meddaugh,	Withey,	
Divine,	Pond,	Woodward,	
Ferry,	Riley,		14

NAYS.

Mr. Crouse,	Mr. Wells,		2

CORPORATIONS OTHER THAN MUNICIPAL.

Mr. Pond moved that,

Article XI., of Corporations other than Municipal, be taken from the table.

Which motion prevailed.

The question being on concurring in the amendments made to the article by the committee of the whole, the same were concurred in, except as to the action by which sections eight and fourteen were striken out.

The action of the committee by which section eight was stricken out, was concurred in, by yeas and nays, as follows:

YEAS.

Mr. Crouse,	Mr. Hatch,	Mr. Withey,	
Devereaux,	Jerome,	Woodward,	
Ferry,	Wells.		8

NAYS.

Mr. Cutcheon,	Mr. Pond,	Mr. Upson,	
Divine,	Riley,	Willits,	
Meddaugh,			7

The action of the committee by which section fourteen was stricken out, was not concurred in, by yeas and nays, as follows:

YEAS.

Mr. Crane,	Mr. Hatch,	Mr. Withey,	
Devereaux,	Jerome,	Woodward,	
Ferry,	Wells,		8

NAYS.

Mr. Crouse,	Mr. Meddaugh,	Mr. Upson,	
Cutcheon,	Pond,	Willits,	
Divine,	Riley,		8

Mr. Upson moved to recommit the article to the committee on corporations, with instructions to insert the following, to stand as section eight:

SEC. 8. No corporation shall issue any stock except in consideration of money, labor, or property actually received by it, equal to the par value of such stock; nor shall it issue any bonds or other evidence of indebtedness except for money, labor, or property actually received by it.

The motion did not prevail, by yeas and nays, as follows:

YEAS.

Mr. Cutcheon,	Mr. Pond,	Mr. Upson,	
Divine,	Riley,	Willits,	
Meddaugh,			7

NAYS.

Mr. Crane,	Mr. Ferry,	Mr. Wells,	
Crouse,	Hatch,	Withey,	
Devereaux,	Jerome,	Woodward,	9

Mr. Withey, leave being granted, moved to insert the following, to stand as section eight:

SEC. 8. All fictitious issue or increase of the bonds or other evidence of indebtedness, or of the capital stock of any corporation, is prohibited.

The motion prevailed, by yeas and nays, as follows:

YEAS.

Mr. Cutcheon,	Mr. Meddaugh,	Mr. Upson,	
Divine,	Pond,	Willits,	
Ferry,	Riley,	Withey,	9

NAYS.

Mr. Crane,	Mr. Hatch,	Mr. Wells,	
Crouse,	Jerome,	Woodward,	
Devereaux,			7

The article being on its final passage, the same was not passed, two-thirds of the members of the Commission not voting therefor, by yeas and nays, as follows:

YEAS.

Mr. Cutcheon,	Mr. Pond,	Mr. Willits,	
Divine,	Riley,	Withey,	
Meddaugh,	Upson,		8

NAYS.

Mr. Crane,	Mr. Ferry,	Mr. Wells,
Crouse,	Hatch,	Woodward,
Devereaux,	Jerome,	8

ADJOURNMENT.

On motion of Mr. Crane,

The Commission adjourned.

THIRTY-FIFTH DAY.

LANSING, *Saturday, October 11, 1873.*

The Commission was called to order at 9 o'clock, by the Chairman.

Roll called: quorum present.

LEAVE OF ABSENCE.

Mr. Jerome asked and obtained leave of absence for Mr Hatch until Tuesday morning.

Mr. Meddaugh asked and obtained leave of absence for himself for the day.

Mr. Upson asked and obtained leave of absence for himself for the day.

MEMORIAL.

Mr. Wells presented the memorial of Dr. I. N. Eldridge, J. W. Begole, and fifty others, relative to the management of the University.

The memorial was ordered printed in the journal and laid on the table.

The memorial is as follows:

To the Hon. Constitutional Commission at Lansing, Mich.:

We, the undersigned, voters and tax-payers of the city of Flint, respectfully ask that no attempt be made by your Honorable Commission to so change the Constitution that the Regents shall have control of the University and its funds, as contemplated by the amendment of Mr. Pond of Wayne. We respectfully express our belief that the University belongs to the people, and the people should have control of it through their representatives, the Legislature. And one among the many reasons why the control of the institution should not be taken from the people is the important one that a part of the funds necessary to carry on the University is derived from a direct tax upon the people, and the Regents depend upon the people for its aid and support.

TIME OF ADJOURNMENT.

Mr. Crane moved that when the Commission adjourn at noon to-day it be until Monday afternoon next at two o'clock.

Mr. Withey moved to amend by making the adjournment from this afternoon until Monday at two o'clock.

Which motion prevailed.

MUNICIPAL INDEBTEDNESS.

Mr. Meddaugh, from the committee on corporations to whom was recommitted

Article X., of Municipal Corporations,

Reported the same back with amendments relative to the limitation of the power to incur indebtedness by municipalities.

Report accepted and committee discharged.

The amendment was amended so as to read as follows, and concurred in:

No city or village shall incur indebtedness, including that incurred by or on behalf of any school district within its corporate limits, so that its aggregate debt at any time shall exceed ten per cent on the valuation of its taxable property, as shown by the assessment roll.

Mr. Withey, leave being granted, moved to amend the article by adding the following to stand as section 3:

SEC. 3. The Board of Supervisors of any county may borrow or raise by tax, not exceeding in any one year two mills upon the dollar of the assessed valuation thereof, for constructing or repairing public buildings, highways, or bridges: *Provided,* The indebtedness of a county shall at no time exceed four mills upon a dollar of such assessed valuation, unless authorized by a majority of the electors of the county, voting thereon as shall be provided by law.

Which motion prevailed.

The article was ordered printed.

FINAL PASSAGE.

The Commission took up the consideration of articles on the order of final passage.

Article XV., of Exemptions,

Was passed, two-thirds of the members of the Commission voting therefor, by yeas and nays, as follows:

YEAS.

Mr. Crane,	Mr. Divine,	Mr. Wells,	
Crouse,	Ferry,	Willits,	
Cutcheon,	Jerome,	Withey,	
Devereaux,	Riley,	Woodward,	12

NAYS. 0

Article XVI., of the Militia,

Was passed, two-thirds of the members of the Commission voting therefor, by yeas and nays, as follows:

YEAS.

Mr. Crane,	Mr. Divine,	Mr. Wells,	
Crouse,	Ferry,	Willits,	
Cutcheon,	Jerome,	Withey,	
Devereaux,	Riley,	Woodward,	12

NAYS. 0

Article XVIII., of Amendment and Revision of the Constitution,

Was passed, two-third of the members of the Commission voting therefor, by yeas and nays, as follows:

YEAS.

Mr. Crane,	Mr. Divine,	Mr. Wells,	
Crouse,	Ferry,	Willits,	
Cutcheon,	Jerome,	Withey,	
Devereaux,	Riley,	Woodward,	12

NAYS. 0

The articles were referred to the committee on phraseology, for engrossment.

FEMALE SUFFRAGE.

Mr. Ferry offered a proposed amendment to the elective franchise, relative to the extension of the right of suffrage to women.

Read twice, ordered printed, referred to the committee of the whole, and placed on the general order.

CORPORATIONS OTHER THAN MUNICIPAL.

Mr. Jerome moved that the vote, by which

Article XI., of Corporations other than Municipal,

Was lost yesterday, be reconsidered;

Which motion prevailed.

The article was laid on the table.

MISCELLANEOUS PROVISIONS.

Article XVII., Miscellaneous Provisions,

Being on the order of final passage, was considered informally as in committee of the whole.

Mr. Withey moved to add the following to section ten:

"This provision shall not be construed to deprive a woman from holding any office to which she may be or become eligible under any law of this State;"

Which motion prevailed.

Mr. Riley moved to amend the article by striking out of section ten the words "county superintendent of schools."

Which motion prevailed.

Mr. Riley moved to further amend the article by inserting after the word "offices," in the last printed line of section ten, the words, "except county superintendent of schools."

The motion did not prevail, by yeas and nays, as follows:

YEAS.

Mr. Devereaux,	Mr. Jerome,	Mr. Woodward,	
Divine,	Riley,		5

NAYS.

Mr. Crouse,	Mr. Ferry,	Mr. Willits,	
Cutcheon,	Wells,	Withey,	6

Mr. Jerome moved that section ten be stricken out and the following inserted as a substitute:

SEC. 10. Every woman above the age of twenty-one years, who shall have resided in the State three months, and in the township or ward ten days, and who is a citizen of the United States, shall be eligible to such offices as may be designated by law.

Which motion prevailed, by yeas and nays, as follows:

YEAS.

Cutcheon,	Jerome,	Mr. Willits,	
Divine,	Riley,	Woodward,	
Devereaux,			7

NAYS.

Mr. Crouse,	Mr. Wells,	Mr. Withey,	
Ferrry,			4

EDUCATION.

Mr. Wells gave notice that at some future day he would move to reconsider the vote by which

Article XIII., of Education,

Was passed, yesterday.

ADJOURNMENT.

On motion of Mr. Crouse,

The Commission adjourned until Monday afternoon, at 2:30 o'clock.

THIRTY-SIXTH DAY.

LANSING, *Monday, October 13, 1873.*

The Commission was called to order at 2.30 o'clock by the Chairman.

Roll called: quorum present.

On motion of Mr Crouse,

Bill No. 59 was taken from the table.

TAXING THE LIQUOR TRAFFIC.

On motion of Mr. Withey,

Bill No. 67, relative to taxing the sale of liquors, was taken from the order of third reading.

Mr. Withey offered the following substitute therefor:

At the election when this amended constitution shall be submitted to the electors of this State, on the first Tuesday after the first Monday of November, in the year one thousand eight hundred and seventy-four, for adoption or rejection, there shall be submitted to such electors the following proposition, to be added, in case of its adoption, to section forty-seven of article four, in the present constitution of this State as it now stands, and to section thirty-six of article four, in said amended constitution, if the latter is adopted, viz.:

An annual tax of three hundred dollars is imposed upon the traffic in intoxicating drinks, to be paid by every person or firm who shall carry on or be engaged in the business of selling or disposing of intoxicating liquors as a beverage, and for each place where such business is carried on. Said tax shall be paid into the treasury of the proper township, city, or village, and be appropriated and applied to the support of primary schools. Every person or firm who shall carry on or engage in such business without having first paid the tax imposed, shall be guilty of a misdemeanor, and on conviction, be punished by fine or imprisonment, or both, as may be prescribed by law. The sale, or other disposition of intoxicating drinks to minors, persons under guardianship, insane and idiotic persons, paupers, and common drunkards, is wholly prohibited, and all necessary laws shall be passed to enforce the provisions of this section. The Legislature may further regulate and restrict the sale, and other disposition of intoxicating drinks, and may increase the annual tax upon said traffic.

Said proposition shall be separately submitted to the electors of this State for their adoption or rejection, in form following, to wit:

A separate ballot may be given by every person having the right to vote, to be deposited in a separate box.

Upon the ballots given for said proposition shall be written, printed, or partly writter, the words, "Restriction and taxation of the liquor traffic,—Yes;" and upon the ballots given against the adoption thereof, in like manner, the words, "Restriction and taxation of the liquor traffic,—No."

If at said election, a majority of the votes for or against said proposition shall contain the words, "Restriction and taxation of the liquor traffic,—Yes," then said proposition shall be added to section 47 in Article IV. of the present constitution, and to section 36 in Article IV. of said amended constitution, if the latter is adopted.

Bills No. 59 and 67 and the substitute were laid on the table, and the substitute ordered printed.

MUNICIPAL CORPORATIONS.

The Commission considered Article X., of Municipal Corporations.

On motion of Mr. Jerome, section 1 was amended by adding after the word "aiding," in line 4:

Enlistments, and in the support of the families of soldiers in time of war.

On motion of Mr. Upson, section 13 was amended by inserting after the word "highways," in line 3, "who shall hold his office three years."

ADJOURNMENT.

On motion of Mr. Withey,

The Commission adjourned.

THIRTY-SEVENTH DAY.

LANSING, *Tuesday, October 14, 1873.*

The Commission was called to order at 9 o'clock, by the Chairman.

Roll called: quorum present.

FINAL PASSAGE.

The Commission took up the consideration of articles on the order of final passage.

Article X., of Municipal Corporations,

Was passed, two-thirds of the members of the Commission voting therefor, by yeas and nays, as follows:

YEAS.

Mr. Crane,	Mr. Jerome,	Mr. Wells,	
Crouse,	Meddaugh,	Willits,	
Cutcheon,	Riley,	Withey,	
Devereaux,	Upson,	Woodward,	
Divine,			13

NAYS. 0

Article XVII., Miscellaneous Provisions,

Was passed, two-thirds of the members of the Commission voting therefor, by yeas and nays, as follows:

YEAS.

Mr. Crane,	Mr. Divine,	Mr. Upson,	
Crouse,	Jerome,	Wells,	
Cutcheon,	Meddaugh,	Willits,	
Deveraux,	Riley,	Withey,	12

NAYS.

Mr. Woodward, 1

CONTROL OF THE AGRICULTURAL COLLEGE.

Mr. Wells, pursuant to his notice given on Saturday, moved to reconsider the vote by which

Article XIII, of Education,

Was passed, in order to place the control of the Agricultural College on a similar basis to that of the University.

On motion of Mr. Withey the subject was made the special order for half past two o'clock this afternoon.

TAXING, RESTRICTING, AND REGULATING THE SALE OF LIQUORS.

Mr. Withey moved to take from the table

Printed bill No. 59,

Printed bill No. 67, and

Printed bill No. 71,

Relative to taxing, restricting, and regulating, the sale of liquors.

Which motion prevailed.

On motion of Mr. Crouse, the Commission resolved itself into committee of the whole, Mr. Woodward in the chair, and proceeded to the consideration of the several propositions above named, and after some time spent therein, the committee rose, and through their chairman, made the following report:

REPORT OF THE COMMITTEE OF THE WHOLE.

The committee of the whole have had under consideration

Printed bill No. 71,

Have made sundry amendments thereto, and have instructed me to report the same back to the Commission, recommending that the amendments be concurred in, and ask to be discharged from the further consideration of the subject.

L. WOODWARD, *Chairman.*

Report accepted and committee discharged.

The amendments were concurred in, except as to the one by which the word "two" was inserted in place of "three," in line one of the proposed section.

The said amendment was concurred in, by yeas and nays, as follows:

YEAS.

Mr. Crane,	Mr. Jerome,	Mr. Wells,	
Ferry,	Meddaugh,	Woodward,	
Hatch,	Upson,		8

NAYS.

Mr. Crouse,	Mr. Devereaux,	Mr. Riley,	
Cutcheon,	Divine,	Willits,	6

Referred to the committee on phraseology.

On motion of Mr. Upson,

Printed bill No. 59, and

Printed bill No. 67,

Were laid on the table.

RECESS.

On motion of Mr. Willitts,

The Commission took a recess until 2:30 P. M.

AFTERNOON SESSION.

The Commission was called to order by the Chairman at 2:30 o'clock.

Roll called: quorum present.

SPECIAL ORDER.

The chair announced the special order to be the motion of Mr. Wells to reconsider the vote by which

Article XIII., of Education

Was adopted.

The motion did not prevail, by yeas and nays, as follows:

YEAS.

Mr. Crane,	Mr. Devereaux,	Mr. Wells,	
Crouse,	Upson,	Woodward,	6

NAYS.

Mr. Cutcheon,	Mr. Jerome,	Mr. Riley,	
Divine,	Meddaugh,	Willits,	
Ferry,	Pond,	Withey,	
Hatch,			10

CORPORATIONS OTHER THAN MUNICIPAL.

Mr. Jerome moved to take from the table

Article XI., of Corporations other than Municipal,

Which motion prevailed.

The article being on its final passage,

Mr. Wells moved that the following be substituted therefor:

ARTICLE XI.

CORPORATIONS OTHER THAN MUNICIPAL.

SECTION 1. Corporations, other than municipal, and those for charitable, educational, penal, and reformatory purposes, under the control of public authority, shall be hereafter created by general laws. The charter of no existing corporation, not embraced in the above exceptions, shall be extended, altered, or amended. All general acts of incorporation, and general laws affecting corporations, may be altered, amended, or repealed.

SEC. 2. No general banking law shall have effect until the same shall, after its passage, be submitted to a vote of the electors of the State, at a general election, and be approved by a majority of the votes cast thereon at such election.

SEC. 3. The stockholders of every corporation or association for banking purposes, issuing bank notes, or paper credits, to circulate as money, shall be individually liable for all debts contracted during the time of their being stockholders of such corporation or association, equally and ratably to the extent of their respective shares of stock in any such corporation or association.

SEC. 4. The Legislature shall provide for the registry of all bills or notes issued or put in circulation as money, by any bank organized under the laws of this State, and shall require security to the full amount of notes and bills so registered, in interest-bearing stocks of this State, or of the United States, which shall be deposited with the State Treasurer, for the redemption of such bills or notes in lawful money of the United States.

SEC. 5. In case of the insolvency of any bank or banking association, the bill-holders thereof shall be entitled to preference in payment, over all other creditors of such bank or association.

SEC. 6. The Legislature shall pass no law authorizing or sanctioning the suspension of payments by any corporation.

SEC. 7. The stockholders in all corporations shall be individually liable for all labor done in behalf of such corporation during the time of their being such stockholders, equally and ratably to the extent of their respective shares in the stock of such corporation.

SEC. 8. No corporation shall hold any real estate for a longer period than ten years from the time of acquiring the same, except such real estate as shall be actually occupied by it in the exercise of its franchises.

SEC. 9. Foreign corporations may be permitted to do business in this State under such limitations and restrictions as may be prescribed by law, but shall be subject to the same restrictions and liabilities that are imposed upon, and shall have no greater rights than are conferred upon domestic corporations of like character, and the stockholders of such foreign corporations shall be subject to like personal liabilities as stockholders in similar domestic corporations. No foreign corporation shall acquire or hold any lands in this State, except such as may be taken in good faith in payment of debts, or such as may be needed for such offices, depots, and warehouses as may be required for its legitimate business; and all lands hereafter acquired or held in violation of this provision shall escheat to the State. Provision shall be made for debarring all foreign corporations which shall violate any law of this State from thereafter being allowed to do business in the State.

SEC. 10. The Legislature may, from time to time, pass laws establishing reasonable maximum rates of charges for the transportation of passengers and freight, and regulating the speed of trains on different railroads in this State, and shall prohibit running contracts between such railroad companies whereby discrimination is made in favor of either of such companies, as against other companies owning connecting or intersecting lines of railroads.

SEC. 11. No railroad corporation shall consolidate its stock, property, or franchises with any other railroad corporation owning a parallel or competing line; and in no case shall any consolidation take place except upon public notice given, of at least sixty days, to all stockholders, in such manner as shall be provided by law.

SEC. 12. No corporation, except for municipal or mining purposes, life insurance, or for the construction of railroads and canals, shall be created for a longer term than thirty years.

SEC. 13. The term corporation, as used in this article, shall be construed to include all associations and joint stock companies having any of the powers or privileges of corporations not possessed by individuals or partnerships.

The motion did not prevail, by yeas and nays, as follows:

YEAS.

Mr. Crane,	Mr. Ferry,	Mr. Wells,	
Crouse,	Hatch,	Woodward,	
Devereaux,	Jerome,		8

NAYS.

Mr. Cutcheon,	Mr. Pond,	Mr. Willits,	
Divine,	Riley,	Withey,	
Meddaugh,	Upson,		8

Mr. Withey moved that the question be taken on the final passage of the article by sections;

Which motion prevailed.

The question being taken on the passage of the first seven sections, the same were passed, two-thirds of the members of the Commission voting therefor, by yeas and nays, as follows

YEAS.

Mr. Crane,	Mr. Ferry,	Mr. Wells,	
Crouse,	Hatch,	Willits,	
Cutcheon,	Jerome,	Withey,	
Devereaux,	Riley,	Woodward,	
Divine,			13

NAYS.

Mr. Meddaugh,	Mr. Pond,	Mr. Upson,	3

The question recurring on the passage of section eight, the

same was not passed, two-thirds of the members of the Commission not voting therefor, as follows:

YEAS.

Mr. Cutcheon,	Mr. Pond,	Mr. Willits,	
Divine,	Riley,	Withey,	
Meddaugh,	Upson,		8

NAYS.

Mr. Crane,	Mr. Ferry,	Mr. Wells,	
Crouse,	Hatch,	Woodward,	
Devereaux,	Jerome,		8

The question recurring on the passage of sections nine and ten, the same were passed, two-thirds of the members of the Commission voting therefor, by yeas and nays, as follows:

YEAS.

Mr. Crane,	Mr. Hatch,	Mr Upson,	
Crouse,	Jerome,	Wells,	
Cutcheon,	Meddaugh,	Willits,	
Devereaux,	Pond,	Withey,	
Ferry,	Riley,	Woodward,	15

NAYS.

Divine, 1

The question recurring on the passage of section eleven, the same was not passed, two-thirds of the members of the Commission not voting therefor, by yeas and nays, as follows:

YEAS.

Mr. Cutcheon,	Mr. Meddaugh,	Mr. Upson,	
Divine,	Pond,	Willits,	
Hatch,	Riley,	Withey,	9

NAYS.

Mr. Crane,	Mr. Ferry,	Mr. Wells,	
Crouse,	Jerome,	Woodward,	
Devereaux,			7

The question recurring on the passage of section twelve, the same was passed, two-thirds of the members of the Commission voting therefor, by yeas and nays, as follows:

YEAS.

Mr. Crane,	Mr. Hatch,	Mr. Upson,
Crouse,	Jerome,	Wells,

Mr. Cutcheon,	Mr. Meddaugh,	Mr. Willits,	
Divine,	Pond,	Withey,	
Ferry,	Riley,	Woodward,	15

NAYS.

Mr. Devereaux, 1

The question recurring on the passage of section thirteen,

Mr. Wells offered the following substitute therefor:

SEC. 13. No railroad corporation shall consolidate its stock, property, or franchises, with any other railroad corporation owning a parallel or competing line. And in no case shall any consolidation take place, except upon public notice given, of at least sixty days, to all stockholders, in such manner as shall be provided by law.

Mr. Pond moved to amend the substitute by adding thereto the following: "Nor shall any such corporation purchase or lease any such parallel or competing line of road."

The motion prevailed, by yeas and nays, as follows:

YEAS.

Mr. Cutcheon,	Mr. Meddaugh,	Mr. Upson,	
Divine,	Pond,	Willits,	
Ferry,	Riley,	Withey,	9

NAYS.

Mr. Crane,	Mr. Hatch,	Mr. Wells,	
Crouse,	Jerome,	Woodward,	
Devereaux,			7

The question recurring on the adoption of the substitute, the same was not adopted, by yeas and nays, as follows:

YEAS.

Mr. Divine,	Mr. Pond,	Mr. Willits,	
Ferry,	Riley,	Withey,	
Meddaugh,	Upson,		8

NAYS.

Mr. Crane,	Mr. Devereaux,	Mr. Wells,	
Crouse,	Hatch,	Woodward,	
Cutcheon,	Jerome,		8

The question recurring on the passage of section thirteen,

Mr. Hatch moved to substitute therefor section two of Article XIX.–A., present Constitution, as follows:

SEC. —. No railroad corporation shall consolidate its stock, property, or franchises, with any other railroad corporation owning a parallel or competing line; and in no case shall any consolidation take place, except upon public notice given, of at least sixty days, to all stockholders, in such manner as shall be provided by law.

Mr. Pond moved to amend the substitute by adding thereto the following:

"Nor shall any such corporation lease any parallel or competing line of road, and no two or more parallel or competing lines of railroad shall be run or operated, directly or indirectly, wholly or in part, under the same management or supervision, or under or subject to any arrangement, agreement, or understanding with reference to rates of fare or freight to be charged, or for the division of earnings;"

Which motion prevailed, by yeas and nays, as follows:

YEAS.

Mr. Cutcheon,	Mr. Pond,	Mr. Willits,	
Divine,	Riley,	Withey,	
Meddaugh,	Upson,		8

NAYS.

Mr. Crane,	Mr. Hatch,	Mr. Wells,	
Crouse,	Jerome,	Woodward,	
Devereaux,			7

The question recurring on the adoption of the substitute, the same was adopted, by yeas and nays as follows:

YEAS.

Mr. Cutcheon,	Mr. Meddaugh,	Mr. Upson,	
Divine,	Pond,	Willits,	
Ferry,	Riley,	Withey,	9

NAYS.

Mr. Crane,	Mr. Hatch,	Mr. Wells,	
Crouse,	Jerome,	Woodward,	
Devereaux,			7

The question recurring on the passage of the substitute, to stand as section thirteen, the same was not passed, two-thirds of the members of the Commission not voting therefor, by yeas and nays, as follows:

YEAS.

Mr. Cutcheon,	Mr. Meddaugh,	Mr. Upson,	
Divine,	Pond,	Willits,	
Ferry,	Riley,	Withey,	9

NAYS.

Mr. Crane,	Mr. Hatch,	Mr. Wells,	
Crouse,	Jerome,	Woodward,	
Devereaux,			7

The question recurring on the passage of section fourteen, the same was not passed, two-thirds of the members of the Commission not voting therefor, by yeas and nays, as follows:

YEAS.

Mr. Crouse,	Mr. Meddaugh,	Mr. Upson,	
Cutcheon,	Pond,	Willits,	
Divine,	Riley,		8

NAYS.

Mr. Crane,	Mr. Hatch,	Mr. Withey,	
Devereaux,	Jerome,	Woodward,	
Ferry,	Wells,		8

Mr. Upson moved to insert the following, to stand as section fourteen:

SEC. 14. No railroad corporation shall issue, or present, or cause to be issued, or presented, directly, or indirectly, to any person holding or exercising any civil office or appointment within this State, any free pass or ticket over its road; nor shall such corporation issue, or cause or permit to be issued, to or for the use of any such person, any commutation pass, or ticket, upon any other or different terms or conditions than the terms and conditions upon which it at the time issues like passes, or tickets, to the public generally.

The motion did not prevail, two-thirds of the Commission not voting therefor, by yeas and nays, as follows:

YEAS.

Mr. Crouse,	Mr. Meddaugh,	Mr. Upson,	
Cutcheon,	Pond,	Willits,	
Divine,	Riley,		8

NAYS.

Mr. Crane,	Mr. Hatch,	Mr. Withey,
Devereaux,	Jerome,	Woodward,
Ferry,	Wells,	8

The question recurring on the passage of section fifteen, the same was not passed, two-thirds of the members of the Commission not voting therefor, by yeas and nays, as follows:

YEAS.

Mr. Cutcheon,	Mr. Pond,	Mr. Upson,
Divine,	Riley,	Willits,
Meddaugh,		7

NAYS.

Mr. Crane,	Mr. Ferry,	Mr. Wells,
Crouse,	Hatch,	Withey,
Devereaux,	Jerome,	Woodward, 9

The question recurring on the passage of sections sixteen and seventeen, the same were passed, two-thirds of the members of the Commission voting therefor, by yeas and nays, as follows:

YEAS.

Mr. Crane,	Mr. Hatch,	Mr. Upson,
Crouse,	Jerome,	Wells,
Cutcheon,	Meddaugh,	Willits,
Devereaux,	Pond,	Withey,
Divine,	Riley,	Woodward,
Ferry,		16

NAYS. 0

Mr. Jerome moved that the vote by which section eleven was not passed be reconsidered;

Which motion prevailed.

Mr. Withey moved the following as a substitute therefor:

Section 11. All domestic corporations, except mining companies in the upper peninsula, shall keep their principal office in this State;

Which motion prevailed.

The question recurring on the passage of the substitute to stand as section eleven, the same was not passed, two-thirds of the members of the Commission not voting therefor, by yeas and nays, as follows:

YEAS.

Mr. Cutcheon,	Mr. Meddaugh,	Mr. Upson,	
Divine,	Pond,	Willits,	
Ferry,	Riley,	Withey,	
Hatch,			10

NAYS.

Mr. Crane,	Mr. Devereaux,	Mr. Wells,	
Crouse,	Jerome,	Woodward,	6

Mr. Pond moved that the following be added as a further section to the article:

Sec. —. No railroad corporation shall consolidate with, or purchase, or lease, any parallel or competing line of road. No agreement for the consolidation of two or more railroad companies shall be entered into, and no lease of the road of one railroad corporation to another shall be made, without the assent of three-fourths of the stockholders of each corporation interested, to be given in such manner as may be provided by law.

Mr. Hatch moved to amend by striking out the words "or purchase," in the second line.

The motion did not prevail, by yeas and nays as follows:

YEAS.

Mr. Crane,	Mr. Hatch,	Mr. Wells,	
Crouse,	Jerome,	Woodward,	
Deveraux,			7

NAYS.

Mr. Cutcheon,	Mr. Meddaugh.	Mr. Upson,	
Divine,	Pond,	Willits,	
Ferry,	Riley,	Withey,	9

The question recurring on the passage of the section as proposed by Mr. Pond, the same was not passed, two-thirds of the members of the Commission not voting therefor, by yeas and nays, as follows:

YEAS.

Mr. Cutcheon,	Mr. Meddaugh,	Mr. Upson,	
Divine,	Pond,	Willits,	
Ferry,	Riley,	Withey,	9

NAYS.

Mr. Crane,	Mr. Hatch,	Mr. Wells,
Crouse,	Jerome,	Woodward,
Devereaux,		7

Mr. Hatch moved that section two, of Art. XIX.-A. of the present Constitution, be added to the article as section eleven, as follows:

SEC. 11. No railroad corporation shall consolidate its stock, property, or franchises, with any other railroad corporation owning a parallel or competing line; and in no case shall any consolidation take place, except upon public notice given, of at least sixty days, to all stockholders, in such manner as shall be provided by law.

Mr. Pond moved that the following be substituted therefor:

"No railroad company shall consolidate with or lease any parallel or competing line of road. No agreement for the consolidation of any two or more railroad companies shall be entered into, and no lease of the road of one railroad corporation to another shall be made without the assent of three-fourths of the stockholders of each corporation interested, to be given in such manner as may be provided by law."

On motion of Mr. Hatch,

The same was laid on the table.

The article was ordered reprinted.

WOMAN SUFFRAGE.

On motion of Mr. Willits,

The Commission resolved itself into committee of the whole on the general order, Mr. Willits in the chair, and, after some time spent therein, the committee rose and, through their chairman, made the following report:

REPORT OF THE COMMITTEE OF THE WHOLE.

The committee of the whole have had under consideration Printed bill No. 69, relative to the Elective Franchise,

Have made sundry amendments thereto, and have directed

me to report the same back to the Commission, recommending that the amendments be concurred in, and ask to be discharged from the further consideration of the subject.

EDWIN WILLITS, *Chairman.*

Report accepted and committee discharged.

The amendments were not concurred in, by yeas and nays, as follows:

YEAS.

Mr. Crouse,	Hatch,	Pond,	
Cutcheon,	Jerome,	Riley,	
Divine,			7

NAYS.

Mr. Ferry,	Mr. Wells,	Mr. Withey,	
Meddaugh,	Willits,	Woodward,	
Upson,			7

On motion of Mr. Ferry,

The bill was laid on the table.

TAXING THE SALE OF LIQUORS.

The committee on phraseology, to whom was referred printed bill No. 71, relative to taxing the sale of liquors,

Respectfully report that they have had the same under consideration, and have directed me to report the same back to the Commission with an amendment thereto, recommending that the amendment be concurred in, and that the section when so amended do pass, and ask to be discharged from the further consideration of the subject.

H. H. HATCH,
For Chairman of Committee.

Report accepted and committee discharged.

On motion of Mr. Withey, the proposed section was laid on the table.

ADJOURNMENT.

On motion of Mr. Withey,

The Commission adjourned.

THIRTY-EIGHTH DAY.

LANSING, *Wednesday, October 15, 1873.*

The Commission was called to order at 2.30 o'clock by the Chairman.

Roll called: quorum present.

WOMAN SUFFRAGE.

Mr. Ferry moved to take from the table,

Printed bill No. 69, relative to the elective franchise;

Which motion prevailed.

Mr. Jerome moved that the proposition be referred back to Mr. Ferry as a special committee, with instructions to modify the same, so as to make it applicable as a proposed amendment to the present constitution;

Which motion prevailed.

CORPORATIONS OTHER THAN MUNICIPAL.

On motion of Mr. Meddaugh,

Article XI., of Corporations other than Municipal,

Was laid on the table.

TAXING THE SALE OF LIQUORS.

Mr. Meddaugh moved to take from the table,

Printed bill No. 71, relative to taxing the sale of liquors;

Which motion prevailed.

Mr. Hatch moved that the following be inserted as a substitute for the substance of printed bill No. 71, to stand as an addition to the provision of the present constitution on the subject:

"But the Legislature shall restrict and regulate the sale of such spirits, and may impose specific taxation upon the traffic therein. The sale, or other disposition of intoxicating liquors to minors, persons under guardianship, insane and idiotic persons, paupers, and common drunkards, is wholly probibited."

Pending the question on the substitute,

Mr. Woodward moved to strike out the word "two," where it occurs in printed bill No. 71, as fixing the amount of the tax to be paid, and to insert the word one in lieu thereof.

The motion did not prevail, by yeas and nays, as follows:

YEAS.

Mr. Crane,	Mr. Hatch,	Mr. Meddaugh,	
Ferry,	Jerome,	Woodward,	6

NAYS.

Mr. Crouse,	Mr. Pond,	Mr. Wells,	
Cutcheon,	Riley,	Withey,	
Divine,	Upson,		8

The question recurring on the adoption of the substitute, the same was not adopted, by yeas and nays, as follows:

YEAS.

Mr. Meddaugh,	Mr. Pond,		2

NAYS.

Mr. Crane,	Mr. Ferry,	Mr. Wells,	
Crouse,	Jerome,	Withey,	
Cutcheon,	Riley,	Woodward,	
Divine,	Upson,		11

The bill being on its final passage, the same was not passed, two-thirds of the members of the Commission not voting therefor, by yeas and nays, as follows:

YEAS.

Mr. Crane,	Mr. Divine,	Mr. Wells,	
Crouse,	Ferry,	Withey,	
Cutcheon,	Jerome,	Woodward,	
Devereaux,	Riley,		11

NAYS.

Mr. Meddaugh,	Mr. Pond,	Mr. Upson,	3

Mr. Upson moved that the vote by which the bill was lost be reconsidered;

Which motion prevailed.

On motion of Mr. Withey,

The bill was laid on the table.

ADJOURNMENT.

On motion of Mr. Crouse,

The Commission adjourned.

AFTERNOON SESSION.

The Commission was called to order by the chairman at 2:30.

Roll called: quorum present.

Mr. Upson moved to take from the table printed bill No. 71, relative to taxing the sale of liquors;

Which motion prevailed.

Mr. Meddaugh moved that the following be substituted for the substance of the proposition, to stand as an addition to the present provision of the constitution on the subject:

"But the Legislature shall restrain and regulate the traffic in such spirits, and impose specific taxation thereon, and the sale, or other disposition of intoxicating drinks, to minors, persons under guardianship, insane and idiotic persons, paupers, and common drunkards, is wholly prohibited;"

Which motion did not prevail.

The question recurring on the final passage of the proposition, the same was passed, two-thirds of the members of the Commission voting therefor, by yeas and nays, as follows:

YEAS.

Mr. Crane,	Mr. Divine,	Mr. Upson,	
Crouse,	Ferry,	Wells,	
Cutcheon,	Jerome,	Withey,	
Devereaux,	Riley,	Woodward,	12

NAYS.

Mr. Hatch,	Mr. Meddaugh,	Mr. Pond,	3

The bill was referred to the committee on phraseology for engrossment.

WOMAN SUFFRAGE.

Mr. Ferry, as the special committee to whom was referred printed bill No. 69, relative to the elective franchise, reported the same back, with an amendment, as instructed.

The question being on its final passage, the same was not passed, two-thirds of the members of the Commission not voting therefor, as follows:

YEAS.

Mr. Crane,	Mr. Upson,	Mr. Withey,	
Ferry,			4

NAYS.

Mr. Crouse,	Mr. Jerome,	Mr. Riley,	
Cutcheon,	Meddaugh,	Wells,	
Divine,	Pond,	Woodward,	
Hatch,			10

CORPORATIONS OTHER THAN MUNICIPAL.

Mr. Hatch moved to take from the table,

Article XI., of Corporations other than Municipal; also, the proposed section offered by him yesterday, being section two of Article XIX.-A., of the present Constitution;

Which motion prevailed.

The question being on Mr. Pond's amendment thereto, the same was not adopted, by yeas and nays, as follows:

YEAS.

Mr. Cutcheon,	Mr. Pond,	Mr. Upson,	
Divine,	Riley,	Withey,	
Meddaugh,			7

NAYS.

Mr. Crane,	Mr. Ferry,	Mr. Wells,	
Crouse,	Hatch,	Woodward,	
Devereaux,	Jerome,		8

The question recurring on the passage of the proposed section, the same

Was passed, two-thirds of the members of the Commission voting therefor, by yeas and nays, as follows:

YEAS.

Mr. Crane,	Mr. Ferry,	Mr. Upson,	
Crouse,	Hatch,	Wells,	
Cutcheon,	Jerome,	Withey,	
Devereaux,	Riley,	Woodward,	12

NAYS.

Mr. Divine,	Mr. Meddaugh,	Mr. Pond,	3

Mr. Upson moved that the vote by which the section was passed be reconsidered;

Which motion did not prevail, by yeas and nays, as follows:

YEAS.

Mr. Meddaugh,	Mr. Riley,	Mr. Upson,	
Pond,			4

NAYS.

Mr. Crane,	Mr. Ferry,	Mr. Wells,	
Crouse,	Hatch,	Withey,	
Cutcheon,	Jerome,	Woodward,	
Devereaux,			10

The article was referred to the committee on phraseology for engrossment.

PREAMBLE.

The Preamble being on its final passage,

Mr. Riley moved the following as a substitute therefor:

We, the people of the State of Michigan, grateful to Almighty God, the Sovereign Ruler of nations, for civil and religious liberty, do ordain and establish this Consititution.

YEAS.

Mr. Cutcheon,	Mr. Divine,	Mr. Wells,	
Devereaux,	Riley,	Withey,	6

NAYS.

Mr. Crane,	Mr. Hatch,	Mr. Pond,	
Crouse,	Jerome,	Upson,	
Ferry,	Meddaugh,	Woodward,	9

The question recurring on the passage of the Preamble, the same was passed, two-thirds of the members of the Commission voting therefor, by yeas and nays, as follows:

YEAS.

Mr. Crane,	Mr. Ferry,	Mr. Riley,	
Crouse,	Hatch,	Upson,	
Cutcheon,	Jerome,	Wells,	
Devereaux,	Meddaugh,	Withey,	
Divine,	Pond,	Woodward,	15

NAYS. 0

The Preamble was referred to the committee on phraseology for engrossment.

On motion of Mr. Hatch,

The Commission proceeded to revise the enrolled bills, as in committee of the whole. Before concluding the revision,

On motion of Mr. Devereaux,

Adjourned till half past 7 p. m.

EVENING SESSION.

The Commission was called to order at 7:30 o'clock, by the Chairman.

Roll called: quorum present.

EDUCATION.

Mr. Jerome moved to reconsider the vote by which the Commission passed

Article XIII., of Education.

The Chairman decided the motion out of order, under the rules governing the Commission.

Mr. Jerome moved that the rules inconsistent with the foregoing motion be suspended;

The motion did not prevail, two-thirds of the members of the Commission not voting therefor, by yeas and nays, as follows:

YEAS.

Mr. Devereaux,	Mr. Jerome,	Mr. Withey,	
Ferry,	Wells,	Woodward,	
Hatch,			7

NAYS.

Mr. Crane,	Mr. Divine,	Mr. Riley,	
Crouse,	Meddaugh,	Upson,	
Cutcheon,	Pond,	Willits,	9

THE SCHEDULE.

Mr. Riley, from the special committee on schedule, reported the schedule back without amendment.

The schedule was considered, and amended by striking out sections 6, 7, 8, 9, and 11. It then passed, two-thirds of the Commission voting therefor, as follows:

YEAS.

Mr. Crouse,	Mr. Hatch,	Mr. Upson,
Cutcheon,	Jerome,	Wells,
Devereaux,	Meddaugh,	Willits,
Divine,	Pond,	Withey,
Ferry,	Riley,	Woodward, 15

NAYS. 0

The schedule was referred to the committee on phraseology for engrossment.

TIME FOR THE CLOSING SESSION.

On motion of Mr. Meddaugh,

Resolved, That when the Commission adjourn to-night it be till to-morrow morning at eight o'clock.

SPECIAL COMMITTEE TO REPORT TO THE GOVERNOR.

On motion of Mr. Hatch,

The chairman of the Commission was appointed a committee to report the work of the Commission to the Governor.

On motion of Mr. Pond,

Mr. Jerome and Mr. Withey were added to said committee.

ADJOURNMENT.

On motion of Mr. Meddaugh,

The Commission adjourned.

THIRTY-NINTH DAY.

LANSING, *Thursday, October 16, 1873.*

The Commission was called to order at 8 o'clock by the Chairman.

Roll called: quorum present.

PRINTING THE CONSTITUTION.

Mr. Hatch moved that the constitution, as amended, be printed in the journal, and that a sufficient number of extra copies be printed to furnish to each of the members and officers of the commission ten copies. Also, that the clerk be directed to forward such copies to the members and officers.

Which motion prevailed.

Mr. Meddaugh moved that the chairman of the committee on phraseology be requested to read the proof of the constitution to be printed in the journal.

Which motion prevailed.

REPORT TO THE GOVERNOR.

Mr. Hatch moved that Mr. Pond be added to the special committee to report the work of the Commission to the Governor;

Which motion prevailed.

CERTIFYING THE WORK OF THE COMMISSION.

Mr. Riley moved that the members of the commission sign the report, certifying their work to the Governor.

Which motion prevailed.

TESTIMONIAL TO THE CHAIRMAN.

Mr. Withey, on behalf of messengers Brown, Barry, and Rice, presented to the chairman a box containing an inkstand and gold pen, accompanied by an appropriate address, which was responded to by the chairman.

Mr. Wells offered the following resolution:

Whereas, The Hon. Sullivan M. Cutcheon has, without fear, and above reproach, served the Constitutional Commission of Michigan ably and well, as its presiding officer; be it therefore

Resolved, That we give to him our thanks for kindness and courtesy extended to us all, throughout the entire session of our deliberations; and that we shall return to our respective homes with the consciousness of having been greatly aided in our deliberations by a chairman who had promptness, parliamentary skill, and a constant desire to be just to all: as we part this day, we wish to closely connect with our farewell to him an honored friend, the words, WELL DONE.

REMARKS BY MR. WITHEY.

Mr. Withey.—I am very glad of the opportunity, through this resolution, of uniting in its spirit. Our deliberations have been presided over by our chairman to our entire satisfaction. His courtesy and urbanity have been constant. We have all witnessed his deference and kindness. His rulings have been impartial and correct; his judgment unbiased; and we have reason, without any qualification, most cordially to unite in the sentiments of that resolution. It has personally my cordial approbation, as well as the gentlemen who has presided over us, my entire confidence and esteem.

The resolution was adopted unanimously by a rising vote.

RESPONSE BY THE CHAIRMAN.

Gentlemen of the Commission—I can only say that I fully appreciate the feeling of good-will you have here expressed towards me; that our sessions have been made pleasant to each other by the uniform friendliness of all the members of the Commission; and that I am grateful for that uniform courtesy that has been manifested toward me, and shall long remember the pleasant associations I have here enjoyed.

COMPILING AND INDEXING THE JOURNAL.

Mr. Riley offered the following resolution:

Resolved, That Henry S. Clubb be allowed the sum of one hundred dollars for his services in preparing and indexing the proceedings of this Commission for publication in book form, and for any other services necessary in closing its work.

The resolution was adopted.

REASSEMBLING OF THE COMMISSION.

Mr. Withey offered the following resolution:

Resolved, That when this Commission adjourn to-day, it be to such time, prior to the 30th day of November next, as shall hereafter be designated by the Chairman of the Commission, and notice thereof given to the members, if occasion requires the body to again convene.

The resolution was adopted.

REPORT OF THE COMMITTEE ON SUPPLIES.

Mr. Willits, chairman of the committee on supplies, submitted the report of the committee, showing the incidental expenses of the Commission, as follows:

F. F. Russell, bill ordered by clerk	$18 17
Richmond & Backus, bill ordered by clerk	7 80
A. Beamer, express,	70
Richmond & Backus, bill ordered by clerk	54 39
Richmond & Backus, bill ordered by clerk	5 40
B. F. Simons, bill ordered by clerk	16 60
W. S. George & Co., printing	28 00
Henry S. Clubb, postage, etc.	92
Grove & Whitney, ordered by doorkeeper	90
Davis & Larned, ordered by doorkeeper	90
A. R. Thayer, ordered by doorkeeper	60
J. Esselstyn & Sons, ordered by doorkeeper	1 70
Samuel F. Cook, arranging scrap books	89 00
Samuel F. Cook, engrossing clerk	30 00
Ferle & Co., ordered by clerk	1 78
S. D. Bingham, P. M., postage	120 26
	$377 12

The report was accepted, the committee discharged, and the several amounts, as reported, were allowed.

FINAL ADJOURNMENT.

On motion of Mr. Crane,

The Commission adjourned *sine die*.

THE CONSTITUTION AS REVISED AND AMENDED.

The following is the communication to be transmitted to the Governor:

To Hon. JOHN J. BAGLEY,

Governor of the State of Michigan:

The undersigned, members of the Constitutional Commission appointed by your Excellency, under, and in accordance with the Joint Resolution of the Legislature of said State, entitled "Joint Resolution to provide for a Commission for the revision of the Constitution of the State of Michigan," approved April 24, 1873, respectfully report that said Commission has performed the duty imposed upon it, and herewith place in the hands of your Excellency the result of its labors, in the form of a revision of the Constitution.

And they report and certify that every proposition contained in said revision is endorsed and recommended by two-thirds of the whole number of members of said Commission.

A committee, appointed by the Commission in that behalf, will, as soon as the same can be prepared, report to your Excellency in detail the principal changes made in the present Constitution, and the reasons which have induced the Commission to recommend such changes.

Dated at Lansing, October 16, 1873.

SULLIVAN M. CUTCHEON, *Chairman.*

ISAAC M. CRANE,	S. C. MOFFATT,
IRA D. CROUSE,	ASHLEY POND,
J. R. DEVEREAUX,	H. H. RILEY,
JOHN DIVINE,	CHAS. UPSON,
WM. M. FERRY,	H. G. WELLS,
H. H. HATCH,	EDWIN WILLITS,
D. H. JEROME,	S. L. WITHEY,
E. W. MEDDAUGH,	L. WOODWARD.

Attest: HENRY S. CLUBB,

Clerk of the Commission.

PROPOSED CONSTITUTION

OF THE

STATE OF MICHIGAN.

The People of the State of Michigan do ordain this Constitution:

ARTICLE I.

BOUNDARIES AND SEAT OF GOVERNMENT.

SECTION 1. The State of Michigan is bounded as follows, to wit: Commencing at a point on the eastern boundary line of the State of Indiana, where a direct line drawn from the southern extremity of Lake Michigan to the most northerly cape of the Maumee Bay, shall intersect the same, said point being the northwest corner of the State of Ohio, as established by an act of Congress entitled, "An act to establish the northern boundary line of the State of Ohio, and to provide for the admission of the State of Michigan into the Union upon the conditions therein expressed," approved June fifteenth, one thousand eight hundred and thirty-six; thence with the said boundary line of the State of Ohio till it intersects the boundary line between the United States and Canada in Lake Erie; thence with the said boundary line between the United States and Canada through the Detroit river, Lake St. Clair, the St. Clair river, Lake Huron, the St. Mary's river and Lake Superior, to a point where the said line last touches Lake Superior; thence in a direct line through Lake Superior to the mouth of the Montreal river; thence through the middle of the main channel of the said Montreal river to the head waters thereof, as marked upon the survey made by Captain Cramm, by authority of the United States; thence in a direct line to the center of the channel between Middle and South Islands, in the Lake of the Desert; thence in a direct line to the southern shore of Lake Brule; thence along said southern shore and down the Brule river to the main channel of the Menominee river; thence down the centre of the main channel of the same, to the center of the most usual ship-channel of the Green Bay of Lake Michigan; thence through the center of the most usual ship-channel of the said bay to the middle of Lake Michigan; thence through the middle of Lake Michigan to the northern boundary of the State of Indiana, as that line was established by the act of Congress, of the nineteenth of April, eighteen hundred and sixteen; thence due east with the north boundary line of the said State of Indiana to the northeast corner thereof; and thence south with the eastern boundary line of Indiana to the place of beginning.

SEC. 2. The seat of government shall remain at Lansing.

ARTICLE II.

BILL OF RIGHTS.

SECTION 1. All political power is inherent in the people. Government is instituted for their equal benefit, security, and protection; they have the right to change or reform the same whenever the public good requires. No special privilege or immunity shall be granted that may not be revoked.

SEC. 2. Every person shall be at liberty to worship God according to the dictates of his own conscience. No person shall be compelled to attend, or, against his consent, to contribute to the erection or support of any place of religious worship, or to pay tithes, taxes, or other rates, for the support of any minister of the gospel, or teacher of religion.

SEC. 3. The civil and political rights, privileges and capacities of no person shall be diminished or enlarged, nor shall any person be incompetent to be a witness, on account of his opinions or belief concerning matters of religion, nor shall any witness be questioned touching his religious belief.

SEC. 4. Every person may freely speak, write, and publish his sentiments on all subjects, being responsible for the abuse of that right; and no law shall be passed to restrain or abridge the liberty of speech or of the press. In all prosecutions for libel, the truth may be given in evidence to the jury, and if it shall appear to the jury that the matter charged as libelous is true, and was published with good motives and for justifiable ends, the accused shall be acquitted; and the jury shall have the right to determine the law and the fact.

SEC. 5. No bill of attainder, *ex post facto* law, or law impairing the obligation of contracts, shall be passed.

SEC. 6. The privilege of the writ of *habeas corpus* shall not be suspended, unless, in case of rebellion or invasion, the public safety may require it.

SEC. 7. The right of trial by jury shall remain, but shall be deemed to be waived in all civil cases, unless demanded by one of the parties in such manner as shall be prescribed by law. The legislature may authorize, in all civil and criminal cases, a trial by jury of a less number than twelve men.

SEC. 8. In every criminal prosecution, the accused shall have the right to a speedy and public trial by an impartial jury, to be informed of the accusation, to be confronted with witnesses against him, to have compulsory process for obtaining witnesses in his favor, and to have the assistance of counsel for his defense.

SEC. 9. Any suitor in any court in this State shall have the right to prosecute or defend his suit, either in person or by attorney.

SEC. 10. The person, houses, papers and possessions of every person shall be secure from unreasonable search and seizure. No warrant to search any place, or to seize any person or thing, shall issue without describing such place, person or thing, nor without probable cause, supported by oath or affirmation.

SEC. 11. No person, after acquittal upon the merits, shall be tried for the same offense. All persons shall, before conviction, be bailable by sufficient sureties, except for murder and treason, when the proof is evident or the presumption great.

SEC. 12. Treason against the State shall consist only in levying war against it, or adhering to its enemies, giving them aid and comfort. No person shall be convicted of treason, unless upon the testimony of two witnesses to the same overt act, or on confession in open court.

SEC. 13. Excessive bail shall not be required; excessive fines shall not be imposed; cruel or unusual punishments shall not be inflicted, nor shall witnesses be unreasonably detained.

SEC. 14. No person shall be deprived of life, liberty or property, without due process of law. No person shall be compelled, in any criminal case, to be a witness against himself. But if any person shall elect to make a statement in his own behalf, he shall be subject to cross-examination relative to the matter of such statement.

SEC. 15. No person shall be imprisoned for debt arising out of or founded on contract, express or implied, except in case of fraud, or breach of trust, or for moneys collected by public officers, or in any professional employment. No person shall be imprisoned for a military fine in time of peace.

SEC. 16. Every person has a right to bear arms for the defense of himself and of the State.

SEC. 17. The military shall be in strict subordination to the civil power.

SEC. 18. No soldier shall, in time of peace, be quartered in any house without the consent of the owner or occupant, nor in time of war, except in a manner prescribed by law.

SEC. 19. The people have the right peaceably to assemble,

to consult for the common good, to instruct their representatives, and to petition the Legislature for redress of grievances.

SEC. 20. Neither slavery nor involuntary servitude, unless for the punishment of crime, shall ever be tolerated in this State.

SEC. 21. Aliens who are, or may hereafter become *bona fide* residents of this State, shall enjoy the same rights in respect to the possession, enjoyment, and inheritance of property, as native-born citizens.

SEC. 22. Private property shall not be taken for public use without just compensation.

ARTICLE III.

DIVISION OF THE POWERS OF GOVERNMENT.

SECTION 1. The powers of government are divided into three departments: Legislative, Executive, and Judicial.

SEC. 2. No person belonging to one department shall exercise power properly belonging to another, except in the cases expressly provided in this Constitution.

ARTICLE IV.

LEGISLATIVE DEPARTMENT.

SECTION 1. The Legislative power is vested in a Senate and House of Representatives.

SEC. 2. The Senate shall consist of thirty-two members. But, after the year one thousand eight hundred and seventy-five, the Legislature may increase the number to thirty-three, by authorizing the election of two Senators in that portion of the State now included within the limits of the Thirty-second Senatorial District. Senators shall be elected for four years, and by single districts. At the first election after the adoption of this amended Constitution, Senators in the odd-numbered districts shall be elected for two years, and in the even-numbered districts for four years. Such districts shall be numbered from one to thirty-three inclusive, each of which shall choose one Senator. No county shall be divided in the formation of Senate districts, unless such county shall be equitably entitled to two or more Senators.

SEC. 3. The House of Representatives shall consist of not more than one hundred and ten members. Representatives shall be chosen for two years, and by single districts. Each representative district shall contain, as nearly as may be, an equal number of inhabitants, and shall consist of convenient and contiguous territory; but every organized county containing a population of not less than four thousand, and every two or more contiguous organized counties, containing a like population, shall constitute a representative district, and be entitled to one Representative. In every county entitled to more than one Representative, the board of supervisors shall assemble at such time and place as may be provided by law, and divide the same into representative districts, equal to the number of Representatives to which such county is entitled by law, and shall cause to be filed in the offices of the Secretary of State and clerk of such county, a description of such representative districts, specifying the number of each district, and the population thereof according to the last enumeration.

SEC. 4. The Legislature shall provide by law for an enumeration of the inhabitants in the year eighteen hundred and eighty-four, and every ten years thereafter; and at the first session after each enumeration so made, and also at the first session after each enumeration by the authority of the United States, the Legislature shall re-arrange the Senate districts, and apportion anew the Representatives among the counties and districts, according to the number of inhabitants. But no re-arrangement of Senate districts shall vacate the seat of any Senator. Each apportionment, and the division into representative districts by any board of supervisors, shall remain unaltered until the return of another enumeration.

SEC. 5. Every Senator and Representative shall be a citizen of the United States, and a qualified elector of the district he represents. A removal from his district shall be deemed a vacation of his office.

SEC. 6. No person holding any elective State office, except that of Regent of the University or Member of the Board of Education, and no person holding the office of probate judge, county clerk, register of deeds, county treasurer, sheriff, county superintendent of schools, prosecuting attorney, or any office to which he was appointed by the President of the United States, by and with the advice and consent of the Senate, shall be allowed to take or hold a seat in either house of the Legislature.

SEC. 7. Senators and Representatives shall not be subject to arrest upon any civil process during the session of the Legislature, or for fifteen days next before the commencement and after the termination of each session; they shall not be questioned in any other place for any speech in either House.

SEC. 8. A majority of each House shall constitute a quorum to do business; but a smaller number may adjourn from day to day, and compel the attendance of absent members in such manner, and under such penalties, as each House may prescribe.

SEC. 9. Each House shall choose its own officers, except as otherwise provided in this constitution; determine the rules of its proceedings, and judge of the qualifications, elections, and returns of its members, and may, with the concurrence of two-thirds of all the members elected, expel a member. The reasons for such expulsion shall be entered upon the journal, with the names of the members voting on the question. No member shall be expelled a second time for the same cause, nor for any cause known to his constituents before his election.

SEC. 10. Each House shall keep a journal of its proceedings, and publish the same, except such parts as may require secrecy. The yeas and nays of the members of either House on any question shall be taken at the request of one-fifth of the members elected. Any member of either House may dissent from and protest against any act, proceeding, or resolution which he may deem injurious to any person or the public, and have the reason of his dissent entered on the journal.

SEC. 11. In all elections by either House, or in joint convention, the votes shall be given *viva voce*. All votes on nominations to the Senate shall be taken by yeas and nays, and published with the journal of its proceedings.

SEC. 12. The doors of each House shall be open, unless the public welfare require secrecy. Neither House shall, without the consent of the other, adjourn for more than three days, nor to any other place than where the Legislature may then be in session.

SEC. 13. Bills may originate in either House, but no bill or new subject of legislation shall be introduced after the expiration of the first fifty days of the session, except on recommendation of the Governor by special message. At extra sessions, legislation shall be confined to the subjects expressly named in the Governor's proclamation, and subjects submitted by special message.

SEC. 14. Every bill and joint resolution passed by the Legislature, and every concurrent resolution appropriating money or property, shall be presented to the Governor, and if he approve, he shall sign it; but if not, he shall return it with his objections, to the House in which it originated, which shall enter the objections at large upon its journal, and reconsider it. On such reconsideration, if two-thirds of the members elected agree to pass such bill or resolution, it shall be sent, with the objections, to the other House, by which it shall be reconsidered. If approved by two-thirds of the members elected to that House, it shall become operative. In such case the vote of both Houses shall be determined by yeas and nays, and the names of the members voting for and against it shall be entered on the journals of each House respectively. If any bill or resolution be not returned by the Governor within ten days (Sundays excepted), after it has been presented to him, the same shall become operative in like manner as if he had signed it, unless the Legislature, by their adjournment, prevent its return; in which case it shall not become operative. The Governor may approve, sign, and file in the office of the Secretary of State, within five days after the adjournment of the Legislature, any act passed during the last five days of the session, and the same shall become operative.

SEC. 15. The compensation of members of the Legislature shall be four dollars a day for actual attendance and when absent on account of sickness. They shall be entitled to ten cents, and no more, for every mile actually traveled going to and returning from the place of meeting, on the usually traveled route; and for stationery and newspapers not exceeding five dollars for each member during any session. Each member shall be entitled to one copy of the laws, journals, and documents of the Legislature of which he was a member; but shall not receive, at the expense of the State, books, newspapers, or other perquisites of office not expressly authorized by this constitution.

SEC. 16. The President of the Senate and Speaker of the House of Representatives shall be entitled to the same per diem compensation and mileage as members of the Legislature, and no more.

SEC. 17. No person elected a member of the Legislature shall receive any civil appointment within this State, or to the Senate of the United States, from the Governor, the Governor and Senate, from the Legislature, or any other State authority, or be eligible to any office which shall have been created, or the emoluments of which shall have been increased by the Legislature during the term for which he is elected. All such appointments, and all votes given for any person so elected, for any such office or appointment, shall be void. No member of the Legislature shall be interested directly or indirectly, in any contract with the State, or any municipal corporation thereof, authorized by any law passed during the time for which he is elected, or for one year thereafter.

SEC. 18. Every bill and joint resolution shall be read three times in each House before the final passage thereof. No bill or joint resolution shall become a law without the concurrence of a majority of all the members elected to each House On the final passage of each bill and joint resolution the vote shall be taken separately, by yeas and nays, and entered on the journal.

SEC. 19. No law shall embrace more than one object, which shall be expressed in its title. No law shall be revised, altered, or amended by reference to its title only; but the act revised, and the section or sections of the act altered or amended, shall be re-enacted and published at length. No public act shall take effect or be in force until the expiration of ninety days from the end of the session at which the same is passed, unless, in case of some emergency to be stated in the act, the Legislature shall otherwise direct, by a two-thirds vote of the members elected to each House, to be taken by yeas and nays.

SEC. 20. The Legislature shall not grant or authorize extra compensation to any public officer, agent, or contractor, after the service has been rendered or the contract entered into.

SEC. 21. The Legislature shall provide by law that the furnishing of fuel and stationery for the use of the State, the printing and binding the laws and journals, all blanks, papers, and printing for the executive department and State offices, and all other printing ordered by the Legislature, shall be let by contract to the lowest competent and responsible bidder or bidders, who shall give adequate and satisfactory security for the performance thereof. The Legislature shall prescribe by law the manner in which the State printing shall be executed, and the accounts rendered therefor, and shall prohibit all charges for constructive labor. It shall not rescind or alter such contract, nor release the person or persons taking the same, or his or their sureties, from the performance of any of the conditions of the contract. No member of the Legislature, or officer of the State, shall be interested, directly or indirectly, in any such contract, or any contract with the State.

SEC. 22. The Legislature shall not pass local or special laws in any of the following enumerated cases:

First, Divorcing any named party, or upon the subject of divorce;

Second, Changing the names of persons or places;

Third, Regulating the practice in courts of justice, or regulating the jurisdiction and duties of justices of the peace, or constables;

Fourth, Providing for changes of venue in civil or criminal cases;

Fifth, Providing for the election or appointment of members of boards of supervisors;

Sixth, Summoning and empaneling grand or petit jurors;

Seventh, Regulating the rate of interest on money;

Eighth, Authorizing the sale, lease, or mortgage of real estate belonging to minors, or by executors or administrators, or by any religious corporation or society;

Ninth, Chartering or licensing ferries or toll bridges;

Tenth, Remitting fines, penalties, or forfeitures;

Eleventh, Creating, increasing, or decreasing fees, percentages, or allowances of public officers;

Twelfth, Changing the law of descent;

Thirteenth, Granting to any corporation, association, or individual any special or exclusive privilege, immunity, or franchise whatever;

Fourteenth, Declaring any named person of age;

Fifteenth, Extending the time for the assessment or collection of taxes, or otherwise relieving any assessor or collector of taxes from the due performance of his official duties;

Sixteenth, Punishing crimes or misdemeanors;

Seventeenth, Adopting by any person any named person as his child or heir;

Eighteenth, Vacating or altering any road laid out by commissioners of highways, or any street, alley, or public ground in any city or village, or in any recorded town plat; or for building or repairing bridges, or for draining swamp or other low lands, except by expenditure of grants to the State;

Nineteenth, Exempting any property from taxation. The Legislature shall provide by general laws for the cases enumerated in this section, and for all other cases which, in its judgment, may be provided for by general laws.

SEC. 23. The Legislature shall not establish a State paper.

SEC. 24. The Legislature may authorize the employment of a chaplain for the State Prison; but no money shall be appropriated for the payment of any religious services in either House of the Legislature.

SEC. 25. No collector, holder, or disburser of public moneys shall have a seat in the Legislature, or be eligible to any office of trust or profit under this State, until he shall have accounted for and paid over, as provided by law, all sums for which he may be liable.

SEC. 26. The Legislature shall not audit or allow any private claim or account.

SEC. 27. The Legislature shall meet at the seat of government on the first Wednesday in January, in the year eighteen hundred and seventy-five, and on the first Wednesday in January in every second year thereafter, and at no other place or time, unless as provided in this Constitution, and shall adjourn without day at such time as the Legislature shall fix by concurrent resolution.

SEC. 28. The Legislature, on the day of final adjournment, shall adjourn at twelve o'clock at noon.

SEC. 29. The election of Senators and Representatives, pursuant to the provisions of this Constitution, shall be held on the Tuesday succeeding the first Monday of November, in the year eighteen hundred and seventy-four, and on the Tuesday succeeding the first Monday of November of every second year thereafter.

SEC. 30. The Legislature shall provide for the speedy publication of all statute laws of a public nature, and of such judicial decisions as it may deem expedient. All laws and judicial decisions shall be free for publication by any person.

SEC. 31. The Legislature may declare the cases in which any office shall be deemed vacant, and also the manner of filling the vacancy, where no provision is made for that purpose in this Constitution.

SEC. 32. The Legislature may confer upon organized townships, incorporated cities, and villages, and upon the board of supervisors of the several counties, such powers of a local, legislative, and administrative character as it may deem proper.

SEC. 33. The Legislature shall not authorize any lottery, or permit the sale of lottery tickets.

SEC. 34. No money shall be appropriated or drawn from the treasury for the benefit of any religious sect or society, theological or religious seminary, or school under private or denominational control, nor shall property belonging to the State be appropriated for any such purpose.

SEC. 35. The assent of two-thirds of the members elected to each House of the Legislature, shall be requisite to every bill appropriating the public money or property, for local or private purposes.

SEC. 36. The Legislature shall not pass any act authorizing the grant of license for the sale of ardent spirits or other intoxicating liquors.

SEC. 37. The style of the laws shall be: "The People of the State of Michigan enact."

ARTICLE V.

EXECUTIVE DEPARTMENT.

SECTION 1. The Executive power is vested in a Governor, who shall hold his office for two years. A Lieutenant Governor shall be chosen for the same term.

SEC. 2. No person shall be eligible to the office of Governor or Lieutenant Governor, who has not been five years a citizen of the United States, a resident of this State two years next preceding his election, and attained the age of thirty years.

SEC. 3. The Governor and Lieutenant Governor shall be elected at the times and places of choosing the members of the Legislature. The person having the highest number of votes for Governor or Lieutenant Governor shall be elected. In case two or more persons shall have an equal and the highest number of votes for Governor or Lieutenant Governor, the Legislature shall, by joint vote, choose one of such persons.

SEC. 4. The Governor shall be commander-in-chief of the military and naval forces, and may call out such forces to execute the laws, to suppress insurrection, and to repel invasion.

SEC. 5. He may require information in writing from officers of the executive department, upon any subject relating to the duties of their respective offices.

SEC. 6. He shall take care that the laws be faithfully executed.

SEC. 7. He may convene the Legislature on extraordinary occasions.

SEC. 8. He shall give to the Legislature, and at the close of his official term, to the incoming Legislature, information by message, of the condition of the State, and recommend such measures to them as he shall deem expedient.

SEC. 9. He may convene the Legislature at some other place, when the seat of government becomes dangerous from disease or a public enemy.

SEC. 10. He shall issue writs of election to fill such vacancies as occur in the Senate or House of Representatives.

SEC. 11. He may grant reprieves, commutations and pardons, after conviction, for all offenses, except treason and cases of impeachment, upon such conditions, and with such restrictions and limitations, as he may think proper; but the Legislature may provide by law as to the manner of hearing applications for pardon. Upon conviction for treason, he may suspend the execution of the sentence until the case shall be reported to the Legislature at its next session, when the Legislature shall either pardon or commute the sentence, direct the execution of the sentence, or grant a further reprieve. He shall communicate to the Legislature at each session, information of each case of reprieve, commutation, or pardon granted, and the reasons therefor.

SEC. 12. In case of the death of the Governor, his removal or suspension from office, inability to perform the duties of the office, resignation, absence from the State, or other disability, the powers and duties of the office shall devolve upon the Lieutenant Governor for the residue of the term, or until the disability cease. But when the Governor shall be absent from the State, at the head of the military forces thereof, he shall continue to be commander-in-chief.

SEC. 13. During the vacancy of the office of Governor, if the Lieutenant Governor die, resign, be displaced, suspended, or be incapable of performing the duties of his office, or absent from the State, the President *pro tempore* of the Senate shall act as Governor until the vacancy be filled or the disability cease.

SEC. 14. The Lieutenant Governor shall, by virtue of his office, be President of the Senate, and when there is an equal division, he shall give the casting vote. In committee of the whole he may debate all questions.

SEC. 15. No member of Congress, or any person holding office under the United States, or this State, shall execute the office of Governor.

SEC. 16. No person elected Governor or Lieutenant Governor shall receive any office or appointment from the Legislature, or either House thereof, during the time for which he was elected.

SEC. 17. The Lieutenant Governor and President of the Senate *pro tempore*, when performing the duties of Governor, shall receive the same compensation as the Governor.

SEC. 18. All official acts of the Governor, his approval of the laws excepted, shall be authenticated by the Great Seal of the State, which shall be kept by the Secretary of State.

SEC. 19. All commissions issued to persons holding office under the provisions of this Constitution shall be "In the name and by the authority of the people of the State of Michigan;" sealed with the Great Seal of the State, signed by the Governor, and countersigned by the Secretary of State.

ARTICLE VI.

JUDICIAL DEPARTMENT.

SECTION 1. The judicial power is vested in a Supreme Court, in circuit courts, probate courts, justices of the peace, and in such other courts, tribunals, and officers as are or shall be established or authorized by law.

SEC. 2. The Supreme Court shall be composed of five judges. Hereafter the judges of said court shall be nominated, and by and with the advice and consent of the Senate, appointed by the Governor; and their term of office shall be ten years. One judge of said Court shall be appointed as soon as practicable after the first day of January, in the year of our Lord one thousand eight hundred and seventy-five, and his term of office shall date from January first, one thousand eight hundred and seventy-four; and one judge of said court shall thereafter be appointed as the terms of the present and future judges shall expire.

SEC. 3. The Supreme Court shall have a general superintending control over all other courts and tribunals; and also such appellate jurisdiction as shall be provided by law; and to that end may issue writs of error, *certiorari*, *mandamus*, *procedendo*, prohibition, and all other appropriate writs and process. It shall also have original jurisdiction in cases of *mandamus*, *habeas corpus*, proceedings in the nature of *quo warranto*, and proceedings by *scire facias*, to vacate letters patent. Its appellate jurisdiction shall not extend to any civil case for the recovery of money or property in which the amount or value of the thing in controversy is less than one hundred dollars, exclusive of costs, except upon the allowance of an appeal, writ of error, or *certiorari*, by the judge who tried such case, or by a judge of the Supreme Court. The concurrence of three judges of said court shall be necessary to a final decision.

SEC. 4. Four terms of the Supreme Court shall be held annually, at such times and places as may be designated by law.

SEC. 5. The Supreme Court shall have power, by general rules, to establish, and from time to time modify the methods of procedure and the practice therein, and to appoint its clerks, and a reporter of its decisions; and said court shall also have power to establish a code or codes of civil procedure, pleading, and practice, including the commencement of suits and proceedings, for all other courts of record, and from time to time to alter and amend such code or codes.

SEC. 6. The Legislature shall divide the State into judicial circuits, and may increase or decrease the number of the same from time to time, for each of which the Governor shall nominate, and, by and with the advice and consent of the Senate, appoint one circuit judge, who shall hold his office for the term of six years, and until his successor is appointed and qualified. No alteration of any circuit shall have the effect to remove a judge from office.

SEC. 7. A circuit court shall be held at least twice in each year in every county organized for judicial purposes, and at least three times in each year in counties containing ten thousand inhabitants. Judges of the circuit court may hold courts for each other, and shall do so when required by law.

SEC. 8. The circuit courts shall have original jurisdiction in all matters civil and criminal, not excepted in this constitution, and not prohibited by law; and such appellate jurisdiction from all inferior courts and tribunals as shall be provided by law, and a supervisory control of the same. They shall also have power to issue writs of injunction, *habeas corpus*, *mandamus*, *quo warranto*, *certiorari*, and other writs necessary to carry into effect their orders, judgments, and decrees, and give them general control over inferior courts and tribunals within their respective jurisdictions. The appellate jurisdiction of said courts shall not extend to any civil case in which the amount or value of the thing in controversy is less than twenty-five dollars, exclusive of costs, except upon allowance of an appeal or writ of *certiorari* by the judge of the court entitled to exercise such appellate jurisdiction.

SEC. 9. The respective circuit courts held in each county, or the judge thereof, shall appoint two circuit court commissioners, who shall be vested with such judicial and ministerial powers as shall be prescribed by law.

SEC. 10. Whenever a judge shall remove beyond the limits of the jurisdiction for which he was appointed or elected, or a justice of the peace from the township in which he was elected, or by a change in the boundaries of such township, shall be placed without the same, he shall be deemed to have vacated his office.

SEC. 11. When a vacancy occurs in the office of judge of the Supreme or circuit court, it shall be filled for the residue of the term by appointment of the Governor, by and with the advice and consent of the Senate; but if the Senate is not in session when such vacancy occurs, the Governor shall fill the same by appointment until the Senate shall assemble, and for thirty days thereafter, when the vacancy shall be filled as hereinbefore provided. When a vacancy occurs in the office of judge of probate or judge of any court of record, other than the Supreme or circuit court, it shall be filled by appointment of the Governor, which appointment shall continue during the residue of the unexpired term, and until a successor is duly qualified.

SEC. 12. The clerk of each county organized for judicial purposes shall be clerk of the circuit court of such county.

The judges of the circuit courts, within their respective jurisdictions, may fill vacancies in the offices of county clerk and prosecuting attorney.

SEC. 13. During their continuance in office, and for one year thereafter, the judges of the supreme and circuit courts shall be ineligible to any other than a judicial office.

SEC. 14. In each county, organized for judicial purposes, there shall be a court of probate. It shall have such probate jurisdiction, powers, and duties as shall be prescribed by law. Other jurisdiction, civil and criminal, may also be conferred on any one or more courts of probate. Judges of probate shall hold their offices for a term of four years, and shall be elected by the electors of their respective counties, as shall be provided by law.

SEC. 15. The Supreme, circuit, and probate courts shall be courts of record, and shall each have a common seal.

SEC. 16. There shall be not exceeding four justices of the peace in each organized township. They shall be elected by the electors of the townships, and shall hold their offices for four years, and until their successors are elected and qualified. At the first election in any township, they shall be classified as shall be prescribed by law. A justice elected to fill a vacancy, shall hold his office for the residue of the unexpired term.

SEC. 17. In civil cases, justices of the peace shall have exclusive jurisdiction to the amount of one hundred dollars, and concurrent jurisdiction to the amount of three hundred dollars, which may be increased to five hundred dollars, with such exceptions and restrictions as may be provided by law. They shall also have such criminal jurisdiction, and perform such duties, as shall be prescribed by the Legislature.

SEC. 18. Judges of the Supreme court, circuit judges, and justices of the peace, shall be conservators of the peace within their respective jurisdictions.

SEC. 19. The style of all process shall be: "In the name of the People of the State of Michigan."

ARTICLE VII.

ELECTIVE FRANCHISE.

SECTION 1. In all elections every person of the age of twenty-one years, who shall have resided in this State three months, and in the township or ward in which he offers to vote, ten days next preceding an election, belonging to either of the following classes, shall be an elector, and entitled to vote:

First, Every male citizen of the United States;

Second, Every male inhabitant of this State, who shall have resided in the United States two years and six months, and declared his intention to become a citizen of the United States pursuant to the laws thereof, six months preceding an election;

Third, Every male inhabitant residing in this State on the twenty-fourth day of June, one thousand eight hundred and thirty-five.

SEC. 2. In time of war, insurrection, or rebellion, the right to vote at such place, and in such manner as shall be prescribed by law, shall be enjoyed by all persons otherwise entitled thereto, who may be in the actual military or naval service of the United States, or of this State, and their votes shall be made to apply to the township or ward of which they are residents. The Legislature may provide by law for allowing townships to hold their elections in any city, wholly or in part, within the limits of such townships.

SEC. 3. All elections shall be by ballot, except of such township officers as may be authorized by law to be otherwise chosen.

SEC. 4. Every elector, in all cases except treason, felony, misdemeanor, or breach of the peace, shall be privileged from arrest during his attendance at election, and in going to and returning from the same. No elector shall be obliged to attend court as a suitor or witness on the day of election, or to do military duty thereon except in time of war or public danger.

SEC. 5. No elector shall be deemed to have gained or lost his residence by reason of absence therefrom in the service of the United States or of this State, nor while engaged in the navigation of the waters of this State or of the United States, or of the high seas, nor while a student at any seminary of learning, nor while kept at any alms-house or other asylum at public expense.

SEC. 6. Laws may be passed to preserve the purity of elections, and guard against the abuses of the elective franchise.

SEC. 7. No soldier, seaman, or marine in the army or navy of the United States shall be deemed a resident of this State, in consequence of being stationed in any place within the same.

SEC. 8. Any inhabitant of this State, who may hereafter be engaged in a duel, shall be disqualified from holding any office, and from voting at any election.

ARTICLE VIII.

STATE OFFICERS.

SECTION 1. There shall be elected at each general biennial election in November, a Secretary of State, a State Treasurer, a Commissioner of the State Land Office, a Superintendent of Public Instruction, and an Auditor General, for the term of two years, each of whom shall keep his office at the seat of government, and shall perform such duties as may be prescribed by law.

SEC. 2. Their term of office shall commence on the first day of January, following their election.

SEC. 3. An Attorney General shall be elected or appointed, as the legislature may by law provide.

SEC. 4. Whenever a vacancy shall occur in any of the State offices, the Governor shall fill the same by appointment, and by and with the advice and consent of the Senate, if in session.

SEC. 5. The Secretary of State, State Treasurer, and Commissioner of the State Land Office, shall constitute a Board of State Auditors, to examine and adjust all claims against the State, not otherwise provided for by law. They shall also constitute a Board of State Canvassers, to determine the result of all elections for Governor, Lieutenant Governor, and State officers, and of such other officers as shall by law be referred to them.

SEC. 6. In case two or more persons have an equal and the highest number of votes for any office, as canvassed by the Board of State Canvassers, the Legislature, in joint convention, shall choose one of said persons to fill such office. When the determination of the Board of State canvassers is contested, the Legislature in joint convention shall decide which person is elected.

ARTICLE IX.

SALARIES.

SECTION 1. The Governor, Lieutenant Governor, Secretary of State, State Treasurer, Commissioner of the State Land Office, Superintendent of Public Instruction, Auditor General, Attorney General, Commissioner of Railroads, Commissioner of Insurance, and all other State officers, shall receive for their services such salaries as shall be provided by law, which shall not be increased or diminished during their official term.

SEC. 2. The judges of the Supreme court, the judges of the circuit courts, and the judges of all other courts of record, shall receive for their services such salaries as shall be provided by law, which shall not be diminished during their official term.

ARTICLE X.

MUNICIPAL CORPORATIONS.

SECTION 1. No county, city, township, or other municipal corporation shall become a stockholder in, or make any loan or gift to, or lend its credit in aid of any person, private corporation, or association, nor shall any county, city, township, or other municipality construct or become the owner of any railroad. The provisions of this section shall not prevent such municipalities from aiding enlistments and in the support of the families of soldiers in time of war; or supporting their poor in such manner as may be provided by law.

Counties.

SEC. 2. Each organized county shall be a body corporate, with such powers and immunities as shall be prescribed by law. All suits and proceedings by or against a county shall be in the name thereof. The power of counties to levy taxes, borrow money, and contract debts, shall be restricted by law.

SEC. 3. The board of supervisors of any county may borrow or raise by tax a sum not exceeding in any one year one and one half mills upon the dollar of the assessed valuation thereof, for constructing or repairing public buildings, highways, or bridges: *Provided,* The indebtedness of a county, incurred under this section, shall at no time exceed three mills upon a dollar of such assessed valuation, unless authorized by a majority of the electors of the county voting thereon as shall be provided by law.

SEC. 4. No organized county shall ever be reduced, by the organization of new counties, to less than sixteen townships, as surveyed by the United States, unless, in pursuance of law, a majority of electors residing in each county to be affected thereby shall so decide. The Legislature may organize any city into a separate county when it has attained a population of twenty thousand inhabitants, without reference to geographical extent, when a majority of the electors of a county in which such city may be situated, voting thereon, shall be in favor of a separate organization. Nothing herein contained shall be so construed as to prevent the Legislature from organizing any county composed wholly of islands within the territory of the State, or discontinuing any such county, and attaching the same to the nearest county or counties on the main land.

SEC. 5. In each organized county there shall be a sheriff, a county clerk, a county treasurer, a register of deeds, and a prosecuting attorney, chosen by the electors thereof once in two years, whose duties and powers shall be prescribed by law; but the Legislature may provide for the appointment, by the Governor, of prosecuting attorneys, by and with the advice and consent of the Senate. The board of supervisors in any county may unite the offices of county clerk and register of deeds in one office, or disconnect the same.

SEC. 6. The sheriff, county clerk, county treasurer, judge of probate, and register of deeds shall hold their offices at the county seat.

SEC. 7. The sheriff shall hold no other office. No person shall be eligible to the office of sheriff for more than four in a period of six years. The county shall never be responsible for his acts.

SEC. 8. A board of supervisors, consisting of one from each organized township, shall be established in each county, with such powers as shall be prescribed by law. Cities and villages shall have such representation in the board of supervisors of the counties in which they are situated as the Legislature may direct.

SEC. 9. No county seat, once established, shall be removed until the place to which it is proposed to be removed shall be designated by two-thirds of the board of supervisors of the county, and a majority of the electors voting thereon shall have voted in favor of the proposed location, in such manner as shall be prescribed by law.

SEC. 10. The board of county auditors in such counties as may be authorized by law to elect county auditors, and in every other county the board of supervisors shall, except as otherwise provided by law, have power to prescribe the compensation for all services rendered for, and adjust all claims against their respective counties, and such determination and adjustment shall be subject to no appeal. Supervisors and county auditors shall receive for their services such compensation as shall be prescribed by law.

SEC. 11. The board of supervisors of each organized county may provide for laying out highways, constructing bridges, and organizing townships, under such restrictions and limitations as shall be prescribed by law.

Townships.

SEC. 12. Each organized township shall be a body corporate, with such powers and immunities as shall be prescribed by law. All suits and proceedings by or against a township shall be in the name thereof.

SEC. 13. There shall be elected in each organized township, annually, on the first Monday of April, or at such other time as the Legislature may provide, one supervisor, one township clerk, who shall be *ex officio* school inspector, one commissioner of highways, who shall hold his office for three years, one township treasurer, one school inspector, not exceeding four constables, and one overseer of highways of each highway district, and such other officers as may be provided by law, whose powers and duties shall be prescribed by law.

Cities and Villages.

SEC. 14. Cities and villages shall hereafter be incorporated only under general laws, in which their powers of taxation, borrowing money, and contracting debts shall be restricted.

SEC. 15. No city or village shall incur indebtedness, including that incurred by or on behalf of any school district within its corporate limits, so that its aggregate debt at any time shall exceed ten per cent on the valuation of its taxable property, as shown by the assessment roll.

SEC. 16. The executive and legislative officers of cities and villages shall be elected, and all other officers shall be elected or appointed, at such time and in such manner as the Legislature may direct.

SEC. 17. Existing charters of cities and villages may be altered and amended.

ARTICLE XI.

CORPORATIONS OTHER THAN MUNICIPAL.

SECTION 1. Corporations, other than municipal, and those for charitable, educational, penal, and reformatory purposes under the control of public authority, shall be hereafter created only by general laws. The charter of no existing corporation, not embraced in the above exceptions, shall be extended, altered, or amended. All general acts of incorporation, and general laws affecting corporations, may be altered, amended, or repealed.

SEC. 2. No general banking law shall have effect until the same shall, after its passage, be submitted to a vote of the electors of the State, at a general election, and be approved by a majority of the votes cast thereon at such election.

SEC. 3. The stockholders of every corporation or association for banking purposes, issuing bank notes, or paper credits, to circulate as money, shall be individually liable for all debts contracted during the time of their being stockholders of such corporation or association, equally and ratably to the extent of their respective shares of stock in any such corporation or association.

SEC. 4. The Legislature shall provide for the registry of all bills or notes issued or put in circulation as money, by any bank organized under the laws of this State, and shall require security to the full amount of notes and bills so registered, in interest-bearing stocks of this State, or of the United States, which shall be deposited with the State Treasurer, for the redemption of such bills or notes in lawful money of the United States.

SEC. 5. In case of the insolvency of any bank or banking association, the bill-holders thereof shall be entitled to preference in payment, over all other creditors of such bank or association.

SEC. 6. The Legislature shall pass no law authorizing or sanctioning the suspension of payments by any corporation.

SEC. 7. The stockholders in all corporations shall be individually liable for all labor done in behalf of such corporation during the time of their being such stockholders, equally and ratably to the extent of their respective shares in the stock of such corporation.

SEC. 8. No corporation shall hold any real estate for a longer period than ten years from the time of acquiring the same, except such real estate as shall be actually occupied by it in the exercise of its franchises.

SEC. 9. Foreign corporations may be permitted to do business in this State under such limitations and restrictions as may be prescribed by law, but shall be subject to the same restrictions and liabilities that are imposed, and shall have no greater rights than are conferred upon domestic corporations of like character, and the stockholders of such foreign corporations shall be subject to like personal liabilities as stockholders in similar domestic corporations. No foreign corporation shall acquire or hold any lands in this State, except such as may be taken in good faith in payment of debts, or such as may be needed for such offices, depots, and warehouses as may be required for its legitimate business; and all lands hereafter acquired or held in violation of this provision shall escheat to the State. Provision shall be made for debarring all foreign corporations which shall violate any law of this State, from thereafter being allowed to do business in the State.

SEC. 10. The Legislature may, from time to time, pass laws establishing reasonable maximum rates of charges for the transportation of passengers and freight, and regulating the speed of trains on different railroads in this State, and shall prohibit running contracts between such railroad companies whereby discrimination is made in favor of either of such companies as against other companies owning connecting or intersecting lines of railroads.

SEC. 11. No railroad corporation shall consolidate its stock, property, or franchises, with any other railroad corporation owning a parallel or competing line; and in no case shall any consolidation take place except upon public notice given of at least sixty days to all stockholders, in such manner as shall be provided by law.

SEC. 12. No corporation, except for municipal or mining purposes, for life insurance, or for the construction of railroads or canals, shall be created for a longer time than thirty years.

SEC. 13. The term corporation, as used in this article, shall be construed to include all associations and joint stock companies having any of the powers or privileges of corporations not possessed by individuals or partnerships.

ARTICLE XII.

IMPEACHMENTS AND REMOVALS FROM OFFICE.

SECTION 1. The House of Representatives shall have the sole power of impeaching civil officers for corrupt conduct in office, or for crimes and misdemeanors; but a majority of the members elected shall be necessary to direct an impeachment.

SEC. 2. Every impeachment shall be tried by the Senate. When the Governor or Lieutenant Governor shall be tried, the Chief Justice of the Supreme Court shall preside. When an impeachment is directed, the members of the Senate shall take an oath or affirmation truly and impartially to try and determine the same according to the evidence. No person shall be convicted without the concurrence of two-thirds of the members elected. Judgment, in case of impeachment, shall not extend further than removal from office; but the party accused, whether acquitted or convicted, shall be liable to trial and punishment according to law.

SEC. 3. When an impeachment is directed, the House of Representatives shall appoint from their own body, a committee, whose duty it shall be to prosecute such impeachment. An impeachment may be tried after the final adjournment of the Legislature.

SEC. 4. No officer shall exercise his office after an impeachment is directed, until he be acquitted, but such disability shall not continue longer than three months, unless the trial of such impeachment shall have been commenced and proceeded with.

SEC. 5. For a reasonable cause, which shall not be a sufficient ground for the impeachment of a judge, the Governor shall remove him on a concurrent resolution of two-thirds of the members elected to each House of the Legislature, after the party accused shall have had an opportunity to be heard in his defense; but the cause for which such removal is required shall be stated at length in such resolution.

SEC. 6. County, township, city, village, or school district officers may be removed in such manner and for such cause as may be provided by law.

SEC. 7. The Governor shall have power, and it shall be his duty, except at such times as the Legislature may be in session, to examine into the condition and administration of any public office, and the acts of any public officer, elective or appointed, to suspend from office for gross neglect of duty, or for corrupt conduct in office, or any other misfeasance or malfeasance therein, either of the following State officers, to wit: The Attorney General, State Treasurer, Commissioner of the State Land Office, Secretary of State, Auditor General, Superintendent of Public Instruction, or Members of the State Board of Education, or any other officer of the State, except legislative and judicial, and to appoint a successor for the remainder of the unexpired term of office, and report the cause of such removal to the Legislature at its next session.

SEC. 8. Whenever, during a recess of the Legislature, it shall, in the opinion of the Governor, become necessary to direct an impeachment of any civil officer, he may, by proclamation, convene the House of Representatives for that purpose; and if the House, when so convened, shall direct an impeachment, he shall in like manner, immediately convene the Senate to try such impeachment; and whenever, in the opinion of the President of the Senate and Speaker of the House of Representatives, it shall, during a recess of the Legislature, become necessary to direct an impeachment of the Governor, they may, by their joint proclamation, convene the House for that purpose; and if the House direct such impeachment, the said President and Speaker shall, in like manner, immediately convene the Senate to try such impeachment.

SEC. 9. The Governor may make a provisional appointment to fill a vacancy occasioned by the suspension of an officer, by impeachment or otherwise, until he shall be acquitted, or until the election or appointment and qualification of a successor.

ARTICLE XIII.

EDUCATION.

SECTION 1. The Superintendent of Public Instruction shall have the general supervision of public instruction, and his duties shall be prescribed by law; and he shall be a member, *ex officio*, of the Boards of all State educational institutions, including the Reform School.

SEC. 2. The regents of the University and their successors in office, shall continue to constitute a body corporate by the name and title of "the Board of Regents of the University of Michigan." Said board shall consist of the two *ex officio* members provided for in this article, and eight elective members. The terms of office of the elective members shall be eight years, and two of such members shall be elected every second year at the time of the annual township election, so as to succeed the regents now in office as their several terms expire.

Said Board of Regents shall, as often as necessary, elect a President of the University, who shall be its chief executive officer, and, *ex officio*, a member and president of said board, with the privilege of speaking, but not of voting. The supervision and control of the University shall be vested in the Board of Regents, and said board shall have the direction and control of all expenditures from the University funds, but all moneys appropriated by the Legislature to the University upon condition, shall, if accepted, be applied as provided in the condition accompanying the appropriation.

SEC. 3. The State Normal School shall continue under the supervision of the State Board of Education, which shall consist of the Superintendent of Public Instruction, *ex officio*, and three elective members. The terms of office of said elective members shall be six years, and one of said members shall be elected every second year, at the time of the election of Governor, and shall enter upon the duties of his office on the first day of January succeeding his election. Said board shall perform such other duties as shall be prescribed by law.

SEC. 4. The duties of the Boards of the State Public School, the Agricultural College, and the Reform School, shall continue as now, or as shall be prescribed by law.

SEC. 5. Any vacancy that shall occur in any of the Boards mentioned in this article shall be filled by appointment of the Governor.

SEC. 6. The Legislature shall provide a system of primary schools, by which a school shall be maintained in each school district in the State, free of charge for tuition, at least three months in the year. The instruction shall, in all cases, be conducted in the English language.

SEC. 7. A school shall be maintained in each school district, at least three months in each year. Any school district neglecting to maintain such school, shall be deprived for the ensuing year, of its proportion of the income of the primary school fund, and of all funds arising from general taxes for the support of schools.

SEC. 8. The proceeds from the sale of all lands that have been or hereafter may be granted by the United States to the State for educational purposes, and the proceeds of all lands or other property given by individuals, or appropriated by the State for like purposes, shall be and remain a perpetual fund, the interest and income of which, together with the rents of all such lands as may remain unsold, shall be inviolably appropriated, and annually applied to the specific objects of the original gift, grant, or appropriation.

SEC. 9. All lands which have heretofore escheated, or which shall hereafter escheat to the State, shall inure to the benefit of the primary school fund, and be held and disposed of as primary school lands.

SEC. 10. The Legislature shall provide for the establishment and maintenance of a library in each township, and of at least one in each city. And all moneys belonging to the public derived from fines, penalties, forfeitures, or recognizances, imposed or taken in the several counties, cities, or townships for any breach of the penal laws of the State, shall be apportioned in the same manner as is the income of the primary school fund, and paid over to the several cities and townships of the county in which such money accrued, for the support of such libraries.

SEC. 11. Institutions for the benefit of those inhabitants who are deaf, dumb, blind, or insane, shall always be fostered and supported.

ARTICLE XIV.

FINANCE AND TAXATION.

SECTION 1. The Legislature shall provide for the collection of specific taxes from banking, railroad, and plank-road corporations, and may, in its discretion, impose specific taxes upon other corporations, and upon any property or business within this State, but when a specific tax is imposed upon a corporation, it shall only apply to such property of the corporation as shall be necessary for the exercise of its corporate franchises.

SEC. 2. All specific State taxes, received from corporations, except mining companies of the Upper Peninsula, shall be applied in paying the interest upon the Primary School, University, and other educational funds, and the interest and principal of the State debt, in the order herein recited, until the extinguishment of the State debt, other than the amounts due to educational funds, when such specific taxes shall be added to and constitute a part of the primary school interest fund.

SEC. 3. The Legislature shall provide for an annual tax, sufficient, with other resources, to pay the estimated expenses of the State government, the interest of the State debt, and such deficiency as may occur in the resources.

SEC. 4. Every law hereafter enacted by the Legislature, creating a debt or authorizing a loan, shall provide a sinking fund for the payment of the same.

SEC. 5. The unfunded debt shall not be funded or redeemed at a value exceeding that established by law in the year one thousand eight hundred and forty-eight.

SEC. 6. The State may contract debts to meet deficits in revenue. Such debts shall not in the aggregate at any time exceed fifty thousand dollars. The moneys so raised shall be applied to the purposes for which they were obtained, or to the payment of the debts so contracted.

SEC. 7. The State may contract debts to repel invasion, suppress insurrection, defend the State, or aid the United States in time of war. The money arising from the contracting of such debts shall be applied to the purposes for which it was raised, or to pay such debts.

SEC. 8. No money shall be paid out of the State treasury, except in pursuance of appropriations made by law. The Legislature shall provide by law for barring all claims against the State, unless presented within a time to be therein fixed.

SEC. 9. The State shall not aid, by gift, or pledge of its credit, any person or corporation, nor shall it subscribe to or become interested in the stock of any corporation, nor assume any indebtedness of a municipal or other corporation. The provisions of this section shall not apply to educational, charitable, reformatory or penal institutions which are or may be under the care and control of the State.

SEC. 10. No scrip, certificate, or other evidence of State indebtedness shall be issued, except for the redemption of stock previously issued, or for such debts as are expressly authorized by this Constitution.

SEC. 11. The State shall not be a party to or be interested in any work of internal improvement, except the Ship Canal at the Sault Ste. Marie, nor engage in carrying on any such work, otherwise than in the expenditure of grants to the State of land or other property.

SEC. 12. The Legislature shall provide a uniform rule of taxation, except on property, business, and corporations paying specific taxes. Taxes shall be levied on all property except such as is or may be exempted by law.

SEC. 13. All assessments hereafter authorized shall be on property at its cash value.

SEC. 14. The Legislature shall provide for an equalization by a State board in the year one thousand eight hundred and fifty-one, and every fifth year thereafter, of assessments on all taxable property except that paying specific taxes.

SEC. 15. Every law which imposes, continues, or revives a tax, shall distinctly state the tax, and the object to which it is to be applied; and it shall not be sufficient to refer to any other law to fix such tax or object.

ARTICLE XV.

EXEMPTIONS.

SECTION 1. The personal property of every resident of this State, to consist of such property only as shall be designated by law, shall be exempted to the amount of not less than five hundred dollars, from sale on execution or other final process of any court, issued for the collection of any debt contracted after the adoption of this Constitution.

SEC. 2. Every homestead of not exceeding forty acres of land, and the dwelling-house thereon, and the appurtenances to be selected by the owner thereof, and not included in any town plat, city, or village, or instead thereof, at the option of the owner, any lot in any city or village, or recorded town plat, or such parts of lots as shall be equal thereto, and the dwelling house thereon, and its appurtenances, owned and occupied by any resident of the State, not exceeding in value two thousand dollars, shall be exempt from forced sale on execution, or any other final process from a court, for any debt contracted after the adoption of this Constitution. Such exemption shall not extend to any mortgage thereon lawfully obtained, but any mortgage not given for purchase money, and any other alienation of such land by the owner thereof, if a married man, shall not be valid without the signature of the wife to the same.

SEC. 3. If the owner of a homestead die, leaving a widow, child, or children, such homestead shall be exempt from the payment of his debts, so long as the widow shall be without other homestead of her own, and during the minority of said child or children.

SEC. 4. The real and personal estate of every woman, acquired before marriage, and all property, real and personal, to which she may afterwards become entitled, shall be and remain the estate and property of such woman, and shall not be liable for the debts, obligations or engagements of her husband, and may be held, controlled, and disposed of by her, in the same manner, and with like effect, as if she were unmarried. And the husband of any married woman shall not be liable for or on account of any debt or obligation of his wife contracted before her marriage, or contracted by her in relation to her sole property after marriage.

ARTICLE XVI.

MILITIA.

SECTION 1. The militia shall be composed of all able-bodied male citizens between the ages of eighteen and forty-five years, except such as are exempted by the laws of the United States or of this State; but all such citizens, of any religious denomination whatever, who from scruples of conscience may be averse to bearing arms, shall be excused therefrom, upon such conditions as shall be prescribed by law.

SEC. 2. The Legislature shall provide by law for organizing, equipping, and disciplining the militia, in such manner as it shall deem expedient, not incompatible with the laws of the United States.

SEC. 3. Officers of the militia shall be elected or appointed, and be commissioned in such manner as may be provided by law.

ARTICLE XVII.

MISCELLANEOUS PROVISIONS.

SECTION 1. Members of the Legislature, and all officers, executive and judicial, shall, before they enter on the duties of their respective offices, take and subscribe the following oath or affirmation: "I do solemnly swear (or affirm) that I will support the Constitution of the United States, and the Constitution of this State, and that I will faithfully discharge the duties of the office of ———, according to the best of my ability."

SEC. 2. Judicial and legislative proceedings shall be conducted, and the laws and public records promulgated and preserved, in the English language.

SEC. 3. Public officers, receiving or having charge of public moneys, are prohibited from using or employing the same in any manner for their private use or benefit, and whenever such moneys are deposited with any person or corporation, the interest thereon shall be paid to the fund to which such moneys belong.

SEC. 4. The Legislature may authorize the taking of private property for the opening of private roads, for use in the improvement of navigable streams, and for flowage when the public interests demand it.

SEC. 5. Before any private property shall be taken without the consent of the owner, for public use, (except for public highways not within any city or village), or for any purpose named in the last above section, the necessity for taking such property, and the compensation to be paid therefor, shall be determined by a jury of freeholders of the vicinity, or by not less than three commissioners, freeholders as aforesaid, appointed by a court of record, as may be provided by law, and such compensation shall be paid or tendered in such manner as shall be prescribed by law.

SEC. 6. The right of the public or of any individual to the free use of any navigable stream, for any purpose for which such stream is capable of use, without improvement, shall not be abridged or obstructed by or under color of any authority which may be given by law to any individual or corporation to improve such stream and charge toll for the use thereof.

SEC. 7. No navigable steam in this State shall be either bridged or dammed without authority from the board of supervisors of the proper county, under the provisions of law. No such law shall prejudice the right of individuals to the free navigation of such streams, or preclude the State from the further improvement of the navigation of such streams.

SEC. 8. An accurate statement of the receipts and expenditures of the public moneys shall be attached to and published with the laws, at every regular session of the Legislature.

SEC. 9. No mechanical trade shall hereafter be taught to convicts in the State Prison of this State, except the manufacture of those articles of which the chief supply for home consumption is imported from other States or countries.

SEC. 10. Any woman above the age of twenty-one years, who shall be a resident of this State, and of the proper township, city or ward, and who is a citizen of the United States, shall be eligible to the office of Register of Deeds, Notary Public, offices connected with schools and libraries, and to such other offices as may be designated by law.

SEC. 11. No lease or grant hereafter of agricultural land for a longer period than twelve years, reserving any rent or service of any kind, shall be valid.

ARTICLE XVIII.

AMENDMENT AND REVISION OF THE CONSTITUTION.

SECTION 1. Any amendment or amendments to this Constitution may be proposed in the Senate or House of Representatives. If the same be agreed to by two-thirds of the members elected to each House, such amendment or amendments shall be entered on their journals respectively, with the yeas and nays taken thereon, and the same shall be submitted to the electors at such time as the Legislature shall prescribe. And if a majority of the electors, qualified to vote for members of the Legislature, voting on the amendment or amendments proposed, shall ratify and approve such amendment or amendments, the same shall become a part of the Constitution, and take effect at the commencement of the year following its adoption.

SEC. 2. At any time after the first day of January, one thousand eight hundred and eighty-five, the Legislature may provide for a convention, to be chosen by the qualified electors of the State, or for a commission to be appointed by the Governor by and with the advice and consent of the Senate, to revise or amend this Constitution. Such revised or amended Constitution shall be submitted to the electors qualified to vote for members of the Legislature, at such time and in such manner as said convention or commission may provide. If a majority of the electors voting on such revised or amended Constitution, shall decide in favor thereof, the same shall take effect at the commencement of the year following its adoption.

SCHEDULE.

That no inconvenience may arise from the changes in the Constitution of this State, and in order to carry the same into operation, it is hereby declared:

SECTION 1. The common law, and the statute laws now in force, not repugnant to this Constitution, shall remain in force until they expire by their own limitation, or are altered or repealed by the Legislature.

SEC. 2. All writs, actions, causes of action, prosecutions, and rights of individuals and of bodies corporate, and of the State, and all charters of incorporation shall continue; and all indictments and informations which shall have been found or filed, or which may hereafter be found or filed, for any crime or offense committed before the adoption of this Constitution, may be proceeded upon as if no change had taken place. The several courts, except as herein otherwise provided shall continue with the like powers and jurisdiction, both at law and in equity, as if this Constitution had not been adopted, and until the organization of the judicial department under this Constitution.

SEC. 3. All fines, penalties, forfeitures, and escheats, accruing to the State under the present Constitution and laws, shall accrue to the use of the State under this Constitution.

SEC. 4. All recognizances, bonds, obligations, and all other instruments entered into or executed before the adoption of this Constitution, to the people of this State, or to any county, or township, or to any public officer, or public body, or which may be entered into or executed under existing laws, to the people of this State, or to any such officer or public body, before the complete organization of the departments of government under this Constitution, shall remain binding and valid, and rights and liabilities upon the same shall continue, and may be prosecuted as provided by law. And all crimes and misdemeanors, and penal actions, shall be prosecuted, tried, and punished as though no change had taken place, until otherwise provided by law.

SEC. 5. All officers, civil and military, now holding any office or appointment, shall continue to hold their respective offices, unless removed by competent authority, until superseded under the laws now in force, or under this Constitution.

SEC. 6. It shall be the duty of the Legislature, at its first session after the adoption of this Constitution, to adapt the present laws to the provisions of this Constitution.

SEC. 7. Any territory attached, or that may be attached to any county for judicial purposes, if not otherwise represented, shall be considered as forming a part of such county, so far as regards elections for the purpose of representation.

TAXATION OF THE LIQUOR TRAFFIC.

[TO BE SEPARATELY SUBMITTED.]

At the election when this amended Constitution shall be submitted to the electors of this State for adoption or rejection, there shall be submitted to such electors the following proposition, to be added, in case of its adoption, to Section 47 of Article IV., in the present Constitution of this State, as it now stands, and to Section 36 of Article IV. in said amended Constitution, if the latter is adopted, viz.:

An annual tax of two hundred dollars is imposed upon the traffic in intoxicating liquors, to be paid by every person or firm who shall carry on or be engaged in the business of selling or disposing of such liquors otherwise than for medicinal, chemical and mechanical purposes, for each place where such business is carried on by such person or firm. Said tax shall be paid into the treasury of the proper township, city, or village, and be applied by the proper authorities to the support of the poor therein, so far as may be necessary, and the residue appropriated as the legislature shall provide. The sale, or other disposition of such liquors, to minors, persons under guardianship, insane, and idiotic persons, paupers, and common drunkards, is wholly prohibited. Every person who shall carry on or engage in the business, or traffic taxed as aforesaid in this section, without having first paid the tax imposed, or otherwise violate any provision of this section, shall be guilty of a misdemeanor, and, on conviction, be punished by fine or imprisonment, or both, as may be prescribed by law, and every sale until the tax is paid shall subject the party to such penalty; and all necessary laws shall be passed to enforce the provisions of this section. The Legislature may further regulate and restrict the sale and other disposition of intoxicating liquors; and may increase the annual tax upon said traffic in any locality.

Said proposition shall be separately submitted to the electors of this State for their adoption or rejection, in form following, to wit:

A separate ballot may be given by every person having the right to vote, to be deposited in a separate box.

Upon the ballots given for said proposition, shall be written, printed, or partly written, or partly printed, the words, "Restriction and taxation of the liquor traffic—Yes;" and upon the ballots given against the adoption thereof in like manner the words, "Restriction and taxation of the liquor traffic—No."

If at said election a majority of the votes given upon said proposition shall contain the words "Restriction and taxation of the liquor traffic—Yes," then said proposition shall be added to Section 47 in Article IV. of the present Constitution, and to Section 36 in Article IV. of said amended Constitution, if the latter is adopted.

INDEX

TO THE

PROPOSED CONSTITUTION.

A.

	ART.	SEC.	PAGE.
Accusation, right to be informed of the	II	8	179
Acquittal upon merit, no person after, to be tried for same offense	II	11	180
Act, emergency requiring immediate effect of, to be stated in	IV	19	186
" when revised to be re-enacted	IV	19	186
Acts, public, when to take effect	IV	19	186
Adjourn, less than a quorum may, from day to day	IV	8	183
Adjournment, without concurrent action, limited to three days	IV	12	184
Adjustments of claims by supervisors and county auditors subject to no appeal	X	10	201
Aliens, resident, property rights of	II	21	181
Alteration of circuit not to remove a judge from office	VI	6	193
Amendment and revision of the constitution, article on	XVIII		214
Appellate jurisdiction of supreme court, limitation of	VI	3	192
Appointment, provisional, during the pending of an impeachment trial	XII	9	206
Appropriations, no money to be paid except in pursuance of	XIV	8	209
" upon condition for university, to be applied as conditioned	XIII	2	207
Arms, right to bear, secured	II	16	180
Arrest, legislators, when exempt from	IV	7	183
Assemble, right to, secured	II	19	180
Assessments to be on property at its cash value	XIV	13	210
Attainder, bill of, passage of, forbidden	II	5	179
Attendance, less than a quorum may compel	IV	8	183
Attorney-general to be elected or appointed	VIII	3	197

B.

	ART.	SEC.	PAGE.
Bill-holders preferred creditors of insolvent banks	XI	5	203
Bills, bank, how secured	XI	4	202
Bills may originate in either house	IV	13	184
Board of agricultural college, duties of to be prescribed by law	XIII	4	207

	ART.	SEC.	PAGE.
Board of regents to have supervision and control of the university	XIII	2	207
Board of state auditors, how constituted	VIII	5	198
Board of state canvassers, how constituted	VIII	5	198
" " " when determination of, is contested	VIII	6	198
Board of supervisors, cities and villages to be represented on	X	8	200
" " how constituted	X	8	200
" " powers of, limited	X	8	199
Boundaries of the state	I	1	177
Bailable before conviction, all persons	II	11	180
Bail, excessive, prohibited	II	13	180
Ballot, all elections by, except of certain township officers	VII	3	196
Banking law, no general, to have effect till approved by a majority of electors at general election	XI	2	202
Banks, stockholders of, to be individually liable	XI	3	202
Barring claims, the legislature to provide for	XIV	8	209

C.

	ART.	SEC.	PAGE.
Census, legislature to provide for taking	IV	4	182
Chaplain may be authorized for the state prison	IV	24	188
Charters of cities and villages may be amended	X	17	202
Charters of incorporation to continue	Sched.	2	215
Circuit court, terms of	VI	7	193
" " vacancy in, how filled	VI	11	194
Circuit courts, appellate jurisdiction of	VI	8	193
" " " " limited	VI	8	194
" " judges of, to hold terms for each other	VI	7	193
" " original jurisdiction of	VI	8	193
" " to appoint circuit court commissioners	VI	9	194
" " to have power to issue writs	VI	8	194
" " " supervisory control of inferior tribunals	VI	8	193
Circuit judges to fill vacancies in office of county clerk and prosecuting attorney	VI	12	195
Circuit judge, when he removes from his circuit vacates his office	VI	10	194
Cities and villages, provisions in regard to	X	14	201
Cities to be incorporated under general laws	X	14	201
City indebtedness, limitation of	X	15	201
City officers, election of	X	16	201
City, when eligible to county organization	X	4	199
Claims against counties, how adjusted	X	10	200
Clerk of county to be clerk of circuit court	VI	12	194
Commissions, by whom signed and countersigned	V	19	192
" to be in the name of the people	V	19	192
" to be sealed with the great seal	V	19	192
Compensation, extra, not to be granted in certain cases	IV	20	186
Competing lines of railroad not to consolidate	XI	11	204
Consolidation of railroad companies, notice required	XI	11	204
Constitutional commission authorized	XVIII	2	214
" convention authorized	XVIII	2	214

	ART.	SEC.	PAGE.
Constitution, how to be amended and revised	XVIII	1	214
Constructive labor, charges for, not to be allowed	IV	21	186
Contracts, certain, to be prohibited by the legislature	XI	10	204
" for fuel and stationery to be provided for by law	IV	21	186
" law impairing obligation of, prohibited	II	5	179
" legislature not to rescind	IV	21	186
Corporation, construed to apply to associations and stock companies	XI	13	204
Corporations, certain, limited to thirty years' duration	XI	12	204
" municipal, legislature to confer powers on	IV	32	189
" other than municipal, article in regard to	XI		202
" " " " to be created by general laws	XI	1	202
Counties, provisions relating to	X	2	199
" suits to be in the name of	X	2	199
" powers of, to be restricted by law	X	2	199
County clerk and register of deeds, offices of, may be united or disconnected	X	5	200
County composed of islands may be organized or attached	X	4	199
" each organized, to be a body corporate	X	2	199
" indebtedness limited	X	3	199
" number of townships of a	X	4	199
" officers prohibited from being legislators	IV	6	183
" " to be elected	X	5	200
" offices to be at county seat	X	6	200
" seat, removal of, how effected	X	9	200
Counsel for defense, right to have	II	8	179
Court of probate in each organized county	VI	14	195
" " " jurisdiction of, may be extended by law	VI	14	195
" " " " " to be prescribed by law	VI	14	195
Court of record, vacancy in, how filled	VI	11	194
Courts of record, the supreme circuit, and probate courts to be	VI	15	195
" " " to have a common seal	VI	15	195
Crimes and misdemeanors unaffected by adopting new constitution	Sched.	4	216
Cross-examination of accused, when allowed	II	14	180

D.

	ART.	SEC.	PAGE.
Debt, imprisonment for, prohibited	II	15	180
" state, limitation of to meet deficits	XIV	6	209
" the unfunded not to be funded at a greater value than that established in 1848	XIV	5	209
Debts, state, authorized for certain purposes	XIV	7	209
Decisions, publication of judicial	IV	30	189
District, representative, description of to be filed	IV	3	182
" " how organized	IV	3	182
Districts, senatorial, when re-arranged	IV	4	182
Duel, penalty for engaging in a	VII	8	197

E.

	ART.	SEC.	PAGE.
Education, article on	XIII		206
Educational purposes, proceeds of lands granted for, how applied	XIII	8	208

	ART.	SEC.	PAGE.
Elective franchise, article on	VII		196
Election-day, no elector obliged to attend court on	VII	4	196
" " " " " do military duty on	VII	4	196
Elector, qualifications of an	VII	1	196
Electors in U. S. service in time of war, allowed to vote	VII	2	196
" privileged from arrest, under certain circumstances	VII	4	196
English language, all proceedings to be recorded in the	XVII	2	212
" " instruction to be conducted in	XIII	6	207
Equalization by state board every fifth year	XIV	14	210
Escheated lands to inure to the benefit of primary school fund	XIII	9	208
Every law creating a state debt to provide for payment thereof	XIV	4	209
Executive department, article on	V		189
" power, in whom vested	V	1	189
Exemption of homestead from execution	XV	2	211
" " personal property from execution	XV	1	211
Exemptions, article on	XV		210
Expenses of state government to be raised by tax	XIV	8	209
Expulsion of members of legislature under certain circumstances, prohibited	IV	9	183
Expulsion of members, reasons for to be entered on journal.	IV	9	183
" " " two-thirds vote required for	IV	9	183
Extra sessions, limitation of legislation at	IV	13	184

F.

	ART.	SEC.	PAGE.
Finance and taxation, article on	XIV		208
Fine, military, no imprisonment for in time of peace	II	15	180
Fines, excessive, imposition of, prohibited	II	13	180
" penalties forfeitures and escheats to be unaffected by adopting new constitution	Sched.	3	215
Flowage, private property, how taken for	XVII	4	213
Foreign corporations, how punished for violation of law	XI	9	203
" " subject to same regulations as domestic	XI	9	203

G.

	ART.	SEC.	PAGE.
General acts of incorporation subject to amendment or repeal.	XI	1	202
Gospel, ministers of, no compulsion to support	II	2	178
Governor, eligibility for office of	V	2	189
" impeachment of, how instituted	XII	8	206
" may call out military and naval forces	V	4	190
" " convene legislature at another place	V	9	190
" " " " on extraordinary occasions.	V	7	190
" may grant reprieves, commutations and pardons in certain cases	V	11	190
" may require information in writing from other executive officers	V	5	190
" may suspend execution of sentence on conviction for treason	V	11	191
" no member of congress, officer of the U. S. or of this state to execute office of	V	15	191
" not to receive appointment from legislature	V	16	191
" official acts of, how authenticated	V	18	192

	ART.	SEC.	PAGE.
Governor, power of, to recommend admission of new legislation	IV	13	184
" term of office of	V	1	190
" to be commander-in-chief	V	4	190
" to examine into the condition and administration of any public office	XII	7	205
" to continue commander-in-chief when in the field	V	12	191
" to inform legislature by message of the condition of the state	V	8	190
" to issue writs of election to fill vacancies in the legislature	V	10	190
" to nominate and appoint a judge for each circuit	VI	6	193
" to recommend to the legislature measures he deems expedient	V	8	190
" to see that the laws are faithfully executed	V	6	190
" when to be elected	V	3	190
" who declared elected	V	3	190
Government, division of powers of, article on	III		181
" seat of	I	2	178
" three departments of	III	1	181
Great seal of state to be kept by the secretary of state	V	18	192

H.

	ART.	SEC.	PAGE.
Habeas corpus, writ of, suspension of the privilege prohibited	II	6	179
Highways and bridges, supervisors to provide for	X	11	201
Homestead, when exempt from deceased's debts	XV	3	211
Husband not liable for wife's debts in certain cases	XV	4	211

I.

	ART.	SEC.	PAGE.
Impeached party to be subject to trial and punishment	XII	2	205
Impeachment, an, may be tried after adjournment of legislature	XII	3	205
" every, to be tried by the senate	XII	2	204
" governor authorized to convene legislature for	XII	8	206
" judgment in, not to extend further than removal from office	XII	2	204
" power of, vested in the house of representatives	XII	1	204
" proceedings under an	XII	3	205
" when directed, to suspend exercise of official functions	XII	4	205
Impeachments and removals from office, article on	XII		204
Indictments and informations, pending, to be unaffected by the adoption of this constitution	Sched.	2	215
Institutions for benefit of deaf, dumb, blind, or insane to be supported	XIII	11	208
Instruction of representatives, right to, secured	II	19	180
Interest on public funds to be added to said funds	XVII	3	218
" " state debt to be raised by tax	XIV	3	209

J.

	ART.	SEC.	PAGE.
Journal, each house to keep a	IV	10	183
Judges and justices to be conservators of the peace	VI	18	195

	ART.	SEC.	PAGE.
Judges of probate, term of office of	VI	14	195
" " supreme and circuit courts ineligible to offices not judicial	VI	13	195
" salaries of, not to be diminished during term of office	IX	2	198
" " to be provided by law	IX	2	198
Judicial department, article on	VI		192
Judicial power vested in the courts authorized by law	VI	1	192
Jury, right of trial by, to remain	II	7	179
" " " " " when waived	II	7	179
" legislature may authorize a, of less than twelve men	II	7	179
Justice of the peace, when office of, is deemed vacated	VI	10	194
" " " " " elected to fill vacancy, to complete the term	VI	16	195
Justices of the peace, classification of, at first election	VI	16	195
" " " " jurisdiction of	VI	17	195
" " " " number of, prescribed	VI	16	195
" " " " to be elected for four years	VI	16	195

L.

	ART.	SEC.	PAGE.
Labor, stockholders individually liable for	XI	7	208
Lands held in violation of law to escheat to the state	XI	9	208
" not to be acquired by foreign corporations, except in payment of debts	XI	9	208
Law and fact, jury to determine in libel cases	II	4	179
Law, each limited to one object	IV	19	186
" " to have its object expressed in its title	IV	19	186
Law, *ex post facto*, passage of, prohibited	II	5	179
Law, no, amended by reference to its title only	IV	19	186
Laws now in force to remain until they expire or are repealed	Sched.	1	215
" speedy publication of all public	IV	30	189
Lease of agricultural land limited to twelve years	XVII	11	214
Legislation, approval of, by governor	IV	14	184
" how to be passed	IV	18	186
" without approval, when operative	IV	14	185
Legislative department, article on	IV		181
Legislators, books allowed to	IV	15	185
" election of, when to take place	IV	29	188
" forbidden to be interested in certain contracts	IV	17	185
" ineligible to certain appointments	IV	17	185
" mileage allowed to	IV	15	185
" not to be interested in any contract with state	IV	21	187
" perquisites to, prohibited	IV	15	185
" stationery, amount allowed for	IV	15	185
Legislature, compensation of members of the	IV	15	185
" hour of final adjournment of the	IV	28	188
" may pardon or commute sentence for treason	V	11	191
" " provide as to manner of hearing applications for pardon	V	11	190
" not to pass special laws in certain cases	IV	22	187
" open to the public	IV	12	184
" to adapt laws to new constitution	Sched.	6	216

	ART.	SEC.	PAGE.
Legislature, to divide the state into judicial circuits	VI	6	193
" to provide by general laws for all cases deemed requisite	IV	22	188
" when and where to meet and when to adjourn	IV	27	188
" when to decide the election of governor or lieutenant governor	V	3	190
Libel, truth may be given in evidence in cases of	II	4	179
Liberty, protection of	II	14	180
Libraries, city and township, how maintained	XIII	10	208
License for sale of intoxicating liquors, not to be authorized	IV	36	189
Lieut. governor, eligibility for office of	V	2	190
" " not to receive appointment from legislature	V	16	191
" " term of office of	V	1	189
" " to be president of the senate	V	14	191
" " when acting as governor to receive same compensation	V	17	191
" " when to be elected	V	3	190
" " " " governor	V	12	191
" " who declared elected	V	3	190
Life, protection of	II	14	180
Lottery, legislature not to authorize any	IV	33	189
" tickets, legislature not to permit the sale of	IV	33	189

M.

	ART.	SEC.	PAGE.
Military subordinate to civil power	II	17	180
Militia, article on	XVI		212
" legislature to provide for organizing and equipping	XVI	2	212
" officers, how commissioned	XVI	3	212
" of whom composed	XVI	1	212
Miscellaneous provisions, article on	XVII		212
Money due the public, holders of, ineligible to seat in legislature or to any state office	IV	25	188
Moneys raised for specific purposes to be devoted thereto	XIV	6-7	209
Mortgage not affected by exemption	XV	2	211
" on homestead not valid without wife's signature	XV	2	211
Municipal and school officers removable according to law	XII	6	205
" corporations, article on	X		198
" " may aid enlistments	X	1	199
" " " support soldiers' families	X	1	199
" " " " their poor	X	1	199
" " not to become stockholders	X	1	198
" " not to lend their credit	X	1	199
" " " own any railroad	X	1	199

N.

	ART.	SEC.	PAGE.
Navigable stream, not to be bridged or dammed except according to law	XVII	7	213
" " public right to, not to be abridged	XVII	6, 7	213
Normal school to be under the control of the state board of education	XIII	8	207

O.

	DIV.	ART.	SEC.	PAGE.
Oath of office		XVII	1	212
Officers, legislative, each house to choose		IV	9	183
" not removed by adoption of new constitution		Sched.	5	216
Offices, legislature to declare when vacant		IV	31	189

P.

	DIV.	ART.	SEC.	PAGE.
Persons belonging to one department not to exercise power belonging to another		III	2	181
Petition, right of, secured		II	19	180
Power, all political, inherent in the people		II	1	178
" legislative, vested in senate and house of representatives		IV	1	181
Preamble to the constitution				177
President of the senate, compensation of		IV	16	185
" " " may debate in committee of the whole		V	14	191
" " " *pro tempore*, when acting as governor to receive same compensation		V	17	191
" " " *pro tempore*, when to act as governor,		V	13	191
" " " to have the casting vote		V	14	191
President of the university, duties and privileges of		XIII	2	207
" " " to be elected by board of regents		XIII	2	207
Press, freedom of, secured		II	4	179
Primary school fund, when withheld from a district		XIII	7	207
Primary schools, free of charge, to be provided for		XIII	6	207
Printing, legislature to prescribe how executed		IV	21	186
Private claims, not to be allowed by the legislature		IV	26	188
" property for roads and streams		XVII	4	213
" " " public use, how taken		XVII	5	213
Privileges, special, none to be granted that may not be revoked		II	1	178
Probate court, vacancy in, to be filled by appointment of the governor		VI	11	194
Probate judges prohibited from being legislators		IV	6	183
Process, style of all		VI	19	195
PROHIBITED SPECIAL LEGISLATION		IV	22	187
bridges, for building or repairing	18	IV	22	188
child or heir, adopting, by any named person	17	IV	22	187
crimes or misdemeanors, punishing	16	IV	22	187
descent, law of, changing the	12	IV	22	187
divorce, on the subject of	1	IV	22	187
divorcing any named person	1	IV	22	187
exempting any property from taxation	19	IV	22	188
fees, percentages, and allowances of public officers, creating	11	IV	22	187
" percentages, and allowances of public officers, decreasing	11	IV	22	187
" percentages, and allowances of public officers, increasing	11	IV	22	187
ferries, licensing or chartering	9	IV	22	187

	DIV.	ART.	SEC.	PAGE.
PROHIBITED SPECIAL LEGISLATION (*Continued*):				
granting exclusive privilege, immunity, or franchise...	13	IV	22	187
jurisdiction and duties of constables, regulating the....	3	IV	22	187
" " " justices of the peace, regulating the........	3	IV	22	187
jurors, summoning........	6	IV	22	187
lease of minors' real estate, permitting........	8	IV	22	187
mortgage of minors' real estate, permitting........	8	IV	22	187
name of any person, changing the........	2	IV	22	187
" " place " "	2	IV	22	187
of age, declaring any named person	14	IV	22	187
practice in courts of justice, regulating the........	3	IV	22	187
rate of interest on money, regulating the	7	IV	22	187
remitting fines, penalties, or forfeitures........	10	IV	22	187
sale of minors' real estate, permitting........	8	IV	22	187
supervisors, providing for election or appointment of..	5	IV	22	187
swamp or low land, for draining of........	18	IV	22	188
taxes, extending time for collection of........	15	IV	22	187
toll-bridges, chartering or licensing........	9	IV	22	187
vacating alley........	18	IV	22	188
" any road........	18	IV	22	188
" " street or public ground........	18	IV	22	188
venue, providing for changes of........	4	IV	22	187
Property, private, not to be taken for public use without compensation........		II	22	181
Property, protection of........		II	14	180
Proposition, if adopted, where to be placed in constitution..				217
" to tax liquor traffic, the........				216
" to tax liquor traffic, to be separately submitted..				217
Prosecute or defend, every suitor to have right to........		II	9	179
Prosecuting attorneys, appointment of authorized........		X	5	200
Protest, right to, secured to legislators........		IV	10	184
Publication of laws and decisions free to all........		IV	30	189
Public officers prohibited from using public funds for private purposes........		XVII	3	212
Punishments, cruel or unusual, prohibited........		II	13	180
Purity of elections, laws to preserve, authorized........		VII	6	197
Purposes to which taxation on liquor traffic shall be applied..				216

Q.

	DIV.	ART.	SEC.	PAGE.
Qualifications of members, each house to judge of........		IV	9	183
Quorum, what shall constitute a........		IV	8	183

R.

	DIV.	ART.	SEC.	PAGE.
Real estate, not to be held by corporations over ten years.....		XI	8	203
Receipts and expenditures, statement of, to be published with the laws........		XVII	8	213
Recognizances, bonds and obligations existing to remain binding and valid........		Sched.	4	215
Reform school, board of, duties of, prescribed by law........		XIII	4	207

	ART.	SEC.	PAGE.
Regents of the university a body corporate	XIII	2	206
" " " election of	XIII	2	206
" " " how constituted	XIII	2	206
Religious sect, no money or property to be appropriated to any	IV	34	189
Removal without impeachment, how to be effected	XII	5	205
Removals by the governor to be reported to the legislature	XII	7	205
Remove from office, governor authorized to, in certain cases	XII	7	205
Representative, removal of, from district deemed vacation of office	IV	5	183
Representatives, house of, number of members of	IV	3	182
" to be United States citizens and electors of the district they represent	IV	5	183
" when re-apportioned	IV	4	182
Residence, no elector to gain or lose by absence for certain reasons	VII	5	197
Rights, bill of, article on	II		178
Rights not abridged on account of religious belief	II	3	179
Rule of taxation, a uniform, legislature to provide	XIV	12	210
Rules, each house to determine its own	IV	9	183

S.

	ART.	SEC.	PAGE.
Salaries, article in regard to	IX		198
Sale of intoxicating liquors prohibited in certain cases			217
Schedule			215
Schools, theological, no money or property to be appropriated for	IV	34	189
" under private or denominational control, no money or property to be appropriated for	IV	34	189
Search warrant not to be issued without probable cause	II	10	180
" " to describe place, person, or thing	II	10	180
Search, unreasonable, protection from	II	10	179
Sections amended to be re-enacted	IV	19	186
Seizure, unreasonable, protection from	II	10	180
Senate, the, how constituted	IV	2	181
Senator, removal from district of, deemed vacation of office	IV	5	183
Senatorial districts, no county to be divided in forming	IV	2	182
Senators, number of, when to be increased	IV	2	181
" terms of office of	IV	2	181
" to be United States citizens and electors of the district they represent	IV	5	183
Services, religious, in legislature, not to be paid for	IV	24	188
Sheriff, county not responsible for his acts	X	7	200
" to be eligible to no other office	X	7	200
" to serve only two consecutive terms	X	7	200
Slavery, prohibition of	II	20	181
Soldiers, quartering of, in any house	II	18	180
Speaker of the house, compensation of	IV	16	185
Specific taxes, collection of	XIV	1	208
" " how appropriated	XIV	2	209
" " to apply only to certain property	XIV	1	209

	ART.	SEC.	PAGE.
Speech, freedom of, secured	II	4	179
" legislators not to be questioned in regard to	IV	7	183
Speed of trains to be regulated by law	XI	10	204
State board of education, how constituted	XIII	3	207
State institutions to be supported by the State	XIV	9	210
State not to aid by gift or by its credit any person or corporation	XIV	9	210
" not to assume municipal indebtedness	XIV	9	210
" not to become a stockholder	XIV	9	210
" not to engage in works of internal improvement	XIV	11	210
" not to issue unauthorized scrip or certificate of indebtedness, except for redemption of stock	XIV	10	210
State officers, article in regard to	VIII		197
" " election and terms of	VIII	1	197
" " prohibited from being legislators	IV	6	183
" " salaries of, not to be increased or diminished during term	IX	1	198
" " salaries of to be established by law	IX	1	198
State offices, vacancy in, how filled	VIII	4	197
" " when terms of, commence	VIII	2	197
State paper not to be established by the legislature	IV	23	188
State prison, mechanical trades taught in, limited	XVII	9	213
State public school, board of, duties of, to be prescribed by law	XIII	4	207
Style of the laws	IV	37	189
Submission of proposition, form of			217
Suits to be in name of township	X	12	201
Superintendent of public instruction *ex officio* member of certain boards	XIII	1	206
Superintendent of public instruction, powers of	XIII	1	206
Supervisors and county auditors, compensation of	X	10	201
Supreme court, concurrence of majority necessary to decision	VI	3	193
" " judges of, how appointed	VI	2	192
" " " " to hold office ten years	VI	2	192
" " " " when to be appointed	VI	2	192
" " " " may issue writs and process	VI	8	192
" " " " to appoint clerks and reporters	VI	5	193
" " to be composed of five judges	VI	2	192
" " to establish and modify its methods of practice	VI	5	193
" " to hold four terms a year	VI	4	193
" " to have a superintending control of all other tribunals	VI	8	192
" " to have original jurisdiction in certain cases	VI	8	192
" " " " power to establish codes for all other courts of record	VI	5	193
" " " " such appellate jurisdiction as provided by law	VI	8	192
" " vacancy in, how filled	VI	11	194
Suspension of payment, legislature not to authorize	XI	9	208

T.

	ART.	SEC.	PAGE.
Taxation of the liquor traffic, proposition in regard to			216
Tax, every law imposing a, to specify object	XIV	15	210
Taxes to be levied on all property except such as are exempt by law	XIV	12	210
Term, a school, to be maintained in each district	XIII	7	207
Terms of office of supreme court judges, when to date from	VI	2	192
Territory attached for judicial purposes to be regarded also attached for election purposes	Sched.	7	216
Testify, no person required to, against himself	II	14	180
Tie vote, how to be determined	VIII	6	198
Time for introduction of legislation limited	IV	13	184
Township, each to be a body corporate	X	12	201
" officers, election of	X	13	201
Townships, provisions in regard to	X	12	201
" supervisors may organize	X	11	201
Transportation rates to be regulated by law	XI	10	203
Treason against the State defined	II	12	180
" two witnesses required to convict of	II	12	180
Trial, right of speedy	II	8	179
Two-thirds vote required for appropriating money for local or private purposes	IV	35	189
Two-thirds vote required for conviction on impeachment	XII	2	204
" " " to give immediate effect to a public act	IV	19	186

U.

	ART.	SEC.	PAGE.
United States officers prohibited from being legislators, when appointed by the President	IV	6	183
" " soldiers and marines acquire no residence from being stationed in the State	VII	7	197

V.

	ART.	SEC.	PAGE.
Vacancies caused by removal in certain cases, how filled	XII	7	205
" in state boards, how filled	XIII	5	207
Vacancy, legislature to declare manner of filling a	IV	31	189
Vacation of seat of senator by re-arrangement, prohibited	IV	4	182
Veto of governor, how to act on	IV	14	184
Village indebtedness, limitation of	X	15	201
" officers, election of	X	16	201
Villages to be incorporated under general laws	X	14	201
Viva voce, when votes shall be given	IV	11	184
Vote on taking immediate effect of public acts to be recorded	IV	19	186

W.

	ART.	SEC.	PAGE.
Witness not to be questioned as to religious belief	II	3	179
Witnesses, right of compulsory process to obtain	II	8	179
" right to be confronted with	II	8	179
" unreasonable detention of, prohibited	II	13	180

	ART.	SEC.	PAGE.
Women, eligible to certain offices	XVII	10	214
" property of, acquired before marriage, to remain theirs	XV	4	211
Worship, liberty to, without restriction	II	2	178
" place of, no compulsion to attend or support	II	2	178
Writs, causes, prosecutions and rights to continue	Sched.	2	215

Y.

	ART.	SEC.	PAGE.
Yeas and nays required on final passage	IV	18	186
" " " " " vetoed legislation	IV	14	184
" " " " separately on each bill or joint resolution	IV	18	186
" " " " on nominations to the senate	IV	11	184
" " " when taken	IV	10	183

GENERAL INDEX.

A.

PAGE.

Absence, leave of, granted to Mr. Crane ... 54, 68
" " " " Crouse ... 63
" " " " Divine ... 18
" " " " Giddings ... 57, 84, 110
" " " " Hatch ... 23, 109, 144
" " " " Jerome ... 109
" " " " Mason ... 23, 27, 42
" " " " Meddaugh ... 23, 37, 48, 84, 144
" " " " Moffatt ... 120
" " " " Pond ... 23, 37, 48
" " " " Riley ... 42, 109
" " " " Willits ... 42
" " " " Withey ... 70, 123
" " " " Woodward ... 37, 60, 77, 89
" " " " Upson ... 23, 37, 93, 144
" " Mr. Withey's resolution in regard to ... 48

ADJOURNMENT OF THE COMMISSION:
Mr. Crane's motion as to the time of ... 145
" " " " Mr. Withey's amendment to ... 145
Mr. Riley's motion as to the ... 78

AGRICULTURAL COLLEGE, THE STATE, CONTROL OF:
Mr. Wells's amendment in regard to ... 151

AMENDMENT AND REVISION OF THE CONSTITUTION:
article in regard to, reported and referred ... 97, 99, 111, 115
" " " " third reading of ... 114
" " " " vote on final passage of ... 146

AMENDMENT OF BILLS ON THIRD READING:
new rule in regard to, proposed by Mr. Moffatt ... 48

AMENDMENT OF THE CONSTITUTION:
Mr. Moffatt's resolution in regard to, negatived ... 28

ANNUAL SESSIONS OF THE LEGISLATURE:
Mr. Devereaux's resolution in regard to, negatived ... 23

Appointment of certain officers of the commission ... 18
Assistant clerk, appointment of ... 18
" " authorized ... 13
Assistants, compensation of ... 4

PAGE.

B.

BILL OF RIGHTS, ARTICLE CONTAINING:
read a third time 106
read twice and referred 58
reported 57, 95, 108
vote on final passage of 129
Blanks, mode of filling 11
BOUNDARIES AND SEAT OF GOVERNMENT, ARTICLE ON:
read third time and referred 70
" twice and referred 59
reported 67, 73, 77
vote on final passage of 129
Business, order of 10

C.

Call of the commission 88
" " " rule in regard to 11
Certificate to the Governor of the work of commission 175
CHAIRMAN OF THE COMMISSION:
duties of the, rule in regard to the 10
Mr. Wells's resolution of thanks to the 172
opening address of the 8
pro tem. address of 6
testimonial to the 172
Chairman's messenger authorized 13
CHURCH PROPERTY, EXEMPTION OF, FROM TAXATION:
amendment prohibiting, adopted 124
Mr. Withey's amendment striking out prohibition clause, vote on 140
prohibitory clause stricken out by committee and concurred in 141
CITIES AND VILLAGES, ARTICLE ON:
read third time and referred 89
" twice and referred 58
reported 76, 109
Clerk, compensation of 8
Closing session, time of meeting of 171
Clubb, Henry S., elected clerk 8
COMMISSION, CONSTITUTIONAL:
eighteenth day of the, September 16, 1873 64
eighth " " " 4, " 28
eleventh " " " 8, " 38
fifteenth " " " 12, " 53
fifth " " " 1, " 20
final adjournment of the 174
first day's session of the, August 27, 1873 5
fourth " " " 30, " 20
journal of 5
" in octavo form, number of to be printed 21
members of, sworn in 5, 7 9, 27
nineteenth day's session of the, September 17, 1873 68
ninth " " " 5, 1873 31

PAGE.

COMMISSION, CONSTITUTIONAL (*Continued*):
postoffice address of officers and members 2
re-assembling of the, Mr. Withey's resolution 173
second day's session of the, August 28, 1873 9
seventeenth day's session of the, September 15, 1873 61
seventh " " " " " 3, " 22
sixteenth " " " " " 13, " 57
sixth " " " " " 2, " 20
tenth " " " " " 6, " 38
third " " " " August 29, 1873 16
thirteenth " " " " September 10, 1873 42
thirtieth " " " " October 2, 1873 120
thirty-eighth " " " " " 15, " 165
thirty-fifth " " " " " 11, " 144
thirty-first " " " " " 3, " 121
thirty-fourth " " " " " 10, " 133
thirty-ninth " " " " October 16, 1873 171
thirty-second " " " " " 8, " 124
thirty-seventh " " " " " 14, " 155
thirty-sixth " " " " " 13, " 148
thirty-third " " " " " 9, " 128
twelfth " " " " September 9, 1873 38
twentieth " " " " " 18, " 71
twenty-eighth " " " " " 30, " 110
twenty-fifth " " " " " 24, " 93
twenty-first " " " " " 19, " 77
twenty-fourth " " " " " 23, " 84
twenty-ninth " " " " October 1, 1873 118
twenty-third " " " " September 20, 1873 83
twenty-second " " " " " 22, " 83
twenty-seventh " " " " " 26, " 109
twenty-sixth " " " " " 25, " 98

COMMISSIONERS OF HIGHWAYS:
Mr. Upson's amendment relating to 150

COMMITTEE OF THE WHOLE:
Proceedings in 14, 15, 17
" " ordered omitted from Journal 30
when to go into, rule in relation to 11

COMMITTEE ON ARRANGEMENT AND PHRASEOLOGY:
all bills to be referred to, rule in relation to 12
" after third reading, to be referred to 49

COMMITTEE ON FINANCE AND TAXATION:
chairman added to 11

Committee on Rules, report of the 9

COMMITTEE, SPECIAL, TO REPORT TO THE GOVERNOR 171
Mr. Jerome added to 171
Mr. Pond " " 172
Mr. Withey " " 171

Compensation for religious services, remonstrance against 62
" of members of the commission 8
" " " legislature 51

PAGE.

CONSTITUTION, AMENDED:
certificate of, signed by members of the commission 172
printing of the 171
proof of the, to be read by Mr. Pond 172
Constitution of 1850 ordered printed 13, 18
" the proposed 177
" " " index to the 219
Continuous sessions, Mr. Withey's resolution 122
Cook, Samuel F., elected Secretary *pro tem* 6
CORPORATIONS, ARTICLE ON:
ordered reprinted 66
read a third time and referred 81
read twice and ordered printed 54
reported 54, 65, 94
Corporations, foreign, Mr. Willits' suggestion 89
CORPORATIONS, OTHER THAN MUNICIPAL, ARTICLE ON:
a special order 124
defeated as a whole 144
first seven sections passed 156
laid on table 147, 165
Mr. Pond's additional section rejected 162
Mr. Hatch's amendment rejected 162
" " additional section 163
" " " " Mr. Pond's substitute for 163
Mr. Pond's amendment rejected 168
Mr. Upson's motion to reconsider vote on Mr. Hatch's additional section lost 169
Mr. Wells's substitute 154
" " " rejected 156
reported 130
" and laid on table 131
section eight rejected 157
" eleven " 157
" " Mr. Withey's substitute for, adopted 161
" fourteen rejected 160
" " Mr. Upson's substitute for 160
" " " " rejected 160
" fifteen rejected 161
" thirteen, Mr. Pond's amendment to 158
" " " " Mr. Hatch's substitute for 158
" " " " " " Pond's amend. to 159
" " " Wells's substitute 158
" " as amended, rejected 160
" twelve passed 157
" nine and ten passed 157
" sixteen and seventeen passed 161
taken from the table 142
vote on article reconsidered 147
vote on section eleven reconsidered 161
" " " rejecting it second time 162

PAGE.

CORPORATIONS, OTHER THAN MUNICIPAL, ARTICLE ON (*Continued*):
vote on sections eight and fourteen 142
" the final passage of article 168
articles on consolidated 113
COUNTIES, ARTICLE ON:
read third time, amended and referred 81
reported, ordered printed, and ordered to third reading 53
" " " " referred 41
Cutcheon, S. M. elected chairman of commission 8

D.

Daily journal, printing of, authorized 13
" " to whom ordered sent 13
Departments of government 6
DIVISION OF POWERS OF GOVERNMENT, ARTICLE ON:
read third time and referred 70
" second " " " 59
reported 67, 73
voted on final passage of 129
Divisions of the constitution referred to committees 19
Doorkeeper, appointment of, authorized 9
Dower, right of conveyable, Mr. Crane's suggestion 78
Double senatorial districts, report on 85

E.

Educational system of Michigan 7
EDUCATION, ARTICLE ON:
amended and ordered printed 31
considered in committee of the whole 29, 30
Mr. Jerome's motion to reconsider, vote on rejected 170
Mr. Wells's " " " " " " 153
Mr. Wells's notice of motion 148
reported 21, 63, 98
read third time 64
read twice 21
re-referred to com. of the whole with substitute 45
vote on final passage of 140
ELECTIVE FRANCHISE, ARTICLE ON:
considered in committee of the whole 40
read third time 105
read twice, ordered printed, and referred 72
reported 72, 95, 108
vote on final passage 137
ELIGIBILITY OF WOMEN FOR OFFICE:
Mr. Jerome's amendment in relation to 148
Mr. Hatch's suggestion in regard to 126
Mr. Riley's amendment in relation to 147
Mr. Wells's amendment " " 128
Mr Willit's suggestion in regard to 89
Mr. Withey's amendment in relation to 147
" " suggestion " " 69

PAGE.

Enrolled bills, revision of ... 170
Enrolling clerk authorized ... 69
EXECUTIVE DEPARTMENT, ARTICLE ON THE:
amended, reprinted, and ordered to third reading ... 33
read third time ... 50
" twice and ordered printed ... 22
reported ... 22, 72
vote on final passage of ... 131
EXEMPTIONS, ARTICLE ON:
read third time and tabled ... 61
read twice, ordered printed and referred ... 43
reported ... 43,55, 96
taken from table and referred ... 97
vote on final passage of ... 146

F.

Ferry, William M., qualified as a member ... 123
Final passage, order of, established ... 73
FINANCE AND TAXATION, ARTICLE ON:
defeated and vote reconsidered ... 141
ordered reprinted ... 57
read third time and referred ... 52
" twice, ordered printed and referred ... 44
re-committed ... 80, 141
reported ... 55, 56, 82, 9
vote on final passage of ... 142
Fines, disposition of, memorial of G. W. Squire ... 61

G.

General election, Mr. Crane's suggestion in regard to ... 84
" " township meeting declared a, report on ... 86, 100
Giddings, E. W., resignation of ... 127
Governor authorized to appoint commission ... 3

H.

Health, memorials of state board of ... 133

I.

IMPEACHMENTS AND REMOVALS FROM OFFICE, ARTICLE ON:
read third time and referred ... 61
" twice, ordered printed and referred ... 43
reported ... 54, 72, 77
vote on final passage of ... 139
Improvement of Streams, article on reported ... 111
Incorporations, committee on, increased to five ... 16
Indebtedness municipal, information called for ... 67
" " report on ... 115
Interests of Michigan, the ... 6

J.

Journal, compiling and indexing the ... 173

PAGE.

Judges, appointment of, Mr. Hatch's resolution................................ 49
" " " Mr. Upson's substitute................................ 49
" " " report on................................ 82
" " " section providing for, reported................................ 59
" " " " " " ordered printed................................ 59

JUDICIAL DEPARTMENT, ARTICLE ON THE:
considered in committee of the whole................................ 47
ordered reprinted................................ 47
placed on order of third reading................................ 97
read third time................................ 104
read twice and referred................................ 32
reported................................32, 108
tabled................................ 65
vote on final passage of................................ 137

Judiciary, an elective, Mr. Woodward's amendment................................ 137
Jury, right of trial by................................ 29
" two-thirds sufficient for a verdict, Mr. Withey's suggestion................................ 29

L.

Land, increased value of................................ 6
Laws of 1873 transmitted to the commission................................ 7
Legislation, special, Mr. Riley's suggestions................................ 24

LEGISLATIVE DEPARTMENT, ARTICLE ON:
considered in committee of the whole................................68, 70, 71
read third time................................ 89
read twice................................ 74
recommitted................................ 74
reported................................74, 96
vote on final passage of................................ 132

LEGISLATIVE PROHIBITIONS:
exempting the Upper Peninsula from, Mr. Devereaux's suggestion................................ 41

Legislature, special or general session of, to consider amendments................................ 4

LICENSING THE SALE OF INTOXICATING LIQUORS:
memorial of the conference of the M. E. church................................ 67
Mr. Crane's suggestions................................24, 94
Mr. Crouse's minority report on................................ 101

LIMITATION, LEGISLATIVE, RESOLUTION ON:
report on from committee of the whole................................ 85

Limitation of jury trials, Mr. Crane's suggestion................................ 97

LIMITATION OF TIME FOR PRESENTATION OF CLAIMS:
Mr. Riley's amendment in regard to................................ 94

LIQUOR TRAFFIC, TAXATION OF, THE ARTICLE ON:
rejected................................ 166
Mr. Hatch's substitute for, rejected................................ 166
Mr. Meddaugh's substitute rejected................................ 166
reconsidered, vote on, and bill tabled................................ 167
Mr. Woodward's amendment rejected................................ 166
minimum reduced to $200 for each sale-room................................ 152
Mr. Withey's bill for separate submission referred................................ 149
" " " " " " reported................................ 152
" " " " " " vote on final passage of................................ 167

PAGE.

Local option in regard to the liquor traffic, report on ... 91
Ludington Lumber Co., memorial of ... 84

M.

McCracken, S. B., appointed assistant clerk ... 18
Male, striking out the word from the constitution, negatived ... 95
Members of the commission, number of ... 3
" " " " from where selected ... 4
" " " " immunities and powers of ... 4
" " " legislature, compensation of the ... 85
Messengers, appointment of, authorized ... 8
" compensation of ... 8
Mileage, Mr. Crane's motion to abolish ... 46
MILITIA, ARTICLE ON:
read third time ... 114
" twice and referred ... 64
reported ... 64, 112
vote on final passage of ... 146
MISCELLANEOUS PROVISIONS, ARTICLE ON:
read third time ... 128
" twice and referred ... 121
reported ... 121, 126, 138
vote on final passage of ... 151
MUNICIPAL CORPORATIONS, ARTICLE ON:
recommitted with instruction ... 139
vote on final passage of ... 151
Municipal corporations, articles on, consolidated ... 120
" indebtedness, Mr. Hatch's suggestion ... 45
" " limitation of ... 139
" " " Mr. Withey's amendment ... 145

N.

Natural history, lecture on, by Prof. Beals ... 14

P.

Pardons, Mr. Hatch's amendment relating to ... 50
" " " suggestions " " ... 44
PARLIAMENTARY PRACTICE:
rules of, in Jefferson's Manual adopted ... 12
Passes on railroads, Mr. Willits' suggestion ... 40
Petitions and memorials, by whom to be presented ... 11
PREAMBLE:
read twice and referred ... 58
Mr. Riley's substitute for, rejected ... 169
reported ... 65, 77
vote on final passage of ... 169
Property, private, for public use, Mr. Willets' suggestion ... 87
" " " " " " " " report on ... 99
Propositions printed in journal ... 23

PAGE.

Power to increase Subjects of Taxation:
 Mr. Jerome's amendment in regard to 60

Q.

Questions in order 10
Quorum, majority to constitute a 19

R.

Railroad consolidation, Mr. Pond's suggestion 88
Railroads, article on:
 amended and recommitted 89
 read third time 89
 read twice and referred 69
 reported 76, 107, 112
Real estate, tenure of, by corporations 84
Remarks of Mr. Withey on vote of thanks to the chairman 178
Report to the Legislature, when to 8
Reports of committees printed in bill form 23
Representation, minority, Mr. Devereaux's suggestion 42
Resolution, joint, providing for the Commission 3
Resolutions and motions, how entered on journal 11
 " " to be in writing 10
Response of chairman to resolution of thanks 173
Restrictions on special legislation, Mr. Wells's suggestion 74
Revision, classification and arrangement, committee on 16
Rule requiring Record of Proceedings in Committee of the Whole:
 rescinded 30
Rules, committee on, appointed 9
 " " " authorized 8
 " printing of the 19
 " suspension of the 11

S.

Salaries, articles on:
 amended and recommitted 46
 read third time 52
 read twice and referred 28
 reported 28, 34, 73
 vote on final passage of 138
Schedule, article on:
 read third time 170
 read twice and referred 100
 reported 100, 111
 sections 6, 7, 8, 9 and 11 stricken out 170
 special committee on 97
 vote on final passage of 171
School laws, communication from Superintendent Briggs on 21
Seat of government, article on read twice and referred 59
Secretary *pro tem.*, choice of 6

PAGE.

SENATORIAL DISTRICTS:
Mr. Crouse's suggestion in regard to 91
Mr. Jerome's proposition relating to 19
Mr. Meddaugh's amendment relating to 131
SENATORIAL TERMS OF OFFICE:
Mr. Jerome's proposition in regard to 19
SENATORS, TWO FOR THE UPPER PENINSULA:
Mr. Devereaux's suggestion 27
SEX, NO DISTINCTION OF IN REGARD TO PROPERTY RIGHTS:
Mr. Crouse's suggestion in regard to 59
Sessions, daily, hours of 16
" evening, Mr. Devereaux's motion 75
SINGLE SENATORIAL DISTRICTS:
Mr. Moffatt's amendment as to, rejected 114
Soldiers' families, Mr. Jerome's amendment 150
Specific taxation, abolition of, Mr. Moffatt's motion 56
Standing committees, announcement of 17
" " designation of 12
" " list of, ordered printed 19
State fair, Mr. Woodward's motion 75
STATE OFFICERS, ARTICLE ON:
read third time 119
read twice and referred 99
reported 98, 111, 119
vote on final passage of 137
State Prison in Upper Peninsula, Mr. Devereaux's suggestion 21
Stationery, purchase of, authorized 13
Stenographer, motion to appoint a, negatived 9
" " " " " tabled 18
STOCKHOLDERS, MUNICIPAL CORPORATIONS, NOT TO BECOME:
Mr. Withey's resolution on 28
Stock, railroad, Mr. Upson's amendment on 143
" " Mr. Withey's " " 143
STREAMS, IMPROVEMENT OF, ARTICLE ON:
read third time and consolidated 119
Mr. Jerome's resolution in regard to 77
report on 98, 121
Supplies, report of committee on 174

T.

TAXATION, EXEMPTION OF CHURCH PROPERTY FROM:
memorial in regard to 78
Taxes, specific, abolition of, Mr. Moffat's suggestion 21
TECHNICAL INSTRUCTION IN THE ARTS:
Mr. Wells's suggestion in regard to 23
Three readings of every article required 12
TOWNSHIPS, ARTICLE ON:
read third time, amended and referred 54
read twice and referred 41
reported 41, 72
Two-thirds vote required on all amendments 4, 12

PAGE.

U.

UNIVERSITY, CONTROL OF:
memorial of Dr. J. N. Eldridge and others.......... 144
Mr. Upson's amendment on.......... 139
University funds, control, of petition on.......... 128
Upper peninsula, senators in the.......... 76

V.

VACANCY IN THE COMMISSION:
to be filled by appointment by the Governor.......... 4

W.

Wells, H. G., elected chairman *pro tem*.......... 5
WIFE'S DEBTS, HUSBAND NOT RESPONSIBLE FOR:
Mr. Crane's suggestion in regard to.......... 63
" " " report on.......... 69
WOMAN'S SUFFRAGE:
adverse report on.......... 72
Mr. Crouse's resolution on, referred.......... 82
" suggestion on.......... 29
Mr. Ferry's amendment for separate submission.......... 147
" bill laid on table.......... 164
" " referred back.......... 165
" " rejected.......... 168
Mr. Willits' suggestions on.......... 26
report of committee of the whole on.......... 163
WORK OF THE COMMISSION:
when to be laid before the governor.......... 4
" " printed.......... 4

Y.

Yeas and nays, may be called for by any member.......... 12

APPENDIX:

CONTAINING

THE REPORT TO THE GOVERNOR,

AN INDEX TO THE CHANGES PROPOSED,

THE CONSTITUTION AS PROPOSED TO BE AMENDED,

THE PRESENT CONSTITUTION.

REPORT TO THE GOVERNOR.

To His Excellency, John J. Bagley, Governor of the State of Michigan:

The commission appointed pursuant to a joint resolution of the legislature, entitled, "Joint Resolution to provide for a Commission for the revision of the Constitution of the State of Michigan," approved April 24, 1873, made a formal report to your excellency on the sixteenth day of October last, communicating the results of its labors.

At the same time you were advised that a committee, appointed by the commission in that behalf, would, as soon as the same could be prepared, report in detail the principal changes made in the present constitution, and the reasons which had induced the commission to recommend such changes. In the performance of this duty, the undersigned, as such committee, beg leave most respectfully to submit the following:

By the terms of the joint resolution under which the commission was appointed, they were authorized "to examine into and report to the next session, either special or general, of the legislature of this State, such amendments and revision of the constitution as in their judgment may be necessary for the best interests of the State and the people." A careful examination of the present constitution showed many ambiguities, as well as some unnecessary and inconvenient restrictions. By incompleteness of arrangement also, different divisions were found to embrace the same subject matter, involving repetitions and inconsistencies. The commission sought to remove the ambiguities and unnecessary restrictions, and, by the re-arrangement and combination of articles and sections, to bring the several provisions into such relationship to each other as to make them the more easily understood. In addition to this, several new and important provisions have been added. The work of the commission therefore has been equivalent to a revision of the constitution, although it is technically recognized in the official records of the commission as the amended constitution.

To exhibit the more intelligibly the changes that are recommended, the committee have deemed it best to repeat the entire constitution as agreed upon by the commission, adding thereto such references and explanations as have seemed necessary. These will appear as an appendix to this, the committee's report, to which is added, for convenience of reference, the full text of the present constitution.

There are some changes in the arrangement and numbering of the several articles, which are explained in their proper places. The present constitution contains twenty-one articles and the schedule, aggregating two hundred and fifty-four sections. The constitution as proposed by the commission contains eighteen articles and the schedule, aggregating two hundred and nine sections. Article XIX of the present constitution, relating to the upper peninsula, is omitted from the revision as obsolete, all necessary special provisions relating to that section being embodied in other parts of the revision.

The preparation of the analysis of the proposed changes involved more labor than any member of the committee could devote to it, and Mr. S. B. McCracken, of Detroit, who acted as assistant clerk of the commission, was employed to do the work. The committee take pleasure in commending the care and method with which his work has been done.

(Signed), S. M. CUTCHEON,
S. L. WITHEY,
D. H. JEROME,
ASHLEY POND,
Committee.

LANSING, December 1, 1873.

INDEX TO CHANGES.

All essential changes proposed are referred to in the index below, by articles and sections. The number of changes is not, however, correctly represented by the number of index lines, as the same subject matter is in many cases referred to under several different heads.

	Art.	Sec.
Agricultural College—duties of board of, to continue	13	4
Amendments to Constitution—when may be submitted	18	1
Appointment—of attorney general, may be authorized	8	3
of circuit judges	6	6
of circuit court commissioners	6	9
of judges of supreme court	6	2
of prosecuting attorney, may be authorized	10	5
Appointments—provisional, to fill vacancies	12	9
Appropriations—to university, upon condition	13	2
Attorney General—appointment of, may be authorized	8	3
Bank, with Branches—clause relating to, omitted—see note to	11	1
Board of Education—members of, eligible to seats in legislature	4	6
Board of Regents of University—to have direction and control of University funds	13	2
Board of Supervisors—allowance of claims by	10	10
power of to raise money for buildings, highways and bridges	10	3
representation of villages on	10	8
Boundaries—of State	1	1
Business—specific tax may be imposed on	14	1
Capital of State	1	2
Changing Names—of persons by legislature, prohibited	4	22
Circuit Court Commissioners—to be appointed	6	9
Circuit Court—three terms of per year in counties having 10,000 inhabitants	6	7
Circuit Courts—appellate jurisdiction of	6	8
Circuit Judges—to be appointed	6	6
to appoint circuit court commissioners	6	9
Cities—limitation of indebtedness in	10	14
not to be divided in formation of representative districts, provision omitted	4	3
only to be incorporated under general laws	10	14
Claims—against State, limitation of	14	8
allowance of by supervisors and auditors	10	10
Compensation—of members of the legislature	4	15
to contestants of seats in legislature—see note to article 4.		
to newspapers for publishing laws—see note to article 4.		
Commission—for revising constitution	18	2
Commissioners of Highways—term of	10	13
Concurrent Resolution—appropriating money or property, to be submitted to governor	4	14
Contestants—of seats in legislature, compensation to—see note to article 4.		
Convention—for revising constitution	18	2
Corporations—charters of, not to be amended	11	1
duration of	11	12
foreign, not to hold lands, except, etc.	11	9
foreign, subject to control of legislature	11	9
liability of stockholders in, for labor	11	7
municipal, not to give aid to private enterprises	10	1
specific and general taxes on property of	14	1
Counties—amount that board of supervisors may raise for buildings, highways and bridges	10	3
having 4,000 inhabitants, to be entitled to representative	4	3
power of, to contract debts, to be restricted	10	2
County Auditors—allowance of claims by	10	10
compensation of	10	10
Court—supreme, to consist of five judges	6	2

	Art.	Sec.
Courts—municipal, clause authorizing, omitted—see note to	6	1
of conciliation, clause authorizing, omitted—see note to	6	1
Courts and tribunals—may be established by law	6	1
Credit of State—not to be pledged in aid of any person or corporation	14	9
Cross-examination—of persons on trial, relative to statements	2	14
Decisions of Supreme Court—clause relating to, omitted—see note to article 6.		
Divorce—legislation upon by special act, prohibited	4	23
Educational boards—duties of, to continue	13	4
Elections—by townships, may be held in cities	7	2
Elective Franchise—see note to article 7.		
Eligibility—of women, to certain offices	14	10
Escheat—of lands, to be held as primary school lands	13	9
Estate—of married women, provisions relating to	15	4
Exemption—of homestead, to value of $2,000	15	2
Extending time for collection of taxes by legislature, prohibited	4	22
Extra Compensation—to members from upper peninsula not allowed	4	15
Extra Sessions—limitation of twenty days removed	4	15
Ferries and toll bridges—chartering or licensing of, prohibited	4	22
Flowage—property may be taken for	17	4
Foreign corporations—provisions relating to	11	9
Forfeiture—of school moneys, if school not maintained	13	7
Homestead—exemption of, to value of $2,000	15	2
House of Representatives—to consist of not more than one hundred and ten members	4	3
Husband—not liable for certain debts of wife	15	4
Immediate effect—public act, how may be given	4	19
Impeachment—how ordered when necessary during recess of legislature	12	8
no officer to exercise office after directed	12	4
to be tried within three months	12	4
Improvement—of streams, property may be taken for	17	4
Incorporation—of cities and villages	10	14
Indebtedness—of corporations, State not to assume	14	9
limitation of, in cities and villages	10	14
Islands—organization of into counties	10	4
Joint Resolution—to be submitted to governor	4	14
Judges—eligibility of, to other office	6	13
of circuit courts, to be appointed	6	6
of supreme court, to be appointed	6	2
salaries of, to be fixed by law	9	2
Judges of Probate—vacancies, how filled	6	11
Jurisdiction—civil and criminal, may be conferred on probate courts	6	14
Jury—trials by, in civil and criminal cases by less than twelve men	2	7
Justices of the Peace—clause relating to, in cities, omitted	6	16
Libraries—certain moneys to go to support of	13	10
to be maintained in cities	13	10
Limitation—of claims against State	14	8
of indebtedness in cities and villages	10	14
Liquors—taxation of traffic in—see separate submission clause.		
Municipal Corporations—not to give aid to private enterprises	10	1
Municipal Courts—clause authorizing, omitted—see note to	6	1
New Bills—may be introduced after fifty days on recommendation of Governor	4	18
Newspapers—compensation of, for publishing laws—see note to art. 4.		
Navigable Streams—property may be taken for improvement of	17	4
right of free use of, not to be abridged	17	6
Oath of Office—clause omitted	17	1
Omitted—clause providing for renewal of sheriff's bond	10	7
clause relative to contested elections—see note to art. 4.		
clause relating to courts of conciliation—see note to	6	1
clause relating to decisions of supreme court—see note to art. 6.		
clause relating to single bank, with branches—see note to	11	1
section prohibiting revision of laws—see note to article 17.		
clause providing pay for publishing laws—see note to art. 4.		
provision against division of cities in formation of representative districts	4	3
Pardons—provisions applicable to	5	11
Postage—clause relative to, omitted—see note to art. 4.		
Private Property—taking of for public use	17	5
Probate Courts—civil and criminal jurisdiction may be conferred upon	6	14
Property—private, taking of for public use	2	22
Prosecuting Attorneys—appointment of, may be authorized	10	5
Public officers—prohibited from using public moneys	17	3
Railway trains—speed of, may be regulated	11	10
Reform School—duties of board of, to continue	13	4
Regents of University—eligible to seats in legislature	4	6
who to be, ex-officio	13	9

	Art.	Sec.
Remitting—of fines, penalties and forfeitures, prohibited	4	22
Religious belief—witness not to be questioned touching	2	3
Religious worship—no person to be compelled to contribute to against his consent	2	3
Representative—in counties of 4,000 inhabitants	4	3
Resolutions—joint and concurrent, to be submitted to governor	4	14
Revision—of constitution, legislature may provide for by convention or commission	18	2
of laws, section prohibiting, omitted—see note to article 17.		
Salaries—of judges, to be fixed by law	9	2
of State officers, to be fixed by law	9	1
Schedule—certain sections of, omitted—see note to schedule.		
School Moneys—forfeiture of, if school not maintained	13	7
Senator—additional, may be authorized in upper peninsula	4	2
Senators—to be elected for four years	4	2
to be elected alternately by even and odd numbered districts	4	2
Senators and Representatives—compensation of	4	15
exempt from arrest on civil process	4	7
Sheriff's bond—clause relative to renewal of, omitted	10	7
Sinking fund—act authorizing loan, shall provide for	14	4
Special legislation—prohibited in certain cases	4	22
Special privileges—prohibition of	4	22
Statement—persons on trial, subject to cross-examination on	2	14
State Normal School—Board of Education to have supervision of	13	3
State Public School—duties of board of, to continue	13	4
Stockholders—liability of, for labor	11	7
Superintendent of Public Instruction—member ex officio of educational boards	13	1
Supervisors—compensation of	10	10
Supreme Court—appellate jurisdiction of	6	3
concurrence of three judges of, necessary to final decision	6	3
decisions of, clause relating to, omitted—see note to article 6.		
to appoint clerks	6	5
to consist of five judges	6	2
to establish rules of practice and code of procedure for courts of record	6	5
Taxation of liquor traffic—see separate submission clause		
Taxes—specific and general, on property of corporations	14	1
specific, may be imposed upon property or business	14	1
Township elections—legislature may prescribe time of holding	10	18
may be held in cities	7	2
Trials—civil and criminal, may be, by less number than twelve jurors	2	7
University Funds—regents to have direction of	13	2
Upper Peninsula—additional senator from, may be authorized	4	2
extra compensation to members from, not allowed	4	15
Vacancies—in educational boards, how filled	13	5
in judicial offices, how filled	6	11
Villages—only to be incorporated under general laws	10	14
limitation of indebtedness in	10	14
may have representation on board of supervisors	10	8
Women—eligibility of to certain offices	14	10
Yeas and nays—on giving public acts immediate effect	4	19
to be taken separately on passage of bills	4	18

THE

AMENDED CONSTITUTION

OF MICHIGAN.

[Those provisions of the amended constitution that are new, are printed in italics. Provisions of the present constitution that are omitted from the revision, are, when practicable, printed with the text of the revision, but enclosed in brackets. In other cases they are explained or embodied in the notes. Mere changes of phraseology are not in all cases noted. All marginal references are to the present constitution.]

The People of the State of Michigan do ordain this Constitution:

ARTICLE I.

BOUNDARIES AND SEAT OF GOVERNMENT.

SECTION 1. The State of Michigan is bounded as follows, to wit: Commencing at a point on the eastern boundary line of the State of Indiana, where a direct line drawn from the southern extremity of Lake Michigan to the most northerly cape of the Maumee Bay shall intersect the same, said point being the northwest corner of the State of Ohio, as established by an act of Congress, entitled "An act to establish the northern boundary line of the State of Ohio, and to provide for the admission of the State of Michigan into the Union upon the conditions therein expressed," approved June fifteenth, one thousand eight hundred and thirty-six; thence with the said boundary line of the State of Ohio till it intersects the boundary line between the United States and Canada, in Lake Erie; thence with the said boundary line between the United States and Canada through the Detroit river, *Lake St. Clair, the St. Clair river*, Lake Huron, the St. Mary's river, and Lake Superior, to a point where the said line last touches Lake Superior; thence in a direct line through Lake Superior to the mouth of the Montreal river; thence through the middle of the main channel of the said Montreal river to the head waters thereof, *as marked upon the survey made by Captain* Art. 1.

*Cramm by authority of the United States;** thence in a direct line to the center of the channel between Middle and South islands, in the Lake of the Desert; thence in a direct line to the southern shore of Lake Brule; thence along said southern shore and down the Brule river to the main channel of the Menominee river; thence down the centre of the main channel of the same to the center of the most usual ship channel of the Green Bay of Lake Michigan; thence through the center of the most usual ship channel of the said bay to the middle of Lake Michigan; thence through the middle of Lake Michigan to the northern boundary of the State of Indiana, as that line was established by the act of Congress of the nineteenth of April, eighteen hundred and sixteen; thence due east with the north boundary line of the said State of Indiana to the northeast corner thereof; and thence south with the eastern boundary line of Indiana to the place of beginning.

Art. 2. SEC. 2. The seat of government shall remain at Lansing.

ARTICLE II. †

BILL OF RIGHTS.

SECTION 1. *All political power is inherent in the people. Government is instituted for their equal benefit, security and protection. They have the right to change or reform the same whenever the public good requires. No special privilege or immunity shall be granted that may not be revoked.*

Art. 4, sec. 39. SEC. 2. Every person shall be at liberty to worship God according to the dictates of his own conscience. No person shall be compelled to attend, *or, against his consent, to contribute to the erection or support of* ‡ any place of religious

---

* The italicised words make no change in the boundary, being only intended to make the description more specific. See enabling act under which the State of Wisconsin was organized, U. S. Statutes at Large, Vol. 9, page 56. See also remarks of Mr. Longyear, Michigan Convention debates, 1867, page 80, and particularly page 82, in his reply to Mr. Withey.

The section fixing the seat of government stands as Article II of the present constitution, which reads as follows: "The seat of government shall be at Lansing, where it is now located."

† There is no corresponding article in the present constitution, but provisions appropriately belonging in a Bill of Rights, found scattered through nearly all articles of the present organic law, have been placed together as Article II, entitled "Bill of Rights." Few changes have been made, only such as seemed desirable to improve the language, or render more clear and certain the right guaranteed.

‡ Constitution of 1850, in place of words italicised, says, "erect or sup

worship, or to pay tithes, taxes, or other rates, for the support of any minister of the gospel or teacher of religion.

SEC. 3. The civil and political rights, privileges and capac- Art. 4, sec.
ities of no person shall be diminished or enlarged, nor shall 41. Art. 6, sec.
any person be incompetent to be a witness, on account of his 34.
opinions or belief concerning matters of religion, *nor shall any witness be questioned touching his religious belief.*

SEC. 4. Every person may freely speak, write and publish Art. 4, sec.
his sentiments on all subjects, being responsible for the abuse 42.
of that right; and no law shall be passed to restrain or abridge the liberty of speech or of the press. In all prosecu- Art. 6, sec.
tions for libel, the truth may be given in evidence to the 25
jury, and if it shall appear to the jury that the matter charged as libelous is true, and was published with good motives and for justifiable ends, the accused shall be acquitted; and the jury shall have the right to determine the law and the fact.

SEC. 5. No bill of attainder, *ex post facto* law, or law impair- Art. 4. sec.
ing the obligation of contracts, shall be passed. 43.

SEC. 6. The privilege of the writ of *habeas corpus* shall not Art. 4, sec.
be suspended [by the legislature] unless, in case of rebellion 44.
or invasion, the public safety may require it.

SEC. 7. The right of trial by jury shall remain, but shall be Art. 6, secs.
deemed to be waived in all civil cases, unless demanded by 27 and 28, and art. 4,
one of the parties in such manner as shall be prescribed by sec. 46.
law. The legislature may authorize, *in all civil and criminal cases,* a trial by jury of a less number than twelve men.*

SEC. 8. In every criminal prosecution the accused shall Art. 6, sec.
have the right to a speedy and public trial by an impartial 28.
jury, to be informed of the accusation, to be confronted with witnesses against him, to have compulsory process for obtaining witnesses in his favor, and to have the assistance of counsel for his defense.

SEC. 9. Any suitor in any court in this State shall have the Art. 6, sec.
right to prosecute or defend his suit either in person or by 24.
attorney.

SEC. 10. The person, houses, papers and possessions of Art. 6, sec.
every person shall be secure from unreasonable search and 26.
seizure. No warrant to search any place, or to seize any person

---

port." The object of the change is, that the constitution may not seem to invalidate specific engagements by persons to contribute to the erection and support of places of worship.

* The corresponding provision of the present constititution relates only to criminal trials in courts not of record. Section 46 of article IV, however, provides that "the legislature may authorize a trial by jury of a less number than twelve men." The present provisions are somewhat ambiguous; the new section is specific.

or thing, shall issue without describing such place, person or thing, nor without probable cause, supported by oath or affirmation.

Art. 6, sec. 29. SEC. 11. No person, after acquittal upon the merits, shall be tried for the same offense. All persons shall, before conviction, be bailable by sufficient sureties, except for murder and treason, when the proof is evident or the presumption great.

Art. 6, sec. 30. SEC. 12. Treason against the State shall consist only in levying war against it, or adhering to its enemies, giving them aid and comfort. No person shall be convicted of treason unless upon the testimony of two witnesses to the same overt act, or on confession in open court.

Art. 6, sec. 31. SEC. 13. Excessive bail shall not be required; excessive fines shall not be imposed; cruel or unusual punishments shall not be inflicted; nor shall witnesses be unreasonably detained.

Art. 6, sec. 32. SEC. 14. No person shall be deprived of life, liberty or property, without due process of law. No person shall be compelled, in any criminal case, to be a witness against himself. *But if any person shall elect to make a statement in his own behalf, he shall be subject to cross-examination relative to the matter of such statement.* *

Art. 6, sec. 33. SEC. 15. No person shall be imprisoned for debt arising out of or founded on contract, express or implied, except in case of fraud, or breach of trust, or for moneys collected by public officers, or in any professional employment. No person shall be imprisoned for a military fine in time of peace.

Art. 18, sec. 7. SEC. 16. Every person has a right to bear arms for the defense of himself and of the State.

Art. 18, sec. 8. SEC. 17. The military shall [in all cases and at all times] be in strict subordination to the civil power.

Art. 18, sec. 9. SEC. 18. No soldier shall, in time of peace, be quartered in any house without the consent of the owner or occupant, nor in time of war, except in a manner prescribed by law.

Art. 18, sec. 10. SEC. 19. The people have the right peaceably to assemble, [together] to consult for the common good, to instruct their representatives, and to petition the legislature for redress of grievances.

Art. 18, sec. 11. SEC. 20. Neither slavery nor involuntary servitude, unless for the punishment of crime, shall ever be tolerated in this State.

Art. 18, sec. 13. SEC. 21. Aliens who are, or may hereafter become, *bona*

---

* This is the present provision of law on the subject. It has been claimed, however, that the present constitution (sec. 32, art. 6), would protect a prisoner on trial from cross-examination as to the matter of his statement. The clause above would do away with any uncertainty.

fide residents of this State, shall enjoy the same rights in respect to the possession, enjoyment and inheritance of property, as native born citizens.

SEC. 22. Private property shall not be taken for public use without just compensation. * Art. 18, sec. 14.

ARTICLE III.

DIVISION OF THE POWERS OF GOVERNMENT.

SECTION 1. The powers of government are divided into three departments: Legislative, Executive, and Judicial. Art. 3, sec. 1.

SEC. 2. No person belonging to one department shall exercise [the] power[s] properly belonging to another, except in the cases expressly provided in this constitution. Art. 3, sec. 2.

ARTICLE IV.

LEGISLATIVE DEPARTMENT.

The sections of this article, to and including section 15, relate respectively to the same subjects as the corresponding sections of the present constitution.

SECTION 1. The legislative power is vested in a Senate and House of Representatives.

SEC. 2. The senate shall consist of thirty-two members. *But, after the year one thousand eight hundred and seventy-five, the legislature may increase the number to thirty-three, by authorizing the election of two senators in that portion of the State now included within the limits of the thirty-second senatorial district.* Senators shall be elected for *four years,* and by single districts. *At the first election after the adoption of this amended constitution, senators in the odd-numbered districts shall be elected for two years, and in the even-numbered districts for four years.* † Such districts shall be numbered from one to thirty-three inclusive, each of which shall choose one senator. No county shall be divided in the formation of senate districts, unless such county shall be equitably entitled to two or more senators.

SEC. 3. The house of representatives shall consist of not [less than sixty-four nor] more than one hundred *and ten* members. * Representatives shall be chosen for two years, and

---

* The remaining provisions of this section of the constitution of 1850 are covered by sections 4 and 5 of article XVII of the revision, which see.

† By this change every senator will hold his office four years, and sit in the senate two regular sessions, thus securing experience at all times in that body. Under the present constitution the entire senate is chosen every second year.

‡ The present constitution makes the house to "consist of not less than sixty-four, nor more than one hundred members." The number is now fixed by law at one hundred.

by single districts. Each representative district shall contain, as nearly as may be, an equal number of inhabitants, [exclusive of persons of Indian descent, who are not civilized, or are members of any tribe] * and shall consist of convenient and contiguous territory; *but every organized county containing a population of not less than four thousand, and every two or more contiguous organized counties, containing a like population, shall constitute a representative district, and be entitled to one representative.* † In every county entitled to more than one representative, the board of supervisors shall assemble at such time and place as may be provided by law, and divide the same into representative districts, equal to the number of representatives to which such county is entitled by law, and shall cause to be filed in the offices of the secretary of state and clerk of such county, a description of such representative districts, specifying the number of each district, and the population thereof according to the last enumeration.

SEC. 4. The legislature shall provide by law for an enumeration of the inhabitants in the year eighteen hundred and [fifty-four] *eighty-four*, and every ten years thereafter; and at the first session after each enumeration so made, and also at the first session after each enumeration by the authority of the United States, the legislature shall re-arrange the senate districts, and apportion anew the representatives among the counties and districts, according to the number of inhabitants. But no re-arrangement of senate districts shall vacate the seat of any senator. Each apportionment, and the division into representative districts by any board of supervisors, shall remain unaltered until the return of another enumeration.

SEC. 5. Every senator and representative shall be a citizen of the United States, and a qualified elector of the district he represents. A removal from his district shall be deemed a vacation of his office.

SEC. 6. No person holding any elective State office, *except*

---

* The words in brackets are obsolete, as all residents of the State are included under the common term "inhabitants."

† The words in italics stand in lieu of the following provisions of the corresponding section and article of the present constitution, which are omitted in the revision, to wit: "But no township or city shall be divided in the formation of a representative district. When any township or city shall contain a population which entitles it to more than one representative, then such township or city shall elect by general ticket the number of representatives to which it is entitled. Each county hereafter organized, with such territory as may be attached thereto, shall be entitled to a separate representative when it has attained a population equal to a moiety of the ratio of representation."

that of regent of the university or member of the board of education, and no person holding the office of probate judge, county clerk, register of deeds, county treasurer, sheriff, county superintendent of schools, prosecuting attorney, or any office to which he was appointed by the president of the United States, by and with the advice and consent of the senate, shall be allowed to take or hold a seat in either house of the legislature. *

SEC. 7. Senators and representatives shall not be subject to arrest upon any civil process during the session of the legislature, or for fifteen days next before the commencement and after the termination of each session. They shall not be questioned in any other place for any speech in either house. †

SEC. 8. A majority of each house shall constitute a quorum to do business; but a smaller number may adjourn from day to day and compel the attendance of absent members, in such manner and under such penalties as each house may prescribe.

SEC. 9. Each house shall choose its own officers, *except as otherwise provided in this constitution*; determine the rules of its proceedings, and judge of the qualifications, elections, and returns of its members, and may, with the concurrence of two-thirds of all the members elected, expel a member. The reasons for such expulsion shall be entered upon the journal, with the names of the members voting on the question. No member shall be expelled a second time for the same cause, nor for any cause known to his constituents before his election.

SEC. 10. Each house shall keep a journal of its proceedings, and publish the same, except such parts as may require secrecy. The yeas and nays of the members of either house on any question shall be taken at the request of one-fifth

---

* There were doubts in the minds of some whether, under the corresponding section of the present constitution, regents of the university and members of the board of education could properly hold seats in the legislature, as there was some question whether the words, "or this State," printed in brackets in the section, were properly there. This doubt is removed by the proposed new section. The corresponding section of the present constitution (sec. 6, art. 4) is given in full:

"No person holding any office under the United States, [or this State,] or any county office, except notaries public, officers of the militia, and officers elected by townships, shall be eligible to or have a seat in either house of the legislature, and all votes given for any such person shall be void."

† The corresponding section of the present constitution, by a manifest inadvertence, exempts members from arrest *in all cases*, except for treason, felony, or breach of the peace. It also exempts them from any *civil* process during, and for fifteen days before and after a session. The new proposed section only exempts them from *arrest* on *civil* process, during the time named, leaving them subject to all other legal process.

of the members elected. Any member of either house may dissent from and protest against any act, proceeding or resolution which he may deem injurious to any person or the public, and have the reason of his dissent entered on the journal.

SEC. 11. In all elections by either house, or in joint convention, the votes shall be given *viva voce*. All votes on nominations to the senate shall be taken by yeas and nays, and published with the journal of its proceedings.

SEC. 12. The doors of each house shall be open, unless the public welfare require secrecy. Neither house shall, without the consent of the other, adjourn for more than three days, nor to any other place than where the legislature may then be in session.

Art. 4, secs. 13 and 28. Art. 4, sec. 15

SEC. 13. Bills may originate in either house, but no bill *or new subject of legislation* shall be introduced after the expiration of the first fifty days of the session, *except on recommendation of the governor by special message.** At extra sessions, legislation shall be confined to the subjects expressly named in the governor's proclamation, and subjects submitted by special message.

SEC. 14. Every bill *and joint resolution* passed by the legislature, and every concurrent resolution *appropriating money or property,* † shall be presented to the governor, and if he approve, he shall sign it; but if not, he shall return it, with his objections, to the house in which it originated, which shall enter the objections at large upon its journal, and reconsider it. On such reconsideration, if two-thirds of the members elected agree to pass such bill or resolution, it shall be sent, with the objections, to the other house, by which it shall be reconsidered. If approved by two-thirds of the members elected to that house, it shall become [a law] *operative.* In such case the vote of both houses shall be determined by yeas and nays, and the names of the members voting for and against it shall be entered on the journals of each house respectively

---

* This clause is added to guard against serious inconveniences that might arise under the otherwise inflexible fifty days' limitation. There have been cases in which measures of vital importance to the State have been overlooked until after the expiration of fifty days, and the oversight has only been remedied by a questionable resort to the form of some other bill before the legislature, which was taken up and adapted to the purpose.

† By the corresponding section of the present constitution, only bills and concurrent resolutions require the approval of the governor. It would seem that joint resolutions, which frequently have all the force of bills, do not. Under the amended section, as will be seen, all bills and joint resolutions, and all concurrent resolutions appropriating money or property, must be presented to the governor.

If any bill or resolution be not returned by the governor within ten days (Sunday excepted), after it has been presented to him, the same shall become [a law] *operative* in like manner as if he had signed it, unless the legislature, by their adjournment, prevent its return, in which case it shall not become [a law] *operative.* The governor may approve, sign, and file in the office of the secretary of state, within five days after the adjournment of the legislature, any act passed during the last five days of the session, and the same shall become [a law] *operative.*

SEC. 15. The compensation of members of the Legislature shall be [three] *four* dollars a day for actual attendance, and when absent on account of sickness. [But the legislature may allow extra compensation to members from the territory of the upper peninsula, not exceeding two dollars per day during the session. When convened in extra session, their compensation shall be three dollars a day for the first twenty days, and nothing thereafter.] They shall be entitled to ten cents, and no more, for every mile actually traveled going to and returning from the place of meeting, on the usually traveled route; and for stationery and newspapers not exceeding five dollars for each member during any session. Each member shall be entitled to one copy of the laws, journals and documents of the legislature of which he was a member; but shall not receive, at the expense of the State, books, newspapers, or other perquisites of office not expressly authorized by this constitution. *

SEC. 16. The president of the senate and speaker of the house of representatives shall be entitled to the same per diem compensation and mileage as members of the legislature, and no more. Art 4, sec. 17.

SEC. 17. No person elected a member of the legislature shall receive any civil appointment within this State, or to the senate of the United States, from the governor, the governor and senate, from the legislature, or any other State authority, *or be eligible to any office which shall have been created, or the emoluments of which shall have been increased by the legislature* during the term for which he is elected. All such appointments, and all votes given for any person so elected, for any such office or appointment, shall be void. No member of the legislature shall be interested, directly or indirectly, in Art. 4, sec. 18.

* This section fixes the compensation of members at four instead of three dollars per day, omits the clause permitting extra compensation to members from the upper peninsula, and removes the limitation of twenty days for extra sessions.

any contract with the State, or any [county] *municipal corporation* thereof, authorized by any law passed during the time for which he is elected, or for one year thereafter.

Art. 4, sec. 19. SEC. 18. Every bill and joint resolution shall be read three times in each house before the final passage thereof. No bill or joint resolution shall become a law without the concurrence of a majority of all the members elected to each house On the final passage of each bill and joint resolution the vote shall be taken *separately*, by yeas and nays, and entered on the journal.

Art. 4, secs. 20 and 25. SEC. 19. No law shall embrace more than one [subject] *object*, which shall be expressed in its title. No law shall be revised, altered or amended, by reference to its title only ; but the act revised, and the section or sections of the act altered or amended, shall be re-enacted and published at length. No public act shall take effect or be in force until the expiration of ninety days from the end of the session at which the same is passed, unless, *in case of some emergency to be stated in the act*, the legislature shall otherwise direct, by a two-thirds vote of the members elected to each house, *to be taken by yeas and nays.* *

Art. 4, sec. 21. SEC. 20. The legislature shall not grant or authorize extra compensation to any public officer, agent or contractor, after the service has been rendered or the contract entered into.

Art. 4, sec. 22. SEC. 21. The legislature shall provide by law that the furnishing of fuel and stationery for the use of the State, the printing and binding the laws and journals, all blanks, paper, and printing for the executive department *and State offices*, and all other printing ordered by the legislature. shall be let by contract to the lowest *competent and responsible* bidder or bidders, who shall give adequate and satisfactory security for the performance thereof. The legislature shall prescribe by law the manner in which the State printing shall be executed, and the accounts rendered therefor, and shall prohibit all charges for constructive labor. It shall not rescind or alter such contract, nor release the person or persons taking the same, or his or their sureties, from the performance of any of the conditions of the contract. No member of the legislature or officer of the State shall be interested, directly or indirectly, in any such contract, *or any contract with the State.*

SEC. 22. *The legislature shall not pass local or special laws in any of the following enumerated cases :*

---

* The changes in this section are intended to place additional restrictions upon the practice of giving immediate effect to important general laws, which is now done upon simple motion by a rising vote.

First—Divorcing any named party, or upon the subject of divorce; Art. 4, sec. 26.

Second—Changing the names of persons or places;

Third—Regulating the practice in courts of justice, or regulating the jurisdiction and duties of justices of the peace, or constables;

Fourth—Providing for changes of venue in civil or criminal cases;

Fifth—Providing for the election or appointment of members of boards of supervisors;

Sixth—Summoning and empaneling grand or petit jurors;

Seventh—Regulating the rate of interest on money;

Eighth—Authorizing the sale, lease or mortgage of real estate belonging to minors, or by executors or administrators, or by any religious corporation or society; Art. 4, sec. 23.

Ninth—Chartering or licensing ferries or toll bridges;

Tenth—Remitting fines, penalties or forfeitures;

Eleventh—Creating, increasing or decreasing fees, percentages or allowances of public officers;

Twelfth—Changing the law of descent;

Thirteenth—Granting to any corporation, association or individual, any special or exclusive privilege, immunity or franchise whatever;

Fourteenth—Declaring any named person of age;

Fifteenth—Extending the time for the assessment or collection of taxes, or otherwise relieving any assessor or collector of taxes from the due performance of his official duties;

Sixteenth—Punishing crimes or misdemeanors;

Seventeenth—Adopting, by any person, any named person as his child or heir;

Eighteenth—Vacating or altering any road laid out by commissioners of highways, or any street, alley or public ground in any city or village, or in any recorded town plat; or for building or repairing bridges, or for draining swamp or other low lands, except by expenditure of grants to the State. Art. 4, sec. 23.

Nineteenth—Exempting any property from taxation. The legislature shall provide by general laws for the cases enumerated in this section, and for all other cases which, in its judgment, may be provided for by general laws. *

---

* The restrictions proposed by some of the subdivisions of this section are now embodied in the constitution. Others of them are already covered by general laws. They are all found in some one or other of the constitutions of the States. It is believed that the adoption of these restrictions will reduce the length and expense of legislative sessions fully one-third, as well as be a safeguard against much hasty, corrupt and partial legislation.

Art. 4, sec. 35. SEC. 23. The legislature shall not establish a State paper.

Art. 4, sec. 24. SEC. 24. The legislature may authorize the employment of a chaplain for the State prison; but no money shall be appropriated for the payment of any religious services in either house of the legislature.

Art. 4, sec. 30. SEC. 25. No collector, holder or disburser of public moneys, shall have a seat in the legislature or be eligible to any office of trust or profit under this State, until he shall have accounted for and paid over, as provided by law, all sums for which he may be liable.

Art. 4, sec. 31. SEC. 26. The legislature shall not audit or allow any private claim or account.

Art. 4, sec. 33. SEC. 27. The legislature shall meet at the seat of government on the first Wednesday in January, in the year eighteen hundred and [sixty-one] *seventy-five*, and on the first Wednesday in January in every second year thereafter, and at no other place or time unless as provided in this constitution, and shall adjourn without day at such time as the legislature shall fix by concurrent resolution.

Art. 4. sec. 32. SEC. 28. The legislature, on the day of final adjournment, shall adjourn at twelve o'clock at noon.

Art. 4, sec. 34. SEC. 29. The election of senators and representatives pursuant to the provisions of this constitution, shall be held on the Tuesday succeeding the first Monday of November, in the year eighteen hundred and [fifty-two] *seventy-four*, and on the Tuesday succeeding the first Monday of November of every second year thereafter.

Art. 4. sec. 36. SEC. 30. The legislature shall provide for the speedy publication of all statute laws of a public nature, and of such judicial decisions as it may deem expedient. All laws and judicial decisions shall be free for publication by any person.

Art. 4, sec. 37. SEC. 31. The legislature may declare the cases in which any office shall be deemed vacant, and also the manner of filling the vacancy, where no provision is made for that purpose in this constitution.

Art. 4, sec. 38. SEC. 32. The legislature may confer upon organized townships, incorporated cities and villages, and upon the board of supervisors of the several counties, such powers of a local, legislative and administrative character as it may deem proper.

Art. 4, sec. 27. SEC. 33. The legislature shall not authorize any lottery, or permit the sale of lottery tickets.

Art. 4, sec. 40. SEC. 34. No money shall be appropriated or drawn from the treasury for the benefit of any religious sect or society, theological or religious seminary, *or school under private or denominational control*, nor shall property belonging to the State be appropriated for any such purpose.

SEC. 35. The assent of two-thirds of the members elected to each house of the legislature shall be requisite to every bill appropriating the public money or property for local or private purposes. Art. 4, sec. 45.

SEC. 36. The legislature shall not pass any act authorizing the grant of license for the sale of ardent spirits or other intoxicating liquors. Art 4, sec. 47.

SEC. 37. The style of the laws shall be: "The People of the State of Michigan enact." Art. 4, sec. 48.

NOTE.—Section 16 of the corresponding article of the present constitution relative to postage, is omitted as obsolete, as all postage is now required to be paid in advance. Section 29, permitting compensation only to the person who may be declared entitled to the seat in case of a contested election, is stricken out, as calculated to work unjustly in some cases where parties hold certificates of election, and in other cases where they are contestants with a reasonably good case. That part of section 55 which allows fifteen dollars to newspapers publishing the general laws of a session, is omitted as absurd in itself, from the smallness of the compensation offered. Under section 30 of this amended article, which requires the legislature to provide for the speedy publication of all statute laws of a public nature, the legislature may provide adequate compensation to newspapers for publishing such laws as they may direct. Sections 39, 41, 42, 43, 44, and 46, of the present article, are embodied in the Bill of Rights, which stands as article II of the amended constitution.

ARTICLE V.*

EXECUTIVE DEPARTMENT.

SECTION 1. The executive power is vested in a Governor, who shall hold his office for two years. A Lieutenant Governor shall be chosen for the same term.

SEC. 2. No person shall be eligible to the office of governor or lieutenant governor who has not been five years a citizen of the United States, a resident of this State two years next preceding his election, [nor shall any person be eligible to either office who has not] *and* attained the age of thirty years.

SEC. 3. The governor and lieutenant governor shall be elected at the times and places of choosing the members of the legislature. The person having the highest number of votes for governor or lieutenant governor shall be elected. In case two or more persons shall have an equal and the highest number of votes for governor or lieutenant governor, the legislature shall, by joint vote, choose one of such persons.

* The changes proposed in this article are few, and generally unimportant. The sections are the same in number, and relate respectively to the same subject matter, with those of the corresponding article of the present constitution.

SEC. 4. The governor shall be commander-in-chief of the military and naval forces, and may call out such forces to execute the laws, to suppress insurrection, and to repel invasion.

SEC. 5. He [shall transact all necessary business with officers of government, and] may require information in writing from officers of the executive department upon any subject relating to the duties of their respective offices.

SEC. 6. He shall take care that the laws be faithfully executed.

SEC. 7. He may convene the legislature on extraordinary occasions.

SEC. 8. He shall give to the legislature, and at the close of his official term to the [next] *incoming* legislature, information by message of the condition of the State, and recommend such measures to them as he shall deem expedient.

SEC. 9. He may convene the legislature at some other place, when the seat of government becomes dangerons from disease or a [common] *public* enemy.

SEC. 10. He shall issue writs of election to fill such vacancies as occur in the senate or house of representatives.

SEC. 11. He may grant reprieves, commutations and pardons, after conviction, for all offenses except treason and cases of impeachment, upon such conditions, and with such restrictions and limitations, as he may think proper; *but the legislature may provide by law as to the manner of hearing applications for pardon.** Upon conviction for treason, he may suspend the execution of the sentence until the case shall be reported to the legislature at its next session, when the legislature shall either pardon or commute the sentence, direct the execution of the sentence, or grant a further reprieve. He shall communicate to the legislature at each session, information of each case of reprieve, commutation or pardon granted, and the reasons therefor.

SEC. 12. In case of the [impeachment] *death* of the governor, his removal *or suspension* from office, [death] inability *to perform the duties of the office*, resignation, absence from the State, *or other disability*, the powers and duties of the office shall devolve upon the lieutenant governor for the residue of the term, or until the disability cease. But when the governor shall be [out of] *absent from* the State, [in time of war] at the head of the military forces thereof, he shall continue to be commander-in-chief.

---

* In place of italics, the present constitution says —" subject to regulations provided by law, relative to the manner of applying for pardons."

SEC. 13. During the vacancy in the office of governor, if the lieutenant governor die, resign, be [impeached] displaced, *suspended*, or be incapable of performing the duties of his office, or absent from the State, the president *pro tempore* of the senate shall act as governor until the vacancy be filled or the disability cease.

SEC. 14. The lieutenant governor shall, by virtue of his office, be president of the senate, and when there is an equal division, he shall give the casting vote. In committee of the whole he may debate all questions.

SEC. 15. No member of congress, or any person holding office under the United States, or this State, shall execute the office of governor.

SEC. 16. No person elected governor or lieutenant governor shall [be eligible to] *receive* any office or appointment from the legislature, or either house thereof, during the time for which he was elected. [All votes for either of them, for any such office, shall be void.]

SEC. 17. The lieutenant governor and president of the senate *pro tempore*, when performing the duties of governor, shall receive the same compensation as the governor.

SEC. 18. All official acts of the governor, his approval of the laws excepted, shall be authenticated by the Great Seal of the State, which shall be kept by the secretary of state.

SEC. 19. All commissions issued to persons holding office under the provisions of this constitution shall be "In the name and by the authority of the people of the State of Michigan," sealed with the Great Seal of the State, signed by the governor, and countersigned by the secretary of state.

ARTICLE VI.

JUDICIAL DEPARTMENT.

SECTION 1. The judicial power is vested in a supreme court, in circuit courts, probate courts, justices of the peace, *and in such other courts, tribunals and officers as are or shall be established or authorized by law.** Art. 6, secs. 1 and 23.

SEC. 2. *The supreme court shall be composed of five judges. Hereafter the judges of said court shall be nominated, and by* Art. 6, sec. 2.

---

* The corresponding section of the present constitution says: "Municipal courts of civil and criminal jurisdiction may be established by the legislature in cities." Section 23, same article, says: "The legislature may establish courts of conciliation, with such powers and duties as shall be prescribed by law." These are both omitted, the powers conferred by them being covered by the words in italics to which this note refers, as also much more comprehensive powers.

*and with the advice and consent of the senate, appointed by the governor; and their term of office shall be ten years. One judge of said court shall be appointed as soon as practicable after the first day of January, in the year of our Lord one thousand eight hundred and seventy-five, and his term of office shall date from January first, one thousand eight hundred and seventy-four; and one judge of said court shall thereafter be appointed as the terms of the present and future judges shall expire.**

Art. 6, sec. 3. SEC. 3. The supreme court shall have a general superintending control over all other courts and tribunals; and also such appellate jurisdiction as shall be provided by law; and to that end may issue writs of error, *certiorari, mandamus, procedendo*, prohibition, and all other appropriate writs and process. It shall also have original jurisdiction in cases of *mandamus, habeas corpus*, proceedings in the nature of *quo warranto*, and proceedings by *scire facias*, to vacate letters patent. *Its appellate jurisdiction shall not extend to any civil case for the recovery of money or property in which the amount or value of the thing in controversy is less than one hundred dollars, exclusive of costs, except upon the allowance of an appeal, writ of error or certiorari by the judge who tried such case, or by a judge of the supreme court. The concurrence of three judges of said court shall be necessary to a final decision.* †

---

* This section does not follow in any manner the language of the corresponding section of the present constitution. That section provided for the *establishment* of a supreme court. The revised section treats of the court as an established and existing fact. The essential changes are—providing for five instead of four judges; providing that they shall be appointed by the governor and senate instead of being elected; and fixing their term of office at ten instead of eight years. The necessity for having the supreme court composed of an odd instead of an even number of judges, is seen in the fact that a number of cases involving important questions of law, have remained practically undecided, owing to an equal division of the court. The extension of the term to ten years is rendered necessary to secure regularity of succession. In proposing the change in the manner of choosing judges, the commission sought to represent what seemed to be the prevailing sentiment with the bar, the press, and the people of the State, so far as an expression was had The proposition on its final passage received the unanimous approval of the members of the commission voting upon it, the only difference of opinion being as to the manner of submission—whether it should be embodied directly in the amended constitution, or submitted separately.

† This section covers the general ground of the corresponding section of the present constitution. Its principal new feature is that restricting the appellate jurisdiction of the court to cases in which the amount in controversy is one hundred dollars or over, etc. The phraseology of the section is generally changed. The last clause, making the concurrence of three judges necessary to a final decision, is in keeping with the provision increasing the number of judges.

SEC. 4. Four terms of the supreme court shall be held annually, at such times and places as may be designated by law.

Art. 6, sec. 4.

SEC. 5. The supreme court shall have power, by general rules, to establish, and from time to time modify, the methods of procedure and the practice therein, *and to appoint its clerks*, and a reporter of its decisions; *and said court shall also have power to establish a code or codes of civil procedure, pleading and practice, including the commencement of suits and proceedings, for all other courts of record, and from time to time to alter and amend such code or codes.**

Art. 6, secs. 5 and 10.

SEC. 6. The legislature shall divide the State into judicial circuits, and may increase or decrease the number of the same from time to time, *for each of which the governor shall nominate, and, by and with the advice and consent of the senate, appoint one circuit judge,* who shall hold his office for the term of six years, and until his successor is appointed and qualified. No alteration of any circuit shall have the effect to remove a judge from office.†

Art. 6, secs. 6 and 7.

SEC. 7. A circuit court shall be held at least twice in each year in every county organized for judicial purposes, and [four] *at least three* times in each year in counties containing ten thousand inhabitants. Judges of the circuit court may hold courts for each other, and shall do so when required by law.

Art. 6. sec. 11.

SEC. 8. The circuit courts shall have original jurisdiction in all matters, civil and criminal, not excepted in this constitution and not prohibited by law, and such appellate jurisdiction from all inferior courts and tribunals as shall be provided by law, and a supervisory control of the same. They shall also have power to issue writs of injunction, *habeas corpus, mandamus, quo warranto, certiorari,* and other writs necessary to carry into effect their orders, judgments and decrees, and give them general control over inferior courts and tribunals within their respective jurisdictions. *The appellate jurisdiction of said courts shall not extend to any civil case in which the amount or value of the thing in controversy is less than twenty-five dollars, exclusive of costs, except upon allowance of an appeal or writ of certiorari by the judge of the court entitled to exercise such appellate jurisdiction.* ‡

Art. 6. sec. 8.

* The following provisions contained in section 5 are omitted: "The legislature shall, as far as practicable, abolish distinctions between law and equity proceedings. The office of master in chancery is prohibited."

† This section covers the general provisions of sections six and seven of the present article. The only material change is from the elective to the appointive system for judges.

‡ The addition to this section is made to relieve the circuit courts from the large number of appeal cases where the amount involved is trivial.

Art. 6, sec. 16. SEC. 9. *The respective circuit courts held in each county, or the judge thereof, shall appoint two circuit court commissioners, who shall be vested with such judicial and ministerial powers as shall be prescribed by law.* *

Art. 6, sec. 22. SEC. 10. Whenever a judge shall remove beyond the limits of the jurisdiction for which he was appointed or elected, or a justice of the peace from the township in which he was elected, or by a change in the boundaries of such township, shall be placed without the same, he shall be deemed to have vacated his office.

Art. 6, sec. 14. SEC. 11. When a vacancy occurs in the office of judge of the supreme or circuit court it shall be filled *for the residue of the term by appointment of the governor, by and with the advice and consent of the senate; but if the senate is not in session when such vacancy occurs, the governor shall fill the same by appointment until the senate shall assemble, and for thirty days thereafter, when the vacancy shall be filled as hereinbefore provided. When a vacancy occurs in the office of judge of probate or judge of any court of record, other than the supreme or circuit court, it shall be filled by appointment of the governor, which appointment shall continue during the residue of the unexpired term, and until a successor is duly qualified.* †

Art. 6, sec. 12. SEC. 12. The clerk of each county organized for judicial purposes shall be clerk of the circuit court of such county [and of the supreme court when held within the same].
Art. 6, sec. 10. The judges of the circuit courts, within their respective jurisdictions, may fill vacancies in the offices of county clerk and prosecuting attorney. ‡

Art. 6, sec. 9. SEC. 13. *During their continuance in office, and for one year thereafter, the judges of the supreme and circuit courts shall be ineligible to any other than a judicial office.* ‖

Art. 6, sec. 13. SEC. 14. In each county organized for judicial purposes there shall be a court of probate. It shall have such probate jurisdiction, powers and duties as shall be prescribed by law.

---

* This is a new section, and is in keeping with other provisions changing the manner of choosing judicial officers.

† Section 14, article VI, of the present constitution, provides that the governor may fill vacancies in supreme, circuit and probate judgeships until a successor is elected.

‡ The present section (sec. 10, art. 6), has a further provision that no judge shall exercise any other power of appointment to public office. This is omitted as unnecessary, and as inconsistent with the power given to appoint circuit court commissioners.

‖ The present provision makes judges ineligible for one year after the expiration of the term for which they are elected. The amended sec.

Other jurisdiction, civil and criminal, may also be conferred on any one or more courts of probate. Judges of probate shall hold their offices for a term of four years, and shall be elected by the electors of their respective counties, as shall be provided by law.*

SEC. 15. The supreme, circuit and probate courts shall be courts of record, and shall each have a common seal. Art. 6, sec. 15.

SEC. 16. There shall be not exceeding four justices of the peace in each organized township. They shall be elected by the electors of the townships, and shall hold their offices for four years, and until their successors are elected and qualified. At the first election in any township they shall be classified as shall be prescribed by law. A justice elected to fill a vacancy shall hold his office for the residue of the unexpired term.† Art. 6, sec. 17.

SEC. 17. In civil cases justices of the peace shall have exclusive jurisdiction to the amount of one hundred dollars, and concurrent jurisdiction to the amount of three hundred dollars, which may be increased to five hundred dollars, with such exceptions and restrictions as may be provided by law. They shall also have such criminal jurisdiction, and perform such duties, as shall be prescribed by the legislature. Art. 6, sec. 18.

SEC. 18. Judges of the supreme court, circuit judges, and justices of the peace, shall be conservators of the peace within their respective jurisdictions. Art 6, sec. 19.

SEC. 19. The style of all process shall be: "In the name of the People of the State of Michigan." Art. 6, sec. 35.

NOTE.—Sections 24 to 34 inclusive, as they stand in article VI of the present constitution, are transferred to the Bill of Rights, which stands as article II of the amended constitution. The following clauses of section 10 of article VI of the present constitution are omitted from the revised article: "The decisions of the supreme court shall be in writing, and signed by the judges concurring therein. Any judge dissenting therefrom, shall give the reasons of such dissent in writing, under his signature. All such opinions shall be filed in the office of the clerk of the supreme court."

---

tion makes the ineligibility to extend only for one year after they cease to hold the office of judge. The clause of the present section declaring void all votes given for a judge for any other than a judicial office, is omitted as superfluous.

* This section is somewhat changed in phraseology, but the clause in italics is the only new feature. This is added for the purpose of giving to the legislature the power to relieve the pressure upon other courts when deemed necessary, by conferring a larger jurisdiction upon probate courts.

† This section is unchanged, but the last clause, providing that the legislature may increase the number of justices in cities, is omitted, all the power conferred by it being covered by the last clause of the first section of this amended article.

ARTICLE VII.

ELECTIVE FRANCHISE.

Art. 7, sec. 1. SECTION 1. In all elections, every person of the age of twenty-one years who shall have resided in this State three months, and in the township or ward in which he offers to vote ten days next preceding an election, belonging to either of the following classes, shall be an elector and entitled to vote:

First—Every male citizen of the United States;

Second—Every male inhabitant of this State, who shall have resided in the United States two years and six months, and declared his intention to become a citizen of the United States pursuant to the laws thereof, six months preceding an election;

Third—Every male inhabitant residing in this State on the twenty-fourth day of June, one thousand eight hundred and thirty-five. *

Art. 7, sec. 1. SEC. 2. In time of war, insurrection or rebellion, the right to vote at such place, and in such manner as shall be prescribed by law, shall be enjoyed by all persons otherwise entitled thereto, who may be in the actual military or naval service of the United States, or of this State, and their votes shall be made to apply to the township or ward of which they are residents. *The legislature may provide by law for allowing townships to hold their elections in any city wholly or in part within the limits of such townships.* †

Art. 7, sec. 2. SEC. 3. All [votes shall be given] *elections shall be* by ballot, except of such township officers as may be authorized by law to be otherwise chosen.

Art. 7, secs. 3 and 4. SEC. 4. Every elector, in all cases except treason, felony, *misdemeanor*, or breach of the peace, shall be privileged from arrest during his attendance at election, and in going to and

---

* The language of this section is changed so as to make it more readily understood, but it does not change the right of the elective franchise. The second subdivision stands in lieu of the following clause of section one of article VII of the present constitution: "Every male inhabitant residing in the State on the first day of January, one thousand eight hundred and fifty, who has declared his intention to become a citizen of the United States, pursuant to the laws thereof, six months preceding an election, or who has resided in this State two years and six months, and declared his intention as aforesaid, and every civilized male inhabitant of Indian descent, a native of the United States, and not a member of any tribe." The omission of the qualifying clause relative to Indians, is because all persons of that class in the State are regarded as civilized and non-tribal.

† The first part of this section is changed in phraseology, as it stands in section 1 of the present article, but not in substance. The last clause is added to remove any doubt as to the legality of the practice which now exists in such cases.

returning from the same. No elector shall be obliged to attend court as a suitor or witness on the day of election, or to do military duty thereon except in time of war or public danger.

SEC. 5. No elector shall be deemed to have gained or lost his residence by reason of absence therefrom in the service of the United States or of this State, nor while engaged in the navigation of the waters of this State or of the United States, or of the high seas, nor while a student at any seminary of learning, nor while kept at any alms-house or other asylum at public expense, [nor while confined in any public prison.] Art. 7, sec. 5.

SEC. 6. Laws may be passed to preserve the purity of elections, and guard against the abuses of the elective franchise. Art. 7, sec. 6.

SEC. 7. No soldier, seaman or marine in the army or navy of the United States, shall be deemed a resident of this State in consequence of being stationed in any place within the same. Art. 7, sec. 7.

SEC. 8. Any inhabitant of this State who may hereafter be engaged in a duel shall be disqualified from holding any office and from voting at any election. * Art. 7, sec. 8.

ARTICLE VIII.

STATE OFFICERS.

SECTION 1. There shall be elected at each general biennial election *in November*, a secretary of state, a state treasurer, a commissioner of the state land office, a superintendent of public instruction, and an auditor general, [an attorney general] for the term of two years, each of whom shall keep his office at the seat of government, and shall perform such duties as may be prescribed by law. † Art. 8, sec. 1.

SEC. 2. Their term of office shall commence on the first day of January following their election. Art. 8, sec. 2.

SEC. 3. *An attorney general shall be elected or appointed, as the legislature may by law provide.* ‡

SEC. 4. Whenever a vacancy shall occur in any of the State offices, the governor shall fill the same by appointment, by by and with the advice and consent of the senate, if in session. Art. 8, sec. 3.

SEC. 5. The secretary of state, state treasurer and com- Art. 8, sec. 4.

* Change in phrascology.

† The order in which the officers are named in the corresponding section is changed.

‡ Should the amended constitution be adopted, the office of attorney general will remain elective, as now, unless changed by the legislature.

missioner of the state land office, shall constitute a board of state auditors, to examine and adjust all claims against the State not otherwise provided for by law. They shall also constitute a board of state canvassers, to determine the result of all elections for governor, lieutenant governor and state officers, and of such other officers as shall by law be referred to them.

Art. 8, sec. 5. SEC. 6. In case two or more persons have an equal and the highest number of votes for any office, as canvassed by the board of state canvassers, the legislature, in joint convention, shall choose one of said persons to fill such office. When the determination of the board of state canvassers is contested, the legislature in joint convention shall decide which person is elected.

ARTICLE IX.

SALARIES.*

SECTION 1. The governor, lieutenant governor, secretary of state, state treasurer, commissioner of the state land office, superintendent of public instruction, auditor general, attorney general, commissioner of railroads, commissioner of insurance, and all other state officers, *shall receive for their services such salaries as shall be provided by law, which shall not be increased or diminished during their official term.*

SEC. 2. The judges of the supreme court, the judges of the circuit courts, and the judges of all other courts of record, *shall receive for their services such salaries as shall be provided by law, which shall not be diminished during their official term.*

---

*The corresponding article of the present constitution fixes the salaries of state officers and circuit judges. The amended article leaves the salaries to be fixed by law, so that they may be modified from time to time, and adjusted to the financial condition of the country. The commission deemed this one of the most needed changes, if not the most important change proposed. It received the unanimous approval of the commission, and is recommended as "deemed necessary for the best interests of the State and the people," in the language of the joint resolution under which the commission was appointed. The frequent resignations of judges, consequent upon the insufficient salary now allowed, involves changes in judgeships, and consequent inexperience, resulting in great expense to parties and to the public at large. Any increase of salaries that might be made would be economy as compared with the present system.

ARTICLE X.

MUNICIPAL CORPORATIONS.*

SECTION 1. *No county, city, township or other municipal corporation, shall become a stockholder in, or make any loan or gift to, or lend its credit in aid of any person, private corporation or association; nor shall any county, city, township or other municipality construct or become the owner of any railroad. The provisions of this section shall not prevent such municipalities from aiding enlistments and in the support of the families of soldiers in time of war; or supporting their poor in such manner as may be provided by law.* †

Counties.

SEC. 2. Each organized county shall be a body corporate, with such powers and immunities as shall be [established] *prescribed* by law. All suits and proceedings by or against a county shall be in the name thereof. *The power of counties to levy taxes, borrow money and contract debts, shall be restricted by law.* ‡ Art. 10, sec. 1.

SEC. 3. *The board of supervisors of any county may borrow or raise by tax a sum not exceeding in any one year one and one half mills upon the dollar of the assessed valuation thereof, for constructing or repairing public buildings, highways or bridges: Provided, The indebtedness of a county incurred under this section shall at no time exceed three mills upon a dollar of such assessed valuation, unless authorized by a majority of the electors of the county voting thereon, as shall be provided by law.* ‖ Art. 10, sec. 9.

---

*In the present constitution the subject of "Counties" is treated of in article X, and of "Townships" in article XI. In the revision the two are combined into a single article, under the title of "Municipal Corporations," to which is also added "Cities and Villages," which have no special place in the present instrument.

† The propriety of this provision was suggested by the experience of some of the western states, where the credit of municipalities has been pledged largely in aid of private corporations.

‡ The present constitution contains a similar provision relative to cities and villages.

‖ Section 9 of the present article limits the amount to one thousand dollars that may be raised in any county in any one year without a vote of the people, but does not limit the aggregate to which the indebtedness may reach by successive yearly appropriations. The amended section limits the amount that may be raised by the board of supervisors in any one year by a per cent upon the assessed valuation, as being more equal in its operation, and also limits the aggregate of indebtedness that may be incurred.

Art. 10, sec. 2. SEC. 4. No organized county shall ever be reduced, by the organization of new counties, to less than sixteen townships as surveyed by the United States, unless, in pursuance of law, a majority of electors residing in each county to be affected thereby shall so decide. The legislature may organize any city into a separate county when it has attained a population of twenty thousand inhabitants, without reference to geographical extent, when a majority of the electors of a county in which such city may be situated, voting thereon, shall be in favor of a separate organization. *Nothing herein contained shall be so construed as to prevent the legislature from organizing any county composed wholly of islands within the territory of the State, or discontinuing any such county and attaching the same to the nearest county or counties on the main land.* *

Art. 10, sec. 3. SEC. 5. In each organized county there shall be a sheriff, a county clerk, a county treasurer, a register of deeds, and a prosecuting attorney, chosen by the electors thereof once in two years, [and as often as vacancies shall happen] † whose duties and powers shall be prescribed by law; *but the legislature may provide for the appointment, by the governor, of prosecuting attorneys, by and with the advice and consent of the senate.* ‡ The board of supervisors in any county may unite the offices of county clerk and register of deeds in one office, or disconnect the same.

Art. 10, sec. 4. SEC. 6. The sheriff, county clerk, county treasurer, judge of probate and register of deeds, shall hold their offices at the county seat.

Art. 10, sec. 5. SEC. 7. The sheriff shall hold no other office. No person shall be eligible to the office of sheriff for more than four in a period of six years. The county shall never be responsible for his acts. ‖

Art. 10, sec. 6. SEC. 8. A board of supervisors, consisting of one from each organized township, shall be established in each county, with

---

* This section is unchanged, except by the addition of the last sentence, which is added to give the section flexibility in the class of cases to which it refers.

† The clause in brackets is omitted, for the reason that provision is made for filling vacancies in county offices by appointment, in most, if not in all cases.

‡ This simply gives the legislature power to provide for the appointment of prosecuting attorneys.

‖ The following clause of the present section is omitted: "He may be required by law to renew his security from time to time, and in default of giving such security his office shall be deemed vacant." The legislature has all necessary power in the premises.

such powers as shall be prescribed by law. Cities *and villages* Art. 10, sec. 7.
shall have such representation in the board of supervisors of the counties in which they are situated as the legislature may direct.

SEC. 9. No county seat, once established, shall be removed, Art. 10, sec. 8.
until the place to which it is proposed to be removed shall be designated by two-thirds of the board of supervisors of the county, and a majority of the electors voting thereon shall have voted in favor of the proposed location, in such manner as shall be prescribed by law.

SEC. 10. The board of county auditors in such counties as Art. 10, sec. 10.
may be authorized by law to elect county auditors, and in every other county the board of supervisors, shall, *except as otherwise provided by law*, have power to prescribe the compensation for all services rendered for, and adjust all claims against their respective counties, and such determination and adjustment shall be subject to no appeal. *Supervisors and county auditors shall receive for their services such compensation as shall be prescribed by law.**

SEC. 11. The board of supervisors of each organized county Art. 10, sec. 11.
may provide for laying out highways, constructing bridges, and organizing townships, under such restrictions and limitations as shall be prescribed by law.

Townships.†

SEC. 12. Each organized township shall be a body corporate, Art. 11, sec. 2.
with such powers and immunities as shall be prescribed by law. All suits and proceedings by or against a township shall be in the name thereof.

SEC. 13. There shall be elected in each organized township, Art. 11, sec. 1.
annually, on the first Monday of April, *or at such other time as the legislature may provide*, one supervisor, one township clerk, who shall be *ex officio* school inspector, one commissioner

---

* There is some verbal change in the first part of this section, but the italicised clauses are the only new features. Supervisors and auditors have in some cases claimed the right to fix their own compensation. The section as amended would be conclusive against such claim.

† The sections of this subdivision are transposed from the order in which they stand in article XI of the present constitution. The italicised clauses are new. The first gives the legislature power to fix some other time than the first Monday of April for the annual township election. The propriety of fixing it in March instead of April, by constitutional provision, was quite strongly urged before the commission, but it was thought best to leave the subject to the legislature. The second clause is intended to remove an ambiguity in the present constitution relative to highway commissioners, and to provide specifically for three commissioners in each township.

of highways, *who shall hold his office for three years,* one township treasurer, one school inspector, not exceeding four constables, and one overseer of highways of each highway district, *and such other officers as may be provided by law,* whose powers and duties shall be prescribed by law.

*Cities and Villages.**

Art. 15, sec. 13. SEC. 14. *Cities and villages shall hereafter be incorporated only under general laws,* in which their powers of taxation, borrowing money, and contracting debts, shall be restricted.

SEC. 15. *No city or village shall incur indebtedness, including that incurred by or on behalf of any school district within its corporate limits, so that its aggregate debt at any time shall exceed ten per cent on the valuation of its taxable property, as shown by the assessment roll.*

Art. 15, sec. 14. SEC. 16. The [judicial] *executive* and legislative officers of cities and villages shall be elected, and all other officers shall be elected or appointed, at such time and in such manner as the legislature may direct.

SEC. 17. *Existing charters of cities and villages may be altered and amended.*

ARTICLE XI.†

CORPORATIONS OTHER THAN MUNICIPAL.

Art 15, sec. 1. SECTION 1. Corporations (other than municipal, and those for charitable, educational, penal and reformatory purposes under the control of public authority), shall be hereafter created only by general laws. *The charter of no existing corpora-*

* There has been a general law for the incorporation of villages for a number of years, but more or less special charters have been granted at every session of the legislature. At the last session, general laws were enacted both for cities and villages. But yet the present constitution (section one, article XV), seems to contemplate special charters for this class of corporations. Section 14, above, is specific in prohibiting special charters. This will relieve the legislature from much labor that would otherwise be demanded of it. Section 15, limiting the amount of indebtedness of cities and villages, was deemed necessary in view of the proneness of this class of corporations to pledge their credit, one or two of the municipalities showing an indebtedness of over 25 per cent on their present assessed valuation. The remaining sections call for no comment.

† This article is the same, with some changes, as article XV of the present constitution, entitled, "corporations." It is made to stand as article XI of the amended constitution, and is entitled, "corporations other than municipal," so as to bring it into a just relationship with the preceding article which treats of "municipal corporations." Article XIX—A, of railroads, adopted as an amendment in 1870, is also embodied in this article as sections 10 and 11.

tion not embraced in the above exceptions, shall be extended, altered or amended. All general acts of incorporation, and general laws affecting corporations, may be altered, amended or repealed.*

SEC. 2. No general banking law shall have effect until the same shall, after its passage, be submitted to a vote of the electors of the State, at a general election, and be approved by a majority of the votes cast thereon at such election. Art. 15, sec. 2.

SEC. 3. The [officers and] stockholders of every corporation or association for banking purposes, issuing bank notes or paper credits to circulate as money, shall be individually liable for all debts contracted during the time of their being [officers or] stockholders of such corporation or association, equally and ratably to the extent of their respective shares of stock in any such corporation or association. Art. 15, sec. 3.

SEC. 4. The legislature shall provide for the registry of all bills or notes issued or put in circulation as money by any bank organized under the laws of this State, and shall require security to the full amount of notes and bills so registered, in interest-bearing stocks of this State, or of the United States, which shall be deposited with the state treasurer, for the redemption of such bills or notes *in lawful money of the United States.* Art. 15, sec. 4.

SEC. 5. In case of the insolvency of any bank or banking association, the billholders thereof shall be entitled to preference in payment over all other creditors of such bank or association. Art. 15, sec. 5.

SEC. 6. The legislature shall pass no law authorizing or sanctioning the suspension of [specie] payments by any [person, association or] corporation. Art. 15, sec. 6.

SEC. 7. The stockholders in all corporations [and joint stock associations] shall be individually liable for all labor [performed for] *done in behalf of* such corporation [or association,] *during the time of their being such stockholders, equally and ratably to the extent of their respective shares in the stock of such corporation.* Art. 15, sec. 7.

SEC. 8. No corporation shall hold any real estate [here- Art. 15, sec. 12.

---

*This section covers the general ground of the section to which it refers, but is changed in phraseology. The following clause of section one of article XV as it now stands, is, however, omitted: "But the legislature may, by a vote of two-thirds of the members elected to each house, create a single bank, with branches." This was adopted as an amendment in 1862. It authorizes the establishment, by special charter, and without submission to the people, of a single bank, with branches permeating the State. The force of the provision could hardly have been understood at the time of its adoption.

after acquired] for a longer period than ten years *from the time of acquiring the same,* except such real estate as shall be actually occupied by it in the exercise of its franchises.

SEC. 9. *Foreign corporations may be permitted to do business in this State under such limitations and restrictions as may be prescribed by law, but shall be subject to the same restrictions and liabilities that are imposed, and shall have no greater rights than are conferred upon, domestic corporations of like character, and the stockholders of such foreign corporations shall be subject to like personal liabilities as stockholders in similar domestic corporations. No foreign corporation shall acquire or hold any lands in this State, except such as may be taken in good faith in payment of debts, or such as may be needed for such offices, depots and warehouses as may be required for its legitimate business, and all lands hereafter acquired or held in violation of this provision shall escheat to the State. Provision shall be made for debarring all foreign corporations which shall violate any law of this State from thereafter being allowed to do business in the State.* *

Art. 19-A, sec. 1. SEC. 10. The legislature may, from time to time, pass laws establishing reasonable maximum rates of charges for the transportation of passengers and freight, *and regulating the speed of trains,* on different railroads in this State, and shall prohibit running contracts between such railroad companies whereby discrimination is made in favor of either of such companies as against other companies owning connecting or intersecting lines of railroads.

Art. 19-A, sec. 2. SEC. 11. No railroad corporation shall consolidate its stock, property or franchises with any other railroad corporation owning a parallel or competing line; and in no case shall any consolidation take place except upon public notice given of at least sixty days to all stockholders, in such manner as shall be provided by law.

Art. 15, sec. 10. SEC. 12. No corporation, except for municipal *or mining* purposes, *for life insurance,* or for the construction of railroads [plank roads] or canals, shall be created for a longer time than thirty years.

Art. 15, sec. 11. SEC. 13. The term corporation, as used in this article, shall be construed to include all associations and joint stock com-

---

* This section is entirely new. It has two leading objects: First, to keep foreign corporations under the control of the legislature; and second, to guard against the absorption in large quantities, by foreign corporations, of land in the State, to the detriment of its interests, or of the interests of the people. See sec. 8 of this article, and sec. 12, art. XV of present constitution, as to restrictions upon all corporations in the matter of holding real estate.

panies having any of the powers or privileges of corporations not possessed by individuals or partnerships.*

NOTE.—Sections 8 and 16 of present article XV, relative to amendments of charters of existing corporations, are omitted, as all such amendments are prohibited by section one of this amended article. Section nine, which provides that "the property of no person shall be taken by any corporation for public use, without compensation being first made or secured in such manner as may be prescribed by law," is omitted, the ground being covered by sec. 22 of article II and sec. 5 of article XVII of the revision.

Sections 13 and 14 of article XV of the present constitution, relating to cities and villages, are embraced in sections 14 and 16 of amended article X, and section 15, relating to the taking of private property for public improvements in cities and villages, is represented in section 5 of amended article XVII, and section 22 of amended article II.

ARTICLE XII.

IMPEACHMENTS AND REMOVALS FROM OFFICE.

Art. 12, sec. 1.

SECTION 1. The house of representatives shall have the sole power of impeaching civil officers for corrupt conduct in office, or for crimes and misdemeanors; but a majority of the members elected shall be necessary to direct an impeachment.

Art. 12, sec. 2.

SEC. 2. Every impeachment shall be tried by the senate. When the governor or lieutenant governor [is] *shall be* tried, the chief justice of the supreme court shall preside. When an impeachment is directed, the *members of the* senate shall take an oath or affirmation truly and impartially to try and determine the same according to the evidence. No person shall be convicted without the concurrence of two-thirds of the members elected. Judgment in case of impeachment shall not extend further than removal from office; but the party *accused, whether acquitted or* convicted, shall be liable to *trial and* punishment according to law.

Art. 12, sec. 3.

SEC. 3. When an impeachment is directed, the house of representatives shall [elect] *appoint* from their own body, [three members] *a committee* whose duty it shall be to prosecute such impeachment. An impeachment may be tried after the final adjournment of the legislature.†

Art. 12, sec. 4.

SEC. 4. No [judicial] officer shall exercise his office after an impeachment is directed, until he be acquitted, *but such disa-*

---

* The last clause of this section, which provides that "all corporations shall have the right to sue and be subject to be sued in all courts, in like cases as natural persons," is omitted as superfluous.

† The last clause of the corresponding section says that "no impeachment shall be tried until after the final adjournment of the legislature, when the senate shall proceed to try the same."

*bility shall not continue longer than three months, unless the trial of such impeachment shall have been commenced and proceeded with.**

Art. 12, sec. 6. SEC. 5. For a reasonable cause, which shall not be a sufficient ground for the impeachment of a judge, the governor shall remove him on a concurrent resolution of two-thirds of the members elected to each house of the legislature, *after the party accused shall have had an opportunity to be heard in his defense ;* but the cause for which such removal is required shall be stated at length in such resolution.

Art. 12. sec. 7. SEC. 6. County, township, city, village or school district officers, may be removed in such manner and for such cause as may be provided by law.

Art. 12, sec. 8. SEC. 7. The governor shall have power, and it shall be his duty, except at such times as the legislature may be in session, to examine into the condition and administration of any public office and the acts of any public officer, elective or appointed, to [remove] *suspend* from office for gross neglect of duty or for corrupt conduct in office, or any other misfeasance or malfeasance therein, either of the following State officers, to wit: The attorney general, state treasurer, commissioner of the state land office, secretary of state, auditor general, superintendent of public instruction, or members of the state board of education, or any other officer of the State, except legislative and judicial, and to appoint a successor for the remainder of [their respective] *the* unexpired term of office, and report the cause of such removal to the legislature at its next session.

SEC. 8. *Whenever, during a recess of the legislature, it shall, in the opinion of the governor, become necessary to direct an impeachment of any civil officer, he may, by proclamation, convene the house of representatives for that purpose ; and if the house, when so convened, shall direct an impeachment, he shall in like manner immediately convene the senate to try such impeachment ; and whenever, in the opinion of the president of the senate and speaker of the house of representatives, it shall, during a recess of the legislature, become necessary to direct an impeachment of the governor, they may, by their joint proclamation, convene the house for that purpose ; and if the*

---

* The corresponding section of the present constitution refers only to judicial officers. By the omission of the word "judicial," it is made applicable to all officers. The italicised portion of the section is added to guard against the contingency of a partisan majority in the legislature virtually removing an officer by directing an impeachment and neglecting to try it.

*house direct such impeachment, the said president and speaker shall, in like manner, immediately convene the senate to try such impeachment.**

SEC. 9. The governor may make a provisional appointment to fill a vacancy occasioned by the suspension of an officer, *by impeachment or otherwise,* until he shall be acquitted, or until the election *or appointment* and qualification of a successor. Art. 12, sec. 5.

ARTICLE XIII.

EDUCATION.

SECTION 1. The superintendent of public instruction shall have the general supervision of public instruction, and his duties shall be prescribed by law; *and he shall be a member, ex-officio, of the boards of all State educational institutions, including the reform school.* Art. 13, sec. 1.

SEC. 2. The regents of the university and their successors in office shall continue to constitute a body corporate by the name and title of "The Board of Regents of the University of Michigan." Said board shall consist of the two *ex-officio* members provided for in this article,† and eight elective members. The terms of office of the elective members shall be eight years, and two of such members shall be elected every second year at the time of the annual township election, so as to succeed the regents now in office as their several terms expire. Said board of regents shall, as often as necessary, elect a president of the university, who shall be its chief executive officer, and, *ex-officio*, a member and president of said board, with the privilege of speaking, but not of voting. *The supervision and control of the university shall be vested in the board of regents, and said board shall have the direction and control of all expenditures from the university funds; but all moneys appropriated by the legislature to the university upon condition, shall, if accepted, be applied as provided in the condition accompanying the appropriation.*‡ Art. 13, secs. 6, 7, and 8.

---

*This new section is regarded as important to meet contingencies that may arise.

†The president of the university and the superintendent of public instruction.

‡This section embraces the subject matter of sections 6, 7, and 8, of article XIII of the present constitution. The only material changes are, the recognition of the superintendent of public instruction as a member *ex-officio* of the board of regents, and the clause relating to the government of the university. The corresponding provision of the present constitution on this subject, (sec. 8, article XIII), is as follows:

Art. 13, sec. 9. SEC. 3. The state normal school shall continue under the supervision of the state board of education, which shall consist of the superintendent of public instruction, *ex-officio*, and three elective members. The terms of office of said elective members shall be six years, and one of said members shall be elected every second year, at the time of the election of governor, and shall enter upon the duties of his office on the first day of January succeeding his election. Said board shall perform such other duties as shall be prescribed by law. *

SEC. 4. *The duties of the boards of the state public school, the agricultural college and the reform school, shall continue as now, or as shall be prescribed by law.*

SEC. 5. *Any vacancy that shall occur in any of the boards mentioned in this article shall be filled by appointment of the Governor.* †

Art. 13, sec. 4. SEC. 6. The legislature shall provide a system of primary schools, by which a school shall be maintained in each school district in the State, free of charge for tuition, at least three months in the year. The instruction shall, in all cases, be conducted in the English language. ‡

Art. 13, sec. 5. SEC. 7. A school shall be maintained in each school district at least three months in each year. Any school district neglecting to maintain such school shall be deprived for the ensuing year of its proportion of the income of the primary school fund, and of all funds arising from *general* taxes for the support of schools.‖

Art. 13, sec. 2. SEC. 8. The proceeds from the sale of all lands that have been or hereafter may be granted by the United States to the State for educational purposes, and the proceeds of all lands or other property given by individuals or appropriated by the

---

"The board of regents shall have the general supervision of the university, and the direction and control of all expenditures from the university interest fund." The change is intended to remove an ambiguity in the present constitution on the subject.

* This section is generally changed in phraseology. The word "general," as a qualifying term before the word "supervision," in the last clause of the existing section, is omitted from the first clause of the amended section.

† This and the preceding section are new. The power of appointment conferred by section five exists at present as to regents only, by section six, article XIII, of the present constitution.

‡ Changed in phraseology only.

‖ The insertion of the word "general," as italicised in this section, is an important change. It relieves from the penalty of forfeiture for default in the maintenance of schools, all funds raised by defaulting districts for special purposes. By the section as it stands in the present constitution all such funds would be forfeited.

State for like purposes, shall be and remain a perpetual fund, the interest and income of which, together with the rents of all such lands as may remain unsold, shall be inviolably appropriated and annually applied to the specific objects of the original gift, grant or appropriation.

SEC. 9. All lands which have heretofore escheated, or which shall hereafter escheat to the State, shall inure to the benefit of the primary school fund, and be held and disposed of as primary school lands.* Art. 13, sec. 8.

SEC. 10. The legislature shall provide for the establishment and maintenance of [at least one] *a* library in each township, *and of at least one in each city.* And all moneys belonging to the public derived from fines, *penalties, forfeitures or recognizances,* imposed or taken in the several counties, *cities* or townships for any breach of the penal laws of the State, shall be apportioned in the same manner as is the income of the primary school fund, and paid over to the several cities and townships of the county in which such money accrued, for the support of such libraries.† Art. 13, sec. 12.

SEC. 11. Institutions for the benefit of those inhabitants who are deaf, dumb, blind or insane, shall always be fostered and supported. Art. 13, sec. 10.

NOTE.—Section 11 of the present article, relating to the encouragement of intellectual, scientific and agricultural improvement, to the establishment of an agricultural school, to the disposition of salt spring lands, etc., is omitted as obsolete.

ARTICLE XIV.

FINANCE AND TAXATION.

SECTION 1. The Legislature [may] *shall* provide for the collection of specific taxes from banking, railroad and plank-road corporations, *and may, in its discretion, impose specific taxes upon other corporations, and upon any property or business within this state; but when a specific tax is imposed upon a* Art. 14, sec. 10.

---

*This section is changed in phraseology. By the section which it stands in lieu of, only lands that escheat "from a defect of heirs," go to the school fund. By the section as amended, all lands escheating to the State take that direction.

† The first clause of this section provides for libraries in cities as well as townships, and the verbal changes are shown by italics and brackets. The balance of the section is changed in phraseology. Instead of "fines," simply, it covers "fines, penalties. forfeitures or recognizances." The present section covers only fines collected in "counties and townships," while the amended section embraces "counties, *cities* and townships."

*corporation it shall only apply to such property of the corporation as shall be necessary for the exercise of its corporate franchises.**

Art. 14, sec. 1. SEC. 2. All specific State taxes *received from corporations*, except mining companies of the upper peninsula, shall be applied in paying the interest upon the primary school, university and other educational funds, and the interest and principal of the State debt, in the order herein recited, until the extinguishment of the State debt other than the amounts due to educational funds, when such specific taxes shall be added to and constitute a part of the primary school interest fund.

Art. 14, sec. 1. SEC. 3. The legislature shall provide for an annual tax, sufficient, with other resources, to pay the estimated expenses of the State government, the interest of the State debt, and such deficiency as may occur in the resources. †

Art. 14, sec. 2. SEC. 4. *Every law hereafter enacted by the legislature, creating a debt or authorizing a loan, shall provide a sinking fund for the payment of the same.*

Art. 14, sec. 2. SEC. 5. The unfunded debt shall not be funded or redeemed at a value exceeding that established by law in the year one thousand eight hundred and forty-eight.

Art. 14, sec. 3. SEC. 6. The State may contract debts to meet deficits in revenue. Such debts shall not in the aggregate at any time exceed fifty thousand dollars. The moneys so raised shall be applied to the purposes for which they were obtained, or to the payment of the debts so contracted.

Art. 14, sec. 4. SEC. 7. The State may contract debts to repel invasion, suppress insurrection, defend the State, *or aid the United States* in time of war. The money arising from the contracting of such debts shall be applied to the purposes for which it was raised, or to pay such debts.

Art. 14, sec. 5. SEC. 8. No money shall be paid out of the State treasury, except in pursuance of appropriations made by law. *The legislature shall provide by law for barring all claims against the State, unless presented within a time to be therein fixed.* ‡

---

* The substance of the first part of this section is found in sec. 10 of article XIV of the present constitution. The italicised portion is new. The last clause is important, as it secures for the purposes of local taxation all property of corporations not necessary for corporate use, as lands held by railroads, etc.

† This and the preceding section constitute section one of article XIV of the present constitution, and are unchanged except by the addition of the words in italics in section two.

‡ This clause is added to bar the presentation of claims after a lapse of years, when the circumstances attending such claims have passed out

SEC. 9. *The State shall not aid, by gift, or pledge of its* Art. 14, secs.
credit, any person or corporation, nor shall it subscribe to or 6 and 8.
*become interested in the stock of any corporation, nor assume any indebtedness of a municipal or other corporation. The provisions of this section shall not apply to educational, charitable, reformatory or penal institutions which are or may be under the care and control of the State.**

SEC. 10. No scrip, certificate or other evidence of State Art. 14, sec.
indebtedness shall be issued, except for the redemption of 7.
stock previously issued, or for such debts as are expressly authorized by this constitution.

SEC. 11. The State shall not be a party to or be interested Art 14, sec.
in any work of internal improvement, *except the ship canal* 9.
at the Sault Ste. Marie, nor engage in carrying on any such work, otherwise than in the expenditure of grants to the State of land or other property.

SEC. 12. The legislature shall provide a uniform rule of Art. 14, sec.
taxation, except on property, *business and corporations* pay- 11.
ing specific taxes. Taxes shall be levied on all property *except such as is or may be exempted by law.* †

SEC. 13. All assessments hereafter authorized shall be on Art. 14, sec.
property at its cash value. 12.

SEC. 14. The legislature shall provide for an equalization Art. 14, sec.
by a State board in the year one thousand eight hundred and 13.
fifty-one, and every fifth year thereafter, of assessments on all taxable property except that paying specific taxes.

SEC. 15. Every law which imposes, continues or revives a Art. 14, sec.
tax, shall distinctly state the tax, and the object to which it 14.
is to be applied; and it shall not be sufficient to refer to any other law to fix such tax or object.

NOTE.—The first part of section two, article XIV of the present constitution, is omitted from the revised article. It is as follows: "The legislature shall provide by law a sinking fund of at least twenty thousand dollars a year, to commence in eighteen hundred and fifty-two, with compound interest at the rate of six per cent per annum, and an annual increase of at least five per cent, to be applied solely to the payment and extinguishment of the principal of the State debt, other than the amounts due to educational funds, and shall be continued until the extinguishment thereof." This clause was regarded as unnecessary, section four of this amended article making all the provision necessary on the subject.

---

of recollection, and evidence that would disprove their validity has been lost.

* This section is substantially new, although embodying the restrictive features of sections six and eight of present article XIV, but being more specific and comprehensive.

† The corresponding clause says, "taxes shall be levied on such property as shall be prescribed by law."

ARTICLE XV.*

EXEMPTIONS.

Art. 16, sec. 1. SECTION 1. The personal property of every resident of this State, to consist of such property only as shall be designated by law, shall be exempted to the amount of not less than five hundred dollars, from sale on execution or other final process of any court, issued for the collection of any debt contracted after the adoption of this constitution.

Art. 16, sec. 2. SEC. 2. Every homestead of not exceeding forty acres of land, and the dwelling-house thereon, and the appurtenances to be selected by the owner thereof, and not included in any town plat, city or village, or instead thereof, at the option of the owner, any lot in any city or village or recorded town plat, or such parts of lots as shall be equal thereto, and the dwelling house thereon and its appurtenances, owned and occupied by any resident of the State, not exceeding in value [fifteen hundred] *two thousand* dollars, shall be exempt from forced sale on execution or any other final process from a court, for any debt contracted after the adoption of this constitution. Such exemption shall not extend to any mortgage thereon lawfully obtained, but [such] *any* mortgage *not given for purchase money, and any* [or] other alienation of such land by the owner thereof, if a married man, shall not be valid without the signature of the wife to the same.

Art. 16, secs. 3 and 4. SEC. 3. If the owner of a homestead die, leaving a widow, child, or children, such homestead shall be exempt from the payment of his debts so long as the widow shall be without other homestead of her own, and during the minority of said child or children.†

Art. 16, sec. 5. SEC. 4. The real and personal estate of every woman, acquired before marriage, and all property, *real and personal,* to which she may afterwards become entitled, [by gift, grant, inheritance or devise] shall be and remain the estate and property of such woman, and shall not be liable for the debts, obligations or engagements of her husband, and may be held, controlled and disposed of by her in the same manner and with like effect as if she were unmarried. *And the husband of any married woman shall not be liable for or on account of*

---

*This article stands as article XVI of the present constitution, and is made article XV of the revision. The most important change is in section two, raising the amount of the homestead exemption to two thousand dollars.

†This section covers the ground of sections three and four of the present article, and is changed in arrangement and phraseology only.

any debt or obligation of his wife contracted before her marriage, or contracted by her in relation to her sole property after marriage. *

ARTICLE XVI.†

MILITIA.

SECTION 1. The militia shall be composed of all able-bodied male citizens between the ages of eighteen and forty-five years, except such as are exempted by the laws of the United States or of this State; but all such citizens of any religious denomination whatever, who from scruples of conscience may be averse to bearing arms, shall be excused therefrom upon such conditions as shall be prescribed by law.

SEC. 2. The legislature shall provide by law for organizing, equipping and disciplining the militia, in such manner as it shall deem expedient, not incompatible with the laws of the United States.

SEC. 3. Officers of the militia shall be elected or appointed, and be commissioned in such manner as may be provided by law.

ARTICLE XVII.‡

MISCELLANEOUS PROVISIONS.

SECTION 1. Members of the legislature, and all officers, executive and judicial, [except such officers as may be by law exempted] shall, before they enter on the duties of their respective offices, take and subscribe the following oath or affirmation: "I do solemnly swear (or affirm) that I will support the constitution of the United States, and the constitution of this State, and that I will faithfully discharge the duties of the office of ——, according to the best of my ability."‖ Art. 18, sec. 1.

---

*In this section the word "woman" is substituted for "female," as used in the corresponding section, and there are other verbal changes, all material ones being indicated in the usual way. The last sentence is new, and is a rational corollary of the preceding provisions, which have become the fixed law of the State, both by constitution and statute.

† This article stands as article XVII of the present constitution. The text is unchanged.

‡ Article XVIII of present constitution.

‖ The following sentence contained in the corresponding section of the present constitution is omitted from the amended section above: "And no other oath, declaration or test, shall be required as a qualification for any office or public trust."

Art. 18, sec. 6.

SEC. 2. Judicial and legislative proceedings shall be conducted, and the laws and public records promulgated and preserved, in the English language.

SEC. 3. *Public officers, receiving or having charge of public moneys, are prohibited from using or employing the same in any manner for their private use or benefit, and whenever such moneys are deposited with any person or corporation, the interest thereon shall be paid to the fund to which such moneys belong.*

Art. 18, sec. 14.

SEC. 4. The legislature may authorize the taking of private property for the opening of private roads, *for use in the improvement of navigable streams, and for flowage when the public interests demand it.**

Art. 18, secs. 2 and 14, and art. 15, sec. 15.

SEC. 5. *Before any private property shall be taken without the consent of the owner, for public use (except for public highways not within any city or village), or for any purpose named in the last above section, the necessity for taking such property, and the compensation to be paid therefor shall be determined by a jury of freeholders of the vicinity, or by not less than three commissioners, freeholders as aforesaid, appointed by a court of record, as may be provided by law, and such compensation shall be paid or tendered in such manner as shall be prescribed by law.*†

Art. 18, sec. 4.

SEC. 6. *The right of the public or of any individual to the free use of any navigable stream for any purpose for which such stream is capable of use, without improvement, shall not be abridged or obstructed by or under color of any authority which may be given by law to any individual or corporation to improve such stream and charge toll for the use thereof.*

Art. 18, sec. 4.

SEC. 7. No navigable stream in this State shall be either bridged or dammed without authority from the board of supervisors of the proper county, under the provisions of law. No such law shall prejudice the right of individuals to the free navigation of such streams, or preclude the State from the further improvement of the navigation of such streams.

---

*It is claimed that the legislature has power already over the new matter of this section relative to streams and flowage. If so, it may operate nevertheless as a limitation on its power, as well as settle the power to the extent given.

† See also section 22 of revised article II, and note to revised article XI. Property condemned for use by certain corporations is, by the construction of courts, regarded as taken for public use. The section to which this note refers is italicised as new matter for the purpose of directing attention to it, and a careful comparison of it with other sections to which reference is made, and especially with section 2 of article XVIII of the present constitution, will give a clearer understanding of it. The clause in parenthesis stands in lieu of the last clause of the last named section, which was adopted as an amendment in 1860.

SEC. 8. An accurate statement of the receipts and expendi- Art. 18, sec. 5.
tures of the public moneys shall be attached to and published
with the laws, at every regular session of the legislature.

SEC. 9. No mechanical trade shall hereafter be taught to Art 18, sec. 8.
convicts in the state prison of this State, except the manufacture of those articles of which the chief supply for home consumption is imported from other states or countries.

SEC. 10. *Any woman above the age of twenty-one years, who shall be a resident of this State, and of the proper township, city or ward, and who is a citizen of the United States, shall be eligible to the office of register of deeds, notary public, offices connected with schools and libraries, and to such other offices as may be designated by law.* *

SEC. 11. No lease or grant hereafter of agricultural land for Art. 18, sec. 12.
a longer period than twelve years, reserving any rent or service
of any kind, shall be valid.

NOTE.—Section 15 of article XVIII of the present constitution, prohibiting a general revision of the laws, is omitted from the revised article, in the belief that legislatures ought to be free to determine whether a revision or compilation of the laws is the more desirable. Sections 7, 8, 9, 10, 11, 13, and the first clause of section 14, are transferred to the Bill of Rights, as being their more appropriate place.

ARTICLE XVIII.

AMENDMENT AND REVISION OF THE CONSTITUTION.

SECTION 1. Any amendment or amendments to this consti- Art. 20, sec. 1.
tution may be proposed in the senate or house of representatives. If the same be agreed to by two-thirds of the members elected to each house, such amendment or amendments shall be entered on their journals respectively, with the yeas and nays taken thereon, and the same shall be submitted to the electors at [the next general election thereafter] *such time as the legislature shall prescribe.* And if a majority of the electors, qualified to vote for members of the legislature, voting [thereon] *on the amendment or amendments proposed,* shall
ratify and approve such amendment or amendments, the same Art. 20, sec. 2.
shall become a part of the constitution, and take effect at the
commencement of the year following its adoption.

SEC. 2. *At any time after the first day of January, one thou-* Art. 20, sec. 2.
sand eight hundred and eighty-five, the legislature may provide for a convention, to be chosen by the qualified electors of the

* This is a new section, and was believed by a majority of the commission to be in accordance with the advanced public sentiment regarding the competency of women for public positions.

State, or for a commission to be appointed by the governor by and with the advice and consent of the senate, to revise or amend this constitution. Such revised or amended constitution shall be submitted to the electors qualified to vote for members of the legislature, at such time and in such manner as said convention or commission may provide. If a majority of the electors voting on such revised or amended constitution shall decide in favor thereof, the same shall take effect at the commencement of the year following its adoption. *

SCHEDULE. †

That no inconvenience may arise from the changes in the constitution of this State, and in order to carry the same into operation, it is hereby declared:

SECTION 1. The common law, and the statute laws now in force, not repugnant to this constitution, shall remain in force until they expire by their own limitation, or are altered or repealed by the legislature.

SEC. 2. All writs, actions, causes of action, prosecutions and rights of individuals and of bodies corporate, and of the State, and all charters of incorporation, shall continue; and all indictments *and informations* which shall have been found *or filed,* or which may hereafter be found *or filed,* for any crime or offense committed before the adoption of this constitution, may be proceeded upon as if no change had taken place. The several courts, except as herein otherwise provided, shall continue with the like powers and jurisdiction, both at law and in equity, as if this constitution had not been adopted, and until the organization of the judicial department under this constitution.

---

* The corresponding section of the present constitution (sec. 2, art. XX, is as follows: "At the general election to be held in the year one thousand eight hundred and sixty-six, and in each sixteenth year thereafter, and also at such other times as the legislature may by law provide, the question of the general revision of the constitution shall be submitted to the electors qualified to vote for members of the legislature; and in case a majority of the electors so qualified voting at such election, shall decide in favor of a convention for such purpose, the legislature, at the next session, shall provide by law for the election of such delegates to such convention. All the amendments shall take effect at the commencement of the year after their adoption."

† Sections one, two, three, four, six, thirteen and fifteen, of the schedule of the present constitution, are reproduced with some verbal changes, as the seven sections of the schedule to the amended constitution. The remaining sections are omitted as inapplicable. The time and manner of submitting the amended constitution to the people are left to be fixed by the legislature.

SEC. 3. All fines, penalties, forfeitures and escheats accruing to the State under the present constitution and laws, shall accrue to the use of the State under this constitution.

SEC. 4. All recognizances, bonds, obligations, and all other instruments entered into or executed before the adoption of this constitution, to the people of [the State of Michigan] *this State*, or to any [State] county or township, or to any public officer or public body, or which may be entered into or executed under existing laws, to the people of [the State of Michigan] *this State or* to any such officer or public body, before the complete organization of the departments of government under this constitution, shall remain binding and valid, and rights and liabilities upon the same shall continue, and may be prosecuted as provided by law. And all crimes and misdemeanors and penal actions shall be prosecuted, tried and punished as though no change had taken place, until otherwise provided by law.

SEC. 5. All officers, civil and military, now holding any office or appointment, shall continue to hold their respective offices, unless removed by competent authority, until superseded under the laws now in force, or under this constitution.

SEC. 6. It shall be the duty of the legislature, at its first session *after the adoption of this constitution*, to adapt the present laws to the provisions of this constitution [so far as may be].

SEC. 7. Any territory attached, *or that may be attached* to any county for judicial purposes, if not otherwise represented, shall be considered as forming a part of such county, so far as regards elections for the purpose of representation.

TAXATION OF THE LIQUOR TRAFFIC.*

At the election when this amended constitution shall be submitted to the electors of this State for adoption or rejection, there shall be submitted to such electors the following proposition, to be added, in case of its adoption, to section 47 of article IV in the present constitution of this State, as it now stands, and to section 36 of article IV in said amended constitution, if the latter is adopted, viz.:

---

* It was felt by the commission that there was a general demand for some proposition relative to the traffic in ardent spirits, upon which a popular expression might be had. While there was much difference of opinion with the commission as to the form in which such proposition should be submitted, the one here proposed was agreed upon as most likely to receive the careful and earnest attention of the people of the State interested in the subject.

An annual tax of two hundred dollars is imposed upon the traffic in intoxicating liquors, to be paid by every person or firm who shall carry on or be engaged in the business of selling or disposing of such liquors otherwise than for medicinal, chemical and mechanical purposes, for each place where such business is carried on by such person or firm. Said tax shall be paid into the treasury of the proper township, city or village, and be applied by the proper authorities to the support of the poor therein, so far as may be necessary, and the residue appropriated as the legislature shall provide. The sale or other disposition of such liquors to minors, persons under guardianship, insane and idiotic persons, paupers and common drunkards, is wholly prohibited. Every person who shall carry on or engage in the business or traffic taxed as aforesaid in this section, without having first paid the tax imposed, or otherwise violate any provision of this section, shall be guilty of a misdemeanor, and, on conviction, be punished by fine or imprisonment, or both, as may be prescribed by law, and every sale until the tax is paid shall subject the party to such penalty; and all necessary laws shall be passed to enforce the provisions of this section. The legislature may further regulate and restrict the sale and other disposition of intoxicating liquors; and may increase the annual tax upon said traffic in any locality.

Said proposition shall be separately submitted to the electors of this State for their adoption or rejection, in form following, to wit: A separate ballot may be given by every person having the right to vote, to be deposited in a separate box. Upon the ballots given for said proposition, shall be written, printed, or partly written or partly printed, the words, "Restriction and taxation of the liquor traffic—Yes;" and upon the ballots given against the adoption thereof, in like manner, the words, "Restriction and taxation of the liquor traffic—No."

If at said election a majority of the votes given upon said proposition shall contain the words "Restriction and taxation of the liquor traffic—Yes," then said proposition shall be added to section 47 in article IV of the present constitution, and to section 36 in article IV of said amended constitution, if the latter is adopted.

THE

PRESENT CONSTITUTION

OF MICHIGAN.

[Those portions of the present constitution in which changes are recommended are repeated entire, with marginal references to the amended constitution. Those portions that are unchanged are omitted, but references are added, showing the position in which they are placed in the amended constitution.]

The People of the State of Michigan do ordain this Constitution.

ARTICLE I.

BOUNDARIES.

[This article is unchanged with the exception of the italics, as shown in the corresponding article of the amended constitution.]

ARTICLE II.

SEAT OF GOVERNMENT.

SECTION 1. The seat of government shall be in Lansing, where it is now established. Art. 1, sec. 2.

ARTICLE III.

DIVISION OF THE POWERS OF GOVERNMENT.

[There is but a slight verbal change in this article, for which reference is had to article III of the amended constitution.]

ARTICLE IV.

LEGISLATIVE DEPARTMENT.

SECTION 1. The legislative power is vested in a senate and house of representatives. Art. 4, sec. 1.

SEC. 2. The senate shall consist of thirty-two members. Senators shall be elected for two years, and by single districts. Such districts shall be numbered from one to thirty-two inclusive; each of which shall choose one senator. No county shall be divided in the formation of senate districts, except such county shall be equitably entitled to two or more senators. Art. 4, sec. 2.

SEC. 3. The house of representatives shall consist of not less than sixty-four, nor more than one hundred members. Representatives shall Art. 4, sec. 3.

be chosen for two years, and by single districts. Each representative district shall contain, as nearly as may be, an equal number of inhabitants, exclusive of persons of Indian descent who are not civilized, or are members of any tribe, and shall consist of convenient and contiguous territory. [But no township or city shall be divided in the formation of a representative district. When any township or city shall contain a population which entitles it to more than one representative, then such township or city shall elect by general ticket the number of representatives to which it is entitled. Each county hereafter organized, with such territory as may be attached thereto, shall be entitled to a separate representative when it has attained a population equal to a moiety of the ratio of representation.]* In every county entitled to more than one representative, the board of supervisors shall assemble at such time and place as the legislature shall prescribe, and divide the same into representative districts, equal to the number of representatives to which such county is entitled by law, and shall cause to be filed in the office of the secretary of state and clerk of such county, a description of such representative districts, specifying the number of each district, and the population thereof, according to the last preceding enumeration.

Art. 4, sec. 4. SEC. 4. The legislature shall provide by law for an enumeration of the inhabitants in the year eighteen hundred and fifty-four, and every ten years thereafter; and at the first session after each enumeration so made, and also at the first session after each enumeration by the authority of the United States, the legislature shall re-arrange the senate districts, and apportion anew the representatives among the counties and districts, according to the number of inhabitants exclusive of persons of Indian descent who are not civilized, or are members of any tribe.† Each apportionment, and the division into representative districts by any board of supervisors, shall remain unaltered until the return of another enumeration.

Art. 4, sec. 5. SEC. 5. Senators and representatives shall be citizens of the United States, and qualified electors in the respective counties and districts which they represent. A removal from their respective counties or districts shall be deemed a vacation of their office.

Art. 4, sec. 6. SEC. 6. No person holding any office under the United States [or this State,] or any county office, except notaries public, officers of the militia, and officers elected by townships, shall be eligible to or have a seat in either house of the legislature, and all votes given for any such person shall be void.

Art. 4, sec. 7. SEC. 7. Senators and representatives shall in all cases, except treason, felony, or breach of the peace, be privileged from arrest. They shall not be subject to any civil process during the session of the legislature, or for fifteen days next before the commencement and after the termination of each session; they shall not be questioned in any other place for any speech in either house.

SEC. 8. [Unchanged. See corresponding section of amended article.]

Art. 4, sec. 9. SEC. 9. Each house shall choose its own officers, determine the rules of its proceedings, and judge of the qualifications, elections and returns of its members, and may, with the concurrence of two-thirds of all the members elected, expel a member. No member shall be expelled a second time for the same cause; nor for any cause known to his constituents antecedent to his election; the reason for such expulsion shall be entered upon the journal, with the names of the members voting on the question.

---

* The words in brackets are omitted from the amended section. See note, foot of page 6.

† The corresponding section of amended article IV has a new provision, that "no re-arrangement of senate districts shall vacate the seat of any senator," which should have been designated by italics.

SEC. 10. [The only change in this section is the substitution of the word "taken" for the words "entered on the journal at," in the second clause. See corresponding section of amended article IV.]

SEC. 11. [Unchanged—see corresponding section of amended article.]

SEC. 12. [Unchanged—see corresponding section.]

SEC. 13. Bills may originate in either house of the legislature. Art. 4, sec. 13.

SEC. 14. Every bill and concurrent resolution, except of adjournment, passed by the legislature, shall be presented to the governor before it becomes a law. Art. 4, sec. 14. If he approve, he shall sign it; but if not, he shall return it with his objections to the house in which it originated, which shall enter the objections at large upon their journal, and reconsider it. On such reconsideration, if two-thirds of the members elected agree to pass the bill, it shall be sent with the objections to the other house, by which it shall be reconsidered. If approved by two-thirds of the members elected to that house, it shall become a law. In such case the vote of both houses shall be determined by yeas and nays; and the names of the members voting for and against the bill shall be entered on the journals of each house respectively. If any bill be not returned by the governor within ten days, Sundays excepted, after it has been presented to him, the same shall become a law in like manner as if he had signed it, unless the legislature, by their adjournment, prevent its return; in which case it shall not become a law. The governor may approve, sign and file in the office of the secretary of state, within five days after the adjournment of the legislature, any act passed during the last five days of the session; and the same shall become a law.

SEC. 15. The compensation of members of the legislature shall be three dollars a day for actual attendance, and when absent on account of sickness. Art. 4, sec. 15. [But the legislature may allow extra compensation to members from the territory of the upper peninsula, not exceeding two dollars per day during the session. When convened in extra session, their compensation shall be three dollars a day for the first twenty days, and nothing thereafter;] * and they shall legislate on no other subject than those expressly stated in the governor's proclamation, or submitted to them by special message. They shall be entitled to ten cents, and no more, for every mile actually traveled going to and returning from the place of meeting, on the usually traveled route; and for stationery and newspapers not exceeding five dollars for each member during any session. Each member shall be entitled to one copy of the laws, journals and documents of the legislature of which he was a member; but shall not receive, at the expense of the State, books, newspapers, or other perquisites of office not expressly authorized by this constitution.

SEC. 16. The legislature may provide by law for the payment of postage on all mailable matter received by its members and officers during the sessions of the legislature, but not on any sent or mailed by them. See note to art. 4, p. 18.

SEC. 17. [Unchanged—stands as section 16 of amended article.]

[Section 18 stands as section 17 of the amended article, and is unchanged except as shown by italics and brackets.]

SEC. 19. Every bill and joint resolution shall be read three times in each house before the final passage thereof. Art. 4, sec. 18. No bill or joint resolution shall become a law without the concurrence of the majority of all the members elected to each house. On the final passage of all bills the vote shall be by ayes and nays, and entered on the journal.

SEC. 20. No law shall embrace more than one object, which shall be expressed in its title. Art. 4, sec. 19. No public act shall take effect or be in force until the expiration of ninety days from the end of the session at which the

---

* The clause in brackets is omitted from the amended article. The succeeding clause is embodied in section 13 of amended article IV.

same is passed, unless the legislature shall otherwise direct, by a two-thirds vote of the members elected to each house.

SEC. 21. [Unchanged—same as sec. 20 of amended article.]

[Section 22 stands as section 21 of the amended article, and is unchanged except by the addition of the words in italics.]

Art. 4, sec. 22. SEC. 23. The legislature shall not authorize, by private or special law, the sale or conveyance of any real estate belonging to any person; nor vacate nor alter any road laid out by commissioners of highways, or any street in any city or village, or in any recorded town plat.

SEC. 24. [Unchanged—same as corresponding section of amended article.]

Art. 4, sec. 19. SEC. 25. No law shall be revised, altered or amended, by reference to its title only; but the act revised, and the section or sections of the act altered or amended, shall be re-enacted and published at length.

Art. 4, sec. 22. SEC. 26. Divorces shall not be granted by the legislature.

SEC. 27. [Unchanged—same as sec. 33 of amended article.]

Art. 4, sec. 13. SEC. 28. No new bill shall be introduced into either house of the legislature after the first fifty days of the session shall have expired.

Note to art. 4, p. 13. SEC. 29. In case of a contested election, the person only shall receive from the state per diem compensation and mileage, who is declared to be entitled to a seat by the house in which the contest takes place.

[Sections 30, 31 and 32 are unchanged, and stand as sections 25, 26 and 28 of amended article IV.]

[Sections 33 and 34 stand as sections 27 and 29 of amended article IV, and are unchanged except in naming the years, as shown by those sections.]

Art. 4, sec. 23, and note, p. 13. SEC. 35. The legislature shall not establish a state paper. [Every newspaper in the state which shall publish all the general laws of any session within forty days of their passage, shall be entitled to receive a sum not exceeding fifteen dollars therefor.]*

[Sections 36, 37 and 38 are unchanged, and stand as sections 30, 31 and 32 of amended article IV.]

Art 2, sec. 2. SEC. 39. The legislature shall pass no law to prevent any person from worshiping Almighty God according to the dictates of his own conscience; or to compel any person to attend, erect or support any place of religious worship, or to pay tithes, taxes or other rates for the support of any minister of the gospel or teacher of religion.

Art. 4, sec. 34. SEC. 40. No money shall be appropriated or drawn from the treasury for the benefit of any religious sect or society, theological or religious seminary; nor shall property belonging to the state be appropriated for any such purposes.

Art. 2, sec. 3. SEC. 41. The legislature shall not diminish or enlarge the civil or political rights, privileges and capacities of any person on account of his opinions or belief concerning matters of religion.

Art. 2, sec. 4. SEC. 42. No law shall be passed to restrain or abridge the liberty of speech or of the press; but every person may freely speak, write and publish his sentiments on all subjects, being responsible for the abuse of such right.

Art. 2, sec. 5. SEC. 43. The legislature shall bass no bill of attainder, *ex post facto* law, or law impairing the obligation of contracts.

Art. 2, sec. 6. SEC. 44. The privilege of the writ of *habeas corpus* remains, and shall not be suspended by the legislature except in case of rebellion or invasion the public safety require it.

SEC. 45. [Unchanged—stands as sec. 35 of amended article IV.]

Art. 2, sec. 7. SEC. 46. The legislature may authorize a trial by jury of a less number than twelve men.

---

* See note to amended article IV, page 13.

SEC. 47. The legislature shall not pass any act authorizing the grant of license for the sale of ardent spirits or other intoxicating liquors.

SEC. 48. The style of the laws shall be: "The people of the State of Michigan enact."*

ARTICLE V.

EXECUTIVE DEPARTMENT.

[The changes proposed to this article are so immaterial, and are so fully set forth by italics and brackets in amended article V. (see page 13) that the repetition of any portion of the article here is deemed unnecessary.]

ARTICLE VI.

JUDICIAL DEPARTMENT.

SECTION 1. The judicial power is vested in one supreme court, in circuit courts, in probate courts, and in justices of the peace. [Municipal courts of civil and criminal jurisdiction may be established by the legislature in cities.]† Art. 6, sec. 1.

SEC. 2. For the term of six years, and thereafter, until the legislature otherwise provide, the judges of the several circuit courts shall be judges of the supreme court, four of whom shall constitute a quorum. A concurrence of three shall be necessary to a final decision. After six years, the legislature may provide by law for the organization of a supreme court, with the jurisdiction and powers prescribed in this constitution, to consist of one chief justice and three associate justices, to be chosen by the electors of the state. Such supreme court, when so organized, shall not be changed or discontinued by the legislature for eight years thereafter. The judges thereof shall be so classified that but one of them shall go out of office at the same time. Their term of office shall be eight years. Art. 6, sec. 2.

SEC. 3. The supreme court shall have a general superintending control over all inferior courts, and shall have power to issue writs of error, *habeas corpus*, *mandamus*, *quo warranto*, *procedendo*, and other original and remedial writs, and to hear and determine the same. In all other cases it shall have appellate jurisdiction only. Art. 6, sec. 3.

SEC. 4. [Unchanged—same as corresponding section of amended article VI.]

SEC. 5. The supreme court shall, by general rules, establish, modify and amend the practice in such court and in the circuit courts, and simplify the same. [The legislature shall, as far as practicable, abolish distinctions between law and equity proceedings. The office of master in chancery is prohibited.]‡ Art. 6, sec. 5.

SEC. 6. The state shall be divided into eight judicial circuits; in each of which the electors thereof shall elect one circuit judge, who shall hold his office for the term of six years and until his successor is elected and qualified. Art. 6, sec. 6

SEC. 7. The legislature may alter the limits of circuits, or increase the number of the same. No alteration or increase shall have the effect to remove the judge from office. In every additional circuit established, Art. 6, sec. 6.

---

* The two last sections are unchanged, and stand as sections 36 and 37 of amended article IV. For proposed addition to the section relating to the sale of liquors, see separate submission clause, page 41.

† Omitted from the amended article.

‡ Omitted from the amended article.

the judge shall be elected by the electors of such circuit, and his term of office shall continue as provided in this constitution for judges of the circuit court.

Art. 6, sec. 8. SEC. 8. The circuit courts shall have original jurisdiction in all matters, civil and criminal, not excepted in this constitution, and not prohibited by law; and appellate jurisdiction from all inferior courts and tribunals, and a supervisory control of the same. They shall also have power to issue writs of *habeas corpus*, *mandamus*, injunction, *quo warranto*, *certiorari*, and other writs necessary to carry into effect their orders, judgments, and decrees, and give them a general control over inferior courts and tribunals within their respective jurisdictions.

Art. 6, sec. 13. SEC. 9. Each of the judges of the circuit courts shall receive a salary, payable quarterly. They shall be ineligible to any other than a judicial office during the term for which they are elected, and for one year thereafter. All votes for any person elected such judge, for any office other than judicial, given either by the legislature or the people, shall be void.

Art. 6, sec. 5. SEC. 10. The supreme court may appoint a reporter of its decisions. [The decisions of the supreme court shall be in writing, and signed by the judges concurring therein. Any judge dissenting therefrom shall give the reasons of such dissent in writing, under his signature. All such opinions shall be filed in the office of the clerk of the supreme court.]* Art. 6, sec. 18. The judges of the circuit court, within their respective jurisdictions, may fill vacancies in the office of county clerk and of prosecuting attorney; [but no judge of the supreme court or circuit court shall exercise any other power of appointment to public office.]*

Art. 6, sec. 7. SEC. 11. A circuit court shall be held at least twice in each year in every county organized for judicial purposes, and four times in each year in counties containing ten thousand inhabitants. Judges of the circuit court may hold courts for each other, and shall do so when required by law.

Art. 6, sec. 12. SEC. 12. The clerk of each county organized for judicial purposes shall be the clerk of the circuit court of such county, and of the supreme court when held within the same.

Art. 6, sec. 14. SEC. 13. In each of the counties organized for judicial purposes, there shall be a court of probate. The judge of such court shall be elected by the electors of the county in which he resides, and shall hold his office for four years, and until his successor is elected and qualified. The jurisdiction, powers and duties of such court shall be prescribed by law.

Art. 6, sec. 11. SEC. 14. When a vacancy occurs in the office of judge of the supreme, circuit or probate court, it shall be filled by appointment of the governor, which shall continue until a successor is elected and qualified. When elected, such successor shall hold his office the residue of the unexpired term.

Art. 6, sec. 15. SEC. 15. The supreme court, the circuit and probate courts of each county, shall be courts of record, and shall each have a common seal.

Art. 6, sec. 9. SEC. 16. The legislature may provide by law for the election of one or more persons in each organized county, who may be vested with judicial powers, not exceeding those of a judge of a circuit court at chambers.

Art. 6, sec. 10. SEC. 17. There shall be not exceeding four justices of the peace in each organized township. These shall be elected by the electors of the township, and shall hold their offices for four years, and until their successors are elected and qualified. At the first election in any township, they shall be classified as shall be prescribed by law. A justice elected

* The clauses in brackets are omitted from the amended article.

to fill a vacancy shall hold his office for the residue of the unexpired term. [The legislature may increase the number of justices in cities.] *

[Sections 18 and 19 stand as sections 17 and 18 of amended article VI, and are unchanged.]

SEC. 20. The first election of judges of the circuit court shall be held on the first Monday in April, one thousand eight hundred and fifty-one, and every sixth year thereafter. Whenever an additional circuit is created, provision shall be made to hold the subsequent election of such additional judges at the regular elections herein provided.†

SEC. 21. The first election of judges of the probate courts shall be held on the Tuesday succeeding the first Monday of November, one thousand eight hundred and fifty-two, and every fourth year thereafter.*

SEC. 22. [Slight change in phraseology. Stands as sec. 10 of amended article.]

SEC. 23. The legislature may establish courts of conciliation, with such powers and duties as shall be prescribed by law.†

SEC. 24. Any suitor in any court in this State shall have the right to Art. 2, sec. 9.
prosecute or defend his suit, either in his own proper person, or by an attorney or agent of his choice.

SEC. 25. In all prosecutions for libels, the truth may be given in evi- Art. 2, sec. 4.
dence to the jury; and if it shall appear to the jury that the matter charged as libelous is true, and was published with good motives and for justifiable ends, the party shall be acquitted. The jury shall have the right to determine the law and the fact.

SEC. 26. The persons, houses, papers and possessions of every person Art. 2, sec.
shall be secure from unreasonable searches and seizures. No warrant to 10.
search any place, or to seize any person or things, shall issue without describing them, nor without probable cause supported by oath or affirmation.

SEC. 27. The right of trial by jury shall remain, but shall be deemed Art. 2, sec. 7.
to be waived in all civil cases, unless demanded by one of the parties in such manner as shall be prescribed by law.

SEC. 28. In every criminal prosecution the accused shall have the Art. 2, sec. 8.
right to a speedy and public trial by an impartial jury, which may consist of less than twelve men in all courts not of record; to be informed of the nature of the accusation; to be confronted with witnesses against him; to have compulsory process for obtaining witnesses in his favor, and have the assistance of counsel for his defense.

[Sections 29, 30 and 31 stand as sections 11, 12, and 13 of amended article II, and are unchanged.]

SEC. 32. No person shall be compelled, in any criminal case, to be a Art. 2, sec.
witness against himself, nor be deprived of life, liberty or property, 14.
without due process of law.

SEC. 33. No person shall be imprisoned for debt arising out of or Art. 2, sec.
founded on a contract, expressed or implied, except in case of fraud or 15.
breach of trust, or of moneys collected by public officers, or in any professional employment. No person shall be imprisoned for a militia fine in time of peace.

SEC. 34. No person shall be rendered incompetent to be a witness on Art. 2, sec.
account of his opinions in matters of religious belief. 3.

SEC. 35. The style of all process shall be: "In the name of the Art. 6, sec.
people of the State of Michigan." [Unchanged.] 19.

---

* Clause in brackets omitted from the revision. See note to sec. 16, amended article VI.

† These sections are all omitted from the amended article as irrelevant and unnecessary. As to sec. 23, see note, foot page 15.

ARTICLE VII.

ELECTIONS.

Art. 7, sec. 1. SECTION 1. In all elections, every male citizen, every male inhabitant residing in the state on the twenty-fourth day of June, one thousand eight hundred and thirty-five; every male inhabitant residing in the state on the first day of January, one thousand eight hundred and fifty, who has declared his intention to become a citizen of the United States, pursuant to the laws thereof, six months preceding an election, or who has resided in this state two years and six months, and declared his intention as aforesaid, and every civilized male inhabitant of Indian descent, a native of the United States and not a member of any tribe, shall be an elector and entitled to vote; but no citizen or inhabitant shall be an elector, or entitled to vote at any election unless he shall be above the age of twenty-one years, and has resided in this state three months, and in the township or ward in which he offers to vote, ten
Art. 7, sec. 2. days next preceding such election: *Provided,* That in time of war, insurrection or rebellion, no qualified elector in the actual military service of the United States, or of this state, in the army or navy thereof, shall be deprived of his vote by reason of his absence from the township, ward or state in which he resides; and the legislature shall have the power, and shall provide the manner in which, and the time and place at which, such absent electors may vote, and for the canvass and return of their votes to the township or ward election district in which they respectively reside, or otherwise.

[Sections 2, 3, 4 and 5 stand as sections 3, 4 and 5 of the amended article (sections 3 and 4 being combined in section 4 of amended article) and are unchanged except as shown in the usual manner. Sections 6 and 7 stand as the corresponding sections of the amended article, and are unchanged. Section 8 is unchanged except in phraseology.]

ARTICLE VIII.

STATE OFFICERS.

Art. 8, sec. 1. SECTION 1. There shall be elected at each general biennial election, a secretary of state, a superintendent of public instruction, a state treasurer, a commissioner of the land office, an auditor general, and an attorney general, for the term of two years. They shall keep their office at the seat of government, and shall perform such duties as may be prescribed by law.

Art. 8, sec. 2. SEC. 2. Their term of office shall commence on the first day of January, one thousand eight hundred and fifty-three, and of every second year thereafter.

[The remaining three sections of this article stand as sections 4, 5, and 6, of amended article VIII, and are unchanged.]

ARTICLE IX.

SALARIES.

Art. 9, secs. 1 and 2. SECTION 1. The governor shall receive an annual salary of one thousand dollars; the judges of the circuit court shall each receive an annual salary of one thousand five hundred dollars; the state treasurer shall receive an annual salary of one thousand dollars; the auditor general shall receive an annual salary of one thousand dollars; the superintendent of public instruction shall receive an annual salary of one thousand dollars; the secretary of state shall receive an annual salary of eight hundred dollars; the commissioner of the land office shall receive an annual salary of eight hundred dollars; the attorney general shall receive an annual salary of eight hundred dollars. They shall receive no fees or perquisites whatever, for the performance of any duties connected with their office. It shall not be competent for the legislature to increase the salaries herein provided.

ARTICLE X.

COUNTIES.

SECTION 1. Each organized county shall be a body corporate, with such powers and immunities as shall be established by law. All suits and proceedings by or against a county shall be in the name thereof. Art. 10, sec. 2.

[Sections 2, 3, 4, 5, 6, 7 and 8 stand as sections 4, 5 6, 7, 8 and 9 of amended article X, (sections 6 and 7 being combined in section 8 of amended article) and are unchanged except as shown in the usual manner.]

SEC. 9. The board of supervisors of any county may borrow or raise by tax one thousand dollars, for constructing or repairing public buildings, highways or bridges; but no greater sum shall be borrowed or raised by tax for such purpose in any one year, unless authorized by a majority of the electors of such county voting thereon. Art. 10, sec. 3.

SEC. 10. The board of supervisors, or in the county of Wayne the board of county auditors, shall have the exclusive power to prescribe and fix the compensation for all services rendered for, and to adjust all claims against their respective counties; and the sum so fixed or defined shall be subject to no appeal. Art 10, sec. 10.

SEC. 11. [Unchanged—stands as corresponding section of amended article.]

ARTICLE XI.

TOWNSHIPS.

[The only changes in this article are shown in sections 12 and 13 of amended article X, and note.]

ARTICLE XII.

IMPEACHMENTS AND REMOVALS FROM OFFICE.

[The sections of this article, to and including section four, stand as the corresponding sections of the amended article. Section five stands as section nine, and sections six, seven and eight as sections five, six and seven of the amended article. The changes are so fully set forth by italics and brackets, that a repetition of any portion of the article is deemed unnecessary. Section seven (section six of amended article) is changed in phraseology.]

ARTICLE XIII.

EDUCATION.

SECTION 1. The superintendent of public instruction shall have the general supervision of public instruction, and his duties shall be prescribed by law. Art. 13, sec. 1.

SEC. 2. [Unchanged—stands as sec. 8 of amended article.]

Art. 13, sec. 9. SEC. 3. All lands, the titles of which shall fail from a defect of heirs, shall escheat to the state; and the interest on the clear proceeds from the sales thereof shall be appropriated exclusively to the support of primary schools.

Art, 13, sec. 6 SEC. 4. The legislature shall, within five years from the adoption of this constitution, provide for and establish a system of primary schools, whereby a school shall be kept without charge for tuition, at least three months in each year, in every school district in the state; and all instruction in said schools shall be conducted in the English language.

Art. 13. sec. 7. SEC. 5. A school shall be maintained in each school district, at least three months in each year. Any school district neglecting to maintain such school shall be deprived for the ensuing year of its proportion of the income of the primary school fund, and of all funds arising from taxes for the support of schools.

Art 13, sec. 2. SEC. 6. There shall be elected in the year eighteen hundred and sixty-three, at the time of the election of a justice of the supreme court, eight regents of the university, two of whom shall hold their office for two years, two for four years, two for six years, and two for eight years. They shall enter upon the duties of their office on the first of January next succeeding their election. At every regular election of a justice of the supreme court thereafter, there shall be elected two regents, whose term of office shall be eight years. When a vacancy shall occur in the office of regent, it shall be filled by appointment of the Governor. The regents thus elected shall constitute the board of regents of the university of Michigan.

Art 13, sec. 2. SEC. 7. The regents of the university and their successors in office shall continue to constitute the body corporate known by the name and title of "The Regents of the University of Michigan."

Art. 13, sec. 2. SEC. 8. The regents of the university shall, at their first annual meeting, or as soon thereafter as may be, elect a president of the university, who shall be *ex-officio* a member of their board, with the privilege of speaking but not of voting. He shall preside at the meetings of the regents, and be the principal executive officer of the university. The board of regents shall have the general supervision of the university, and the direction and control of all expenditures from the university interest fund.

Art. 13, sec. 8. SEC. 9. There shall be elected at the general election in the year one thousand eight hundred and fifty-two, three members of a state board of education; one for two years, one for four years, and one for six years; and at each succeeding biennial election there shall be elected one member of such board, who shall hold his office for six years. The superintendent of public instruction shall be *ex-officio* a member and secretary of such board. The board shall have the general supervision of the state normal school, and their duties shall be prescribed by law.

Art. 13, sec. 11. SEC. 10. Institutions for the benefit of those inhabitants who are deaf, dumb, blind or insane, shall always be fostered and supported.

Omitted—see note to amended article 13. SEC. 11. The legislature shall encourage the promotion of intellectual, scientific and agricultural improvement; and shall, as soon as practicable, provide for the establishment of an agricultural school. The legislature may appropriate the twenty-two sections of salt-spring lands now unappropriated, or the money arising from the sale of the same, where such lands have been already sold, and any land which may hereafter be granted or appropriated for such purpose, for the support and maintenance of such school, and may make the same a branch of the university, for instruction in agriculture and the natural sciences connected therewith, and place the same under the supervision of the regents of the university.

Art 13, sec. 10. SEC. 12. The legislature shall also provide for the establishment of at least one library in each township; and all fines assessed and collected in the several counties for any breach of the penal laws shall be exclusively applied to the support of such libraries.

ARTICLE XIV.

FINANCE AND TAXATION.

SECTION 1. All specific state taxes, except those received from the Art. 14, sec.
mining companies of the upper peninsula, shall be applied in paying 2.
the interest upon the primary school, university, and other educational funds, and the interest and principal of the state debt, in the order herein recited, until the extinguishment of the state debt, other than the amounts due to educational funds, when such specific taxes shall be added to, and constitute a part of the primary school interest fund. The leg- Art. 14, sec.
islature shall provide for an annual tax, sufficient, with other resources, 3.
to pay the estimated expenses of the state government, the interest of the state debt, and such deficiency as may occur in the resources.

SEC. 2. The legislatnre shall provide by law a sinking fund of at least Art. 14, sec.
twenty thousand dollars a year, to commence in eighteen hundred and 4.
fifty-two, with compound interest at the rate of six per cent per annum, and an annual increase of at least five per cent, to be applied solely to the payment and extinguishment of the principal of the state debt, other than the amounts due to educational funds, and shall be continued until the extinguishment thereof. The unfunded debt shall not be Art. 14, sec.
funded or redeemed at a value exceeding that established by law in one 5.
thousand eight hundred and forty-eight.

[Sections 3 and 4 stand as sections 6 and 7 of amended article XIV, and are unchanged except by the addition of the words in italics in the last named section.]

SEC. 5. No money shall be paid out of the treasury except in pursu- Art. 14, sec.
ance of appropriations made by law. 8.

SEC. 6. The credit of the state shall not be granted to or in aid of any Art. 14, sec.
person, association or corporation. 9.

SEC. 7. [Unchanged—stands as section 10 of amended article.]

SEC. 8. The state shall not subscribe to or be interested in the stock Art. 14, sec.
of any company, association or corporation. 9.

SEC. 9. The state shall not be a party to or interested in any work of Art. 14, sec.
internal improvement, nor engaged in carrying on any such work, 11.
except in the expenditure of grants to the state of land or other property.

SEC. 10. The state may continue to collect all specific taxes accruing Art. 14, sec.
to the treasury under existing laws. The legislature may provide for 1.
the collection of specific taxes from banking, railroad, plank road and other corporations hereafter created.

SEC. 11. The legislature shall provide an uniform rule of taxation, Art. 14, sec.
except on property paying specific taxes; and taxes shall be levied on 12.
such property as shall be prescribed by law.

[Sections 12, 13 and 14 stand as sections 13, 14 and 15 of the amended article, and are unchanged.]

ARTICLE XV.

CORPORATIONS.

SECTION 1. Corporations may be formed under general laws, but shall Art. 11, sec.
not be created by special act, except for municipal purposes. All laws 1.
passed pursuant to this section may be amended, altered or repealed.

[But the legislature may, by a vote of two-thirds of the members elected to each house, create a single bank with branches.]*

[Sections 2 and 3 stand as the corresponding sections of amended article XI, and are unchanged except by the omission of the words in brackets in section 3.]

Art. 11, sec. 4. SEC. 4. For all banks organized under general laws, the legislature shall provide for the registry of all bills or notes issued or put in circulation as money, and shall require security to the full amount of notes and bills so registered, in state or United States stocks, bearing interest, which shall be deposited with the state treasurer for the redemption of such bills or notes in specie.

[Sections 5 and 6 stand as the corresponding sections of amended article XI, and are unchanged except by the omission of the words in brackets in section 6.]

Art. 11, sec. 7. SEC. 7. The stockholders of all corporations and joint stock associations shall be individually liable for all labor performed for such corporation or association.

See clause in italics, art. 11, sec. 1. SEC. 8. The legislature shall pass no law altering or amending any act of incorporation heretofore granted, without the assent of two-thirds of the members elected to each house; nor shall any such act be renewed or extended. This restriction shall not apply to municipal corporations.

See note to art. 11, p. 29. SEC. 9. The property of no person shall be taken by any corporation for public use, without compensation being first made or secured, in such manner as may be prescribed by law.

Art. 11. sec. 12. SEC. 10. No corporation, except for municipal purposes, or for the construction of railroads, plank roads and canals, shall be created for a longer term than thirty years.

[Section 11 stands as section 13 of amended article XI, and is unchanged except as shown by the note to that section.]

Art. 11, sec. 8. SEC. 12. No corporation shall hold any real estate hereafter acquired for a longer period than ten years, except such real estate as shall be actually occupied by such corporation in the exercise of its franchises.

Art. 10, sec. 14. SEC. 13. The legislature shall provide for the incorporation and organization of cities and villages, and shall restrict their powers of taxation, borrowing money, contracting debts and loaning their credit.

Art. 10, sec. 16. SEC. 14. Judicial officers of cities and villages shall be elected, and all other officers shall be elected or appointed at such time and in such manner as the legislature may direct.

Art. 17, sec. 5. SEC. 15. Private property shall not be taken for public improvements in cities and villages without the consent of the owner, unless the compensation therefor shall first be determined by a jury of freeholders, and actually paid or secured in the manner provided by law.

Omitted from revision. SEC. 16. Previous notice of any application for an alteration of the charter of any corporation shall be given in such manner as may be prescribed by law.

ARTICLE XVI.

EXEMPTIONS.

[Sections 1 and 2 of this article are made the corresponding sections of amended article XV. The only changes are in section 2, which are fully set forth by italics and brackets, and explained in note.]

Art. 15, sec. 3. SEC. 3. The homestead of a family, after the death of the owner thereof, shall be exempt from the payment of his debts, contracted after the adoption of this constitution, in all cases, during the minority of his children.

---

* Words in brackets omitted from amended article.

SEC. 4. If the owner of a homestead die, leaving a widow, but no children, the same shall be exempt, and the rents and profits thereof shall accrue to her benefit during the time of her widowhood, unless she be the owner of a homestead in her own right. Art. 15, sec 3.

SEC. 5. The real and personal estate of every female, acquired before marriage, and all property to which she may afterwards become entitled by gift, grant, inheritance or devise, shall be and remain the estate and property of such female, and shall not be liable for the debts, obligations or engagements of her husband, and may be devised or bequeathed by her as if she were unmarried. Art. 15, sec 4.

ARTICLE XVII.

MILITIA.

[This article stands as article XVI of the amended constitution, and is unchanged.]

ARTICLE XVIII.

MISCELLANEOUS PROVISIONS.

SECTION 1. Members of the legislature, and all officers, executive and judicial, except such officers as may by law be exempted, shall, before they enter on the duties of their respective offices, take and subscribe the following oath or affirmation: "I do solemnly swear (or affirm) that I will support the constitution of the United States, and the constitution of this state, and that I will faithfully discharge the duties of the office of ——— according to the best of my ability." [And no other oath, declaration or test shall be required as a qualification for any office of public trust.]* Art. 17, sec. 1.

SEC. 2. When private property is taken for the use or benefit of the public, the necessity for using such property and the just compensation to be made therefor, except when to be made by the state, shall be ascertained by a jury of twelve freeholders, residing in the vicinity of such property, or by not less than three commissioners, appointed by a court of record, as shall be prescribed by law: *Provided*, The foregoing provision shall in no case be construed to apply to the action of commissioners of the highways in the official discharge of their duties as highway commissioners. Art. 17, sec. 5.

SEC. 3. [Unchanged—stands as sec. 9 of amended article XVII.]

[Sections 3, 4 and 5 stand respectively as sections 9, 7 and 8 of amended article XVII, and are unchanged.]

SEC. 6. The laws, public records, and the written, judicial and legislative proceedings of the state shall be conducted, promulgated and preserved in the English language. Art. 17, sec. 2.

[Sections 7, 8, 9, 10, 11 and 13 stand as sections 16 to 21 inclusive, of amended article II. All changes are noted in the usual way.]

SEC. 12. No lease or grant hereafter, of agricultural land, for a longer period than twelve years, reserving any rent or service of any kind, shall be valid. Art. 17, sec. 11.

SEC. 14. The property of no person shall be taken for public use without just compensation therefor. Private roads may be opened in the manner to be prescribed by law; but in every case the necessities of the road, and the amount of all damages to be sustained by the opening thereof, shall be first determined by a jury of freeholders, and such Art. 17, sec. 5.

---

* Clause omitted from the revision.

amount, together with the expenses of proceeding, shall be paid by the person or persons to be benefited.

Omitted—see note to amended art. 17. SEC. 15. No general revision of the laws shall hereafter be made. When a reprint thereof becomes necessary, the legislature, in joint convention shall appoint a suitable person to collect together such acts and parts of acts as are in force, and without alteration arrange them under appropriate heads and titles. The laws so arranged shall be submitted to two commissioners appointed by the governor, for examination, and if certified by them to be a correct compilation of all general laws in force, shall be printed in such manner as shall be prescribed by law.

ARTICLE XIX.

UPPER PENINSULA.

[The general provisions of this article are obsolete. All necessary special provisions relating to the upper peninsula are embodied in other portions of the amended constitution.]

ARTICLE XIX—A

OF RAILROADS

[The two sections of this article stand as sections 10 and 11 of amended article XI. The only change is the addition of the clause relating to the speed of railway trains, as shown by italics in section 10.]

ARTICLE XX.

AMENDMENT AND REVISION OF THE CONSTITUTION

[The changes in this article will appear by reference to amended article XVIII.]

SCHEDULE

[The schedule contains 29 sections, but most of its provisions are obsolete. See note to schedule of amended constitution.]

www.ingramcontent.com/pod-product-compliance
Lightning Source LLC
LaVergne TN
LVHW020238110826
845151LV00003B/961